D1332463

YEOVIL COLLEGE
LIBRARY

£ 27·00
D
BW

A Manager's Guide to
RECRUITMENT & SELECTION

2nd edition

Margaret Dale

RECOMMENDED BY
INSTITUTE OF DIRECTORS

KOGAN PAGE

London and Sterling, VA

Yeovil College

Y0059369

This book has been endorsed by the Institute of Directors.

The endorsement is given to selected Kogan Page books which the IoD recognises as being of specific interest to its members and providing them with up-to-date, informative and practical resources for creating business success. Kogan Page books endorsed by the IoD represent the most authoritative guidance available on a wide range of subjects including management, finance, marketing, training and HR.

First published in 1995
Second edition 2003

Apart from any fair dealing for the purposes of research or private study, or criticism or review, as permitted under the Copyright, Designs and Patents Act 1988, this publication may only be reproduced, stored or transmitted, in any form or by any means, with the prior permission in writing of the publishers, or in the case of reprographic reproduction in accordance with the terms and licences issued by the CLA. Enquiries concerning reproduction outside these terms should be sent to the publishers at the undermentioned addresses:

120 Pentonville Road
London N1 9JN
UK
www.kogan-page.co.uk

22883 Quicksilver Drive
Sterling VA 20166-2012
USA

© Margaret Dale, 1995, 2003

The right of Margaret Dale to be identified as the author of this work has been asserted by her in accordance with the Copyright, Designs and Patents Act 1988.

The views expressed in this book are those of the author and are not necessarily the same as those of the Institute of Directors.

ISBN 0 7494 3896 7

British Library Cataloguing-in-Publication Data

A CIP record for this book is available from the British Library.

Library of Congress Cataloging-in-Publication Data

Dale, Margaret.
    A manager's guide to recruitment and selection / Margaret Dale.-- 2nd ed.
        p. cm. -- (MBA masterclass series)
Includes bibliographical references and index.
    ISBN 0-7494-3896-7
    1. Employees--Recruiting. 2. Employee selection. I. Title. II. Series.
    HF5549.5.R44D29 2003
    658.3'11--dc21

                                                                2003008163

Typeset by JS Typesetting Ltd, Wellingborough, Northants
Printed and bound in Great Britain by Biddles Ltd, Guildford and King's Lynn
www.biddles.co.uk

Contents

Acknowledgements   *vii*
The series editor   *ix*

Introduction: successful recruitment and selection   **1**

1 Describing the job   **15**
Designing the job   17
Scientific management   18
Human relations school   19
Work design   23
Return of Taylorism   26
Alternatives to traditional job design   28
Jobs or roles   30
Expectations   32
The work   32
Relationships   33
Job descriptions   35
Employee specification   44
Summary   47

2 Attracting the right person   **48**
Marketing the job   51
Recruitment methods   66
How to know you have succeeded   90
Summary   91

3 Making decisions   **93**
Information flow   93
What information is needed to make decisions   95
The difficulties in making decisions   100

Providing additional information   108
Obtaining information   120
Summary   121

4   Applications   **124**
How to short-list   125
Decision frames   129
Forms of application   134
Screening methods   143
Short-listing matrix   153
Summary   156

5   Selection methods   **157**
Whether selection methods can predict success in post   159
Errors and biases   160
Selection methods   164
Factors influencing the choice of selection method   190
Decision making   191
Summary   193

6   Impact on the candidates   **195**
Candidates' personal considerations   197
Unfair discrimination   204
The consequences of not considering the candidates   213
Improving the treatment of candidates   219
Summary   228

7   After the offer   **230**
Making win/win decisions   231
Making an offer of employment   235
Negotiations after the offer   239
Treating unsuccessful candidates well   242
Giving feedback   245
Correcting mistakes   250
Words of caution   258
Summary   259

8   Induction and inclusion   **261**
Needs of new employees   261
Starting with recruitment   263
Induction methods   266
Inclusion   273
Celebrating the new employee's appointment   276
Probation and temporary contracts   277

Initial training 279
Development 286
Summary 289

9 Evaluation **291**
Evaluating the techniques 292
Evaluating the appointment 296
Outcome measures 303
Using the need to fill a post as a strategic opportunity 312
Summary 313

References *315*
Index *321*

Acknowledgements

My thanks go to Liz and Linda who helped enormously to complete the revisions to time. I must also acknowlege the work of my former colleagues at Sheffield Hallam University with whom I trialled many of the approaches described on the following pages. From and with them I learnt about the realities of recruitment and selection.

Roger's determined efforts as a job seeker increased my awareness of the effect recruiters can have. He continues, tirelessly, to tolerate my writing and provides moral support.

Most of all I must pay tribute to Bruce, his love and the joyfulness of his spirit.

The series editor

Philip Sadler is a Vice President of the Ashridge Business School where he was Chief Executive for 20 years. He now divides his time between writing, speaking, consultancy and voluntary service. He is a Fellow of the International Academy of Management, a Board Member of the International Leadership Association, a Companion of the Institute of Management, a Fellow of the Institute for Personnel and Development, a Fellow of the Institute of Directors, and a Patron of the Centre for Tomorrow's Company.

He has been awarded the honorary degrees of DSc (City University) and DBA (De Montfort University). He holds the Burnham Gold Medal of the Institute of Management and was appointed CBE in 1986.

His recent books include *Managing Change* (1995), *Leadership* (2003), *The Seamless Organization* (2001) and *Building Tomorrow's Company* (2002).

Introduction: successful recruitment and selection

The primary purpose of the recruitment and selection process is to achieve one desired end: appointing the right person to the right job. This is a critical task for any manager, and one that is more difficult when there is a shortage of the needed skills and experience in the labour market. Some would say that appointment decisions are the most important ones a manager has to make: they affect the manager's ability to achieve targets, the quality of services or products delivered to the customer and the well-being of the whole team.

Appointment decisions are comparatively common; the size of the recruitment industry and amount of money spent on vacancy advertising shows this. Yet despite the frequency of making appointments and the importance of selecting the best candidate, many managers only learn how to make these decisions from their own experience and watching others. Some may receive training, but usually this is only in interviewing techniques. It is not that common for them to be trained in all aspects of what, in reality, is a complex process fraught with pitfalls.

It should therefore surprise no one when the wrong appointment is made, possibly more often than we like to admit. Each time this happens it is an indication of a poor decision on the part of either the selector or the candidate. Those on both sides of the decision take part in a lengthy, complicated process which presents as many opportunities for making wrong decisions as there are for making the right one.

The effect of poor decisions on the organization and manager

A poor or wrong selection decision can have catastrophic consequences for an organization as well as the individual manager. Even at the basic entry level, a poor trainee, not in tune with the organization's ethos and aims, can damage production, relationships with suppliers, spoil relationships with customers, and affect the overall quality of service. The new appointee can adversely affect the morale and commitment of co-workers and negate efforts to foster team working. For managers, whose performance is frequently assessed on the basis of their staff, a poor selection decision can reflect very badly on their subsequent achievement.

Correcting these decisions can be costly. Even if it is possible to dismiss the new member of staff quickly, appointment costs will have already been incurred. There is also the cost associated with the time needed to make another appointment. If a poor appointment decision cannot be remedied by ending the individual's contract, living with the consequences can have long-term repercussions. We can all recount stories from our own experience that demonstrate just how expensive and painful living with a poor appointment can be.

The effects of poor decisions on the individual

For an individual appointed to the wrong job, there is no easy way out. Trying to be effective in the wrong job can rapidly lead to a loss of self-esteem. It is easy for individuals to blame themselves and assume that they are not up to the job, that their skills are not adequate or that they over-estimated their own level of capability when making the original application. It can be hard for individuals to attribute the cause of their difficulties, especially in the early days, to a badly constructed post, undefined selection criteria, or lack of clarity among members of the appointment panel.

Finding a respectable way out can be more difficult for the individual than for the employer. Resignation soon after appointment can be risky even when levels of unemployment are low. When these levels are high, finding another job can take months. In any case, appointment mistakes are usually taken as a reflection of the individual's level of competence. Living with the situation can lead to a loss of morale and self-confidence, which in turn can lower future performance levels further, thus making it even harder for the individual to find another job.

Reducing the risk

Treating a selection decision as a risk can be an aid to finding a way of reducing the chance of making a poor decision. The first step is to recognize that the end decision is, in fact, two-way. First, the employer offers a contract of employment then the individual decides whether to accept or reject it. The factors influencing the decision are complex. The employer's decision is usually made on the basis of a judgement – which candidate is the 'best' (whatever this means). Second, the individual's decision has to take account of the post in question, the effect it will have on subsequent jobs and the rest of the person's life. The decision at the end of the selection process, therefore, should be seen from the perspective of both parties if the resultant contract is to be mutually beneficial.

Long-term investment rather than short-term solution

The risk of making a poor decision can also be reduced if an appointment, even for a short-term contract, is treated as if it thousands of pounds were to be spent on a capital project or invested in a speculative venture, shares, stocks or bonds. Even the most risk-seeking entrepreneur considers ways of reducing the chances of losing money and increasing the possibility of increasing the value of the investment.

Examples of ways of doing this will be described later. For now, the most important point to remember is that rectifying a bad or poor decision can be time-consuming and costly. Making a good decision, on the other hand, can lead to rewards and pay-offs that far outstrip initial expectations of the parties involved. Investing in people can be far more rewarding than playing the Stock Exchange. People can blossom and grow in surprising ways. An individual who fits in with the organization, its culture and other employees, and is prepared and encouraged to develop and improve personal and organizational perform-ance, can bring unpredictable benefits.

Picking the right person does not have to cost a lot of money. Many of the actions that can be taken do not require highly developed skills of experienced professional practitioners. Rather, like moving to a new building, buying new plant or investing, the decision needs to be based on information gathered in a planned, systematic process that is prepared and organized.

WHAT IS TO COME

This book aims to provide practical insights, suggestions and examples of simple cost-effective ways of improving every stage of the recruitment and selection process. While it is intended primarily for managers and personnel practitioners, it will also help those applying for jobs. It will be particularly useful for those entering the labour market for the first time.

Most people involved in the appointment process are aware of the import-ance of making the right decision. Therefore it is likely that it will be a tense, stressful experience. This book aims to reduce this stress by demystifying the process and explaining the different stages and methods available for use. This will be done through the provision of examples based on known good and bad practices.

Underpinning theories will be outlined, where necessary, as this will help to explain the rationale beneath some of the practices, and may be useful for those currently involved in recruitment and selection and seeking to improve their practice. Unless one is employed by a large organization or one with a high turnover of staff, appointing people is not an everyday activity. Inevitably skills become rusty, and busy managers and personnel professionals get out of touch with current thinking and practice. Various devices such as checklists and highlighted points will accompany the examples and explanations so that busy people can find their way through the different stages of the process.

This book does not claim to be an exclusive textbook, so references will be given to other works and there are suggestions for further reading. Case law, tribunal decisions and the influences of European legislation continue to bring about changes to employment law, and demand different and new approaches to employment practice. Because these changes are occurring constantly as judgements redefine and interpret statute and new directives are made, details will not be given. Rather than risk misleading the reader, some suggestions will be given about general good practice and pointers given on how to find out the latest legal position.

Describing the job and the best person

Chapter 1 will outline how to build and describe the job. Often a collection of tasks are bundled together, called a job, and a person is sought to do it. It is assumed that these tasks must be carried out by one individual who will work full time to achieve a satisfactory standard of performance and the desired objectives. Job-sharing possibilities are sometimes thought about, but more often, the consideration of part-time working is restricted to areas of work where large numbers of the same type of worker (frequently women or young people) are employed. In the case of more specialist jobs or senior manager posts, normally it is assumed the post-holder will work five days, if not more.

Whether that job can realistically be performed by a single human being is even more rarely considered – until, that is, that human begins to fail in some way. But usually the human is faulted rather than the 'design' of the job.

In some occupations and organizations, there has been a move away from the idea of employees holding jobs to the concept of people occupying roles. This change recognizes that the individual does more than simply complete the tasks or achieve the stated objectives. The role-holder makes a broader contribution to the organization and plays a part in the wider community. This change is probably happening more in the sort of organization that employs profession- ally qualified staff or 'knowledge' workers.

Regardless of whether the discussion is about job- or role-holders, the pro- cesses used for analysing the organizational requirements are similar. The desired output is a useful description of what the individual needs to be able to do and what he or she needs to know to do it. The methods used for this analysis include considering the factors that influence whether the role or job is doable. Elements that lead to satisfaction for employees and enable their development will also be covered.

The description should not be a static record. It should be not only tight enough to provide an accurate outline of the job or role's purpose and its main responsibilities and objectives, but also broad enough to allow for change, growth and contraction.

The employee specification

Once it has been drawn up, the job description can be the basis for a person or employee specification. This describes the attributes needed by the person best suited to perform the duties of the job or fill the role. It should not, however, be a stereotypical picture; rather it is an indication of the attainment, achievements, abilities and aptitudes needed to enable an individual perform the tasks to the required standard and achieve the desired objectives. The specification is the foundation, along with the job description, for any recruitment activity, and establishes the competency statements against which candidates will be assessed. It can also be used to identify the initial training needed by individuals appointed and inform their subsequent development plans.

The compilation of the description and specification can also be used to check against bias and the inappropriate use of assumptions and stereotypes. Especially when a post previously occupied is being filled, it is easy to build the characteristics of the previous holder into the specification. Alternatively it can lead to a total turnaround, with the opposite traits are being sought. This practice can be dangerous, as it can lead either to the appointment of clones, or to bringing in a person who is so different that the organization is not able to assimilate him or her.

The task of compiling the specification provides the opportunity for a forward look at the attainments, achievements, abilities and aptitudes that are needed for acceptable performance in the future. The creation of a vacancy, be it from the termination of an existing contract or the creation of a new post, is a chance to either draw up a new specification or validate the existing description. Regardless of the prompt for doing so, when compiling the description and specification, the overriding question should be, 'What does the organization really need now?'

Attracting candidates

Chapter 2 discusses attracting the right person for the job. Knowing what to look for makes the search for the right person somewhat easier. Recruitment is about attracting candidates who are qualified and capable of carrying out the job, in the context of the employing organization. This is when potential candidates are told about the vacancy, and possibly the organization, and encouraged to express their interest in the job. In effect, it is the same as any sales task, but instead of selling a product or service, we are selling a job.

Even at this preliminary stage, the potential candidates have the power – it is they who decide whether to submit an application or to ignore the vacancy. This applies to search just as much as to advertisements placed in newspapers.

How to obtain the right person's attention and interest is the main challenge for the recruiter. When levels of unemployment are high, recruitment is generally straightforward – it is an employers' market. The biggest difficulty can be shifting through a large number of applications from people equally well qualified and who are apparently capable of doing the job. However when levels of unemployment are low, the employer can be faced with a very different task. Power then lies with the applicants, and the major challenge for the recruiter is selling the job and the employer. Even finding the basic level of competency required to do the job at the most elementary level can prove difficult. Skill shortages and gaps are presented in a number of sectors as major impediments to growth and business development.

We will explore the different ways of recruiting applicants, including some novel approaches. Because recruitment contains many elements similar to other sales activities, we will draw on the principles used in marketing products and services. One of the most recent developments has been the use of the Internet for advertising vacancies and disseminating the CVs of individuals seeking employment. This can be a fast and comparatively inexpensive way of recruiting, particularly for organizations with high numbers of vacancies. Time and money are needed to set up Web pages, although these are recompensed by the later savings.

Inevitably, a lot of time, effort and money is taken when recruiting to a vacancy, and research shows that many people find a new job through a person who already works for the organization. Some of the outlay, therefore, may not be necessary. However, in saying this, all recruiters need to aware of their responsibilities for equal treatment of all groups in the whole community. This means ensuring that access to jobs is open. Restricting the media where the vacancy is advertised can be one way in which certain groups are discriminated against unfairly.

The Equal Opportunities Commission and Council for Race Equality have produced guidance on how to ensure that jobs are made available to people suitably qualified from all sections of the community regardless of race, marital status and gender. Increasingly concern is being expressed about age discrimination, and the Disability Discrimination Act has drawn attention to the importance of avoiding unjustifiable discrimination against people with disabilities. Ways of promoting vacancies fairly to all sectors of the community need to be uppermost when deciding how to recruit.

Making decisions

Chapter 3 discusses decision making in the recruitment and selection process. This process is punctuated by decisions, yet human decision making is known to be flawed. The errors and biases affect both parties. They influence the ways in which recruiters and selectors make judgements about applicants, and how potential applicants decide whether to submit and continue with their application. As these decisions are central to each of the stages in the process, some of the more common biases and sources of error will be outlined.

Two of the main factors that influence how decisions are made are the information available to the individual making the decision, and the media used to communicate that information. The initial medium used to communicate the existence of the job is the advertisement or another form of public announcement. This is supplemented by supporting information such as packs. These tend to be used mainly by larger employers who recruit significant numbers of employees, and more widespread use can be beneficial to employers and employers in ways other than merely attracting candidates. The infinite capacity of the Internet to hold data and provide links between different pages and sources makes it easy to provide as much information as the employer wishes to give for little additional cost.

The information about the job and organization helps applicants decide whether to express their interest. It also influences the way in which they frame their application. As well as guiding the applicant, detailed information can save the time of the person short-listing the applications. It will go some way towards ensuring that the applications are formatted in a way that makes it easier to find the evidence needed to decide whether to progress them.

The presentation, as well as the content, of the application influences the recruiter when making short-listing decisions. Research suggests that if good quality information is given to the candidates before the start of the appointment, the chances of the appointment being successful are increased. Creating an accurate impression of the organization and job in the mind of candidates contributes to their eventual induction and early training.

Submitting an application

Job applications are the subject of Chapter 4. There are a number of means by which candidates are expected to express their interest. Each sector tends to have its own preferred way of doing this, which can influence how an uninitiated candidate's application is received. This simple lack of knowledge of what is expected, which may have nothing to do with their ability to perform the job, can inhibit people moving between industrial sectors. This barrier can work to the detriment of individuals and the economy as a whole, as it prevents the development of generic competencies and the transfer of skills and approaches.

The different methods in common use will be explored to explain how different expectations can be best met, and applications can be assessed in terms of best fit against the specification and job requirements instead of conformity to specific norms. The exploration should prove useful to those appointing applicants from other sectors and employers. It should also help applicants decide how best to present their application.

Assessing applications

Assessment of the application is normally the first stage of selection – a process of discrimination aimed at picking the 'best' candidate. It is at this stage that prejudices and stereotypes begin to be shown. Interestingly, very little research has been conducted into the decisions made during short-listing. This opportunity, therefore, will be taken to consider what might be taking place in the short-listers' minds. Suggestions will be made to explain what is happening, to help both selectors and those putting themselves forward for selection understand better the possible factors influencing their decisions. This will lead to proposals about ways of improving current practice and make the subconscious, hidden decisions more transparent.

Selection

Selection methods are the subject of Chapter 5. A selection event is usually the first time when applicants and potential employers formally meet in person. The interview is by far the most common selection method used, and continues to be so despite much evidence that as a predicator of performance it is weak. Some organizations have rejected the interview and have experimented with other ways of assessing applicants' skills and attributes, which have better predictive validity.

Some of these have attracted controversy of their own, and have been the subject of heated debate at professional conferences and in the press. There is a popular belief that these methods are high-cost and do not necessarily justify the expenditure involved. This may be a valid argument if recruitment and selection are seen in terms of costs alone. However, if the process is evaluated in terms of its contribution to creating an organization, made up of people able and motivated to do the job to the standards required and capable of further development, the expenditure can be seen more as a long-term investment.

Even so, the full cost of the process should be accounted for, so that each stage can be assessed to ensure that it is adding value. The accounting should include the time spend by the individuals involved, and be focused on the impact the post will have on the overall effectiveness of the organization. Even a low-paid receptionist can have a major impact on levels of customer satisfaction. Therefore deciding who to appoint can be of major importance. Thus it is worth spending more than half an hour, having a chat with a few likely candidates, to make sure the right and best person is appointed.

However there is no point in creating a sophisticated multi-stage selection event if there are other simpler, cheaper ways available that are equally effective in predicting which candidate is most likely to perform to the desired standard. We will consider some of the more common approaches and discuss practical ways of implementing them. References will also be made to some of the less well-known techniques. The choice of method should always have the over-riding reason for using it clearly in mind – and it should be clear how will it help managers and personnel specialists reduce the odds of making a poor decision.

The chapter will also help those facing selection events to prepare themselves for what may be a new experience. A well-run selection event, even if the application is not successful, can be very helpful for the individual applicants. It is easy for those making the decision to forget what the applicants go through when submitting their application. If the job has been done thoroughly, the person will have considered his or her skills, experience and potential against the job description and specification. Applicants will have considered whether getting the job will be beneficial for both their future and that of the organization, and they know they will be putting themselves forward for scrutiny. After the event, individuals not appointed may feel disappointed and sometimes angry. Sensitively supplied and constructive feedback can help them overcome these emotions, and provide guidance on how to remedy any shortfalls so that the chances of future applications being successful are increased.

The impact on applicants

The impact of the process on applicants is discussed in Chapter 6. Once the selection events have been held, those with the responsibility for the appointment have to make the decision. No matter how sophisticated the techniques used during selection, the human beings involved cannot absolve themselves of the final decision. But the decision to appoint is not the only issue. The selected candidate has some say in the matter, and there are other questions to be discussed in addition to 'Do you want the job – yes or no?'

The need to engage in these discussions can take all the attention of the managers involved. And of course there is the wish to congratulate the successful candidate and begin to make that person feel welcome. This can lead to those not appointed being forgotten.

These people will be told the outcome, often in terms of a simple letter thanking them for their application and telling them a more suitable person has been offered the job. Their perceptions of the process and full recognition of the efforts they have made in submitting their application are not acknowledged. How often are unsuccessful candidates asked to give feedback on how they feel their application has been handled?

It is sad but true that there are examples of selection events having a negative effect on candidates. Some have caused damage to individuals. It is rare for employers to examine their recruitment and selection processes from the perspective of individual applicants, especially those currently not employed by the organization. In addition to being time-consuming, putting oneself forward for critical appraisal is stressful and requires the individual to make an investment of energy and emotion. Applicants engage in a period of self-examination and have to imagine different future scenarios which could involve major changes for themselves, partners and families.

They enter the process in good faith and most do so honestly, with no intention of wasting anyone's time. They will expect the selection process to be challenging and testing but there is not need for it to, nor should it, be destructive. Some selectors believe that a potentially damaging selection process is valid, to see how applicants will withstand pressure and aggression. But what is the point in putting candidates through gruelling, traumatic activities just to see if they are up to 'it' when 'it' is not a true requirement of the job?

We will therefore consider the ways in which an organization engages with and affects applicants and candidates. Much can be done to improve the interaction and reduce unnecessary stress without removing the challenge, and the thorough examination of skills and attributes.

As both the successful and unsuccessful candidates expend time and effort in applying for the job, they deserve something in return. This can be given in the form of useful feedback. However, if the feedback is given ineptly it can also lead to unnecessary damage to an individual's self-esteem, and possibly give grounds for complaint where otherwise there would have been none.

When designing the recruitment and selection process, it should always be remembered that applicants have the right to complain to an employment tribunal if they believe they have been treated unfairly. Some employers see this as a justification for not giving out any information about the decision, believing that it will simply add fuel to a smouldering fire and provide evidence that could be used against the organization.

This argument is not a valid excuse for not giving feedback. Nor is it justification from wrapping up helpful, but possibly critical, information in generalities. Rather it is a reason for making sure that feedback is provided in a constructive manner, providing enough information to help individuals learn while leaving their self-confidence intact. If the feedback is given against the profile required for the job and grounded on evidence, it may reduce the chance of a complaint being made rather than providing support to the complainant.

Induction and inclusion

Chapters 7 and 8 discuss the induction and inclusion processes that take place just after the final selection decisions have been made and an offer of employment made. Changes to employment practice mean that it is not uncommon for an individual contract between the employer and employee to be created. This can include a package of benefits to recompense individuals for the application of their skills, expertise and effort. This package can include pay and other monetary rewards and a range of non-pay benefits selected from a 'basket'. For some senior appointments, this basket could include complex financial options and contractual terms, such as payments on the termination of the contract. Therefore the offer of employment can be far more complex than, 'We would like to offer you the job. Do you accept? Yes or no?'

A period of negotiation can be entered into, during which the details of the employment contract will be settled. This will include agreement on the explicit terms and the implicit ones. The appointed person will want to clarify details of his or her reward package and other matters such as future career development opportunities. He or she may also want to discuss personal matters such as housing, relocation reimbursements, schools, and employment prospects for a partner.

Frequently, employers do not realize the importance of these discussions, particularly how they relate to the implicit terms of the contract. The understandings of both parties formed during this phase create further expectations and interpretations about the job, the standards required and the conditions surrounding the employment. Misinformation and misleading discussions can cause problems later on.

Despite all the efforts to get the appointment right, occasionally wrong decisions are made. Remedying such a situation can be time-consuming, painful and costly, if handled badly. There is often pressure on the appointers to make an appointment rather than make the right appointment. It can be hard to say that none of the candidates are up to the standard required and start the process again. But sometimes this decision is better, in the longer term, than putting someone into a job when there are doubts about his or her abilities to succeed in it.

Selection mistakes can be hard to acknowledge, partly because it is not easy to rectify them. We will therefore look at some simple ways in which remedial action can be taken. It should be possible to find ways that allow the employer and the newly appointed employee to get out of the situation and admit a genuine error of judgement has been made without either party losing too much face.

Increasingly access to training and development is being seen as a part of an individual's broader reward package. Every employee has the right to expect to be adequately trained to carry out duties to the required standard. Even those with considerable experience need some initial training to orientate them to the new organization's ways of working and induct them into its culture.

The early days of employment – the induction period – are known to be critical of the long-term success of the appointment. This phase is not often seen as part of the recruitment and selection process. Yet how the new employee is treated during recruitment, selection and induction can make or break the achievement of the predicted outcomes. If induction is done badly, all the effort and expenditure spend on the recruitment and selection process can be squandered.

There is a temptation to see the newly appointed person as perfect. Even outstanding candidates need help to fit into the organization. The assessments carried out during selection will include a thorough appraisal of the new appointee's abilities and achievements. It can be argued that this is the most rigorous assessment employees undergo in the course of their employment with any one organization. Therefore, it makes sense to make full use of the results.

It is rare for a person appointed to a new job to meet every aspect of the requirements to the standards needed at the outset. The assessment will have identified specific areas seen as less strong than others. Some help will therefore be needed to enable the comparatively weak aspects to be improved. We will explore various ways of using the induction phase of employment to rectify these areas of shortfall. We will discuss these bearing in mind what can reasonably be expected of someone new in a job, and equally important, what should not be expected.

Employees have the right to access training to help them do the job to the required standard and longer-term development to equip them for the changes the future is guaranteed to bring. The period just after appointment presents an ideal opportunity to create an individual development plan. By this time, an individual's skills will have been assessed rigorously against a carefully considered job description and specification, and compared to other suitably qualified individuals. In the euphoria of success, individuals will be as open as ever they are likely to be to constructive feedback and positive guidance.

The employee is on the other side of the contract. A poor decision during selection can have far more devastating consequences for individuals than organizations, particularly if they have relocated home and family. In the past, generally when employees realized they had made a mistake and resigned during the first year after appointment, employers tended to shrug their shoulders and hope that the next post-holder would stay a little longer. More recently the attitude has changed. The lack of skills in certain areas has meant that employers have been forced to examine their turnover more critically and understand why employees leave. Retention of key staff has become a new challenge for managers and HR professionals.

Evaluation

We will discuss the importance of evaluating the success of the process in the final chapter. Obtaining feedback from those involved in the process is one of the best ways of assessing its quality. It is comparatively easy to ask the person appointed to a job to express his or her views on how well he or she was treated during the selection process. However, it will be no surprise to find that often, in the glow of success, individuals feel somewhat positive about the events that led to their achievement. Asking those candidates who were not successful can be more difficult, but can nevertheless be a source of valuable information. But again, it should be of no surprise that their perceptions may not be so positive.

This is a normal reaction. Nevertheless, it is possible to organize a recruitment and selection process that may leave some of the participants feeling disappointed, but with the view that they had had a fair chance to demonstrate their abilities.

Even if at the end of the process the post has not been filled, the recruitment and selection activities in themselves should have contributed to the organization's operations in some of the following ways:

▌ The need to outline the current and future requirements of the job and the sort of person to occupy it will have given the opportunity to consider how the organization's requirements translate into these terms.

▌ Every exposure to the outside world has an impact on an organization's image. Bringing people in for the purposes of selection says something publicly about the way the employer treats people. Therefore, it is worth using an appointment process as part of the organization's overall marketing and promotion effort.

▌ The appointment process can produce useful lessons for the next time a post needs to be filled. Market testing the skills and attributes thought to be needed against those available can be salutary. It also provides a real test of comparative pay rates.

▌ It allows the value and performance levels of existing staff to be compared to those of others. There is always a temptation to see those outside as 'better' than one's current employees. Sometimes this is an illusion.

▌ If the recruitment and selection process has been expensive, it may be necessary to justify the outlay. The utility of the process can be calculated and the result used to demonstrate longer-term value to the organization. If an appointment is paralleled to other forms of investment it becomes possible for the recruitment and selection process to demonstrate its value in strategic terms and claim its successes.

Once an appointment has been made, it is easy to forget the effort that went into getting it right. The lessons can be forgotten, and the people who worked hard for its success neglected, when the bouquets are handed out. A thorough evaluation can help to ensure that responsibility and praise are fairly attributed.

FINALLY

This book has been written to aid those wishing to understand more about the process and wanting to make improvements. Its contents are based on personal experiences of applying for jobs, running recruitment and selection activities, and reflecting on these and the experiences of others. It does not aim to be a thorough compendium of techniques or methods, nor does it aim to outline current legislation. This is a specialist area in its own right, and changes rapidly. Those with recruitment and selection responsibilities as a key part of their role should take steps to ensure they remain up to date. Others will need to rely on the advice and guidance of appropriate professionals. Leighton and Proctor (2002) have produced a short but useful guide to the law relating to recruitment and selection.

From all accounts, going through a recruitment and selection process can have a major impact on all the individuals involved and the employing organizations. The process can be stressful for everyone concerned, and contains a lot of risk. As it is complex and lengthy, it provides plenty of opportunities for getting things wrong. Even when the very best methods are used, the ways in which they are applied can result in good appointments and a positive experience, or lead to disastrous mistakes. Yet getting it right need not be difficult or costly. In fact making use of good practice can actually reduce cost as well as increase the chances of picking the right person for the job.

1

Describing the job

Appointing the right person for the job is more than simply making the right decision after an interview. Several stages have to occur before this final decision can be made. To start the process, suitably qualified and appropriately experienced applicants must be attracted, but what is meant by 'suitably qualified' and 'experienced'? If this definition is not clear and communicated, people will not know whether to apply or not – and if there is doubt, the chances are they will not.

Deciding who is the right person will also be rather difficult. Without a set of clear and explicit criteria, those making the decision will have no framework against which to compare candidates. The lack of such criteria is one of the failings often found by employment tribunals, yet it is so easy to identify the criteria and it makes the work of selectors simpler, for the criteria are used to assess the candidates and indicate how the best person will be recognized.

Many recruiters are aware of the need to identify desirable and essential qualifications and experience, but specifying the qualifications and experience required is only one part of describing the most suitable candidate. The job that person is to do must also be defined. There has been a shift away from preparing job descriptions and specifications comprising detailed lists of tasks and vague personal characteristics. The more recent approaches recognize that employees have to be flexible and capable of multitasking, and that expertise can be obtained in ways other than through formal qualifications and years in work. Increasingly employers are defining roles as outlines, descriptions of main responsibilities accompanied by the specification of the competencies required for effective performance.

Nevertheless job descriptions and employee specifications continue to be used widely, and will probably be familiar to those who have some experience of recruitment and selection. If they (and role profiles) are to be useful fully, they need to be written in such a way that both the requirements and candidates are assessed factually and comparatively.

The job description contains activities, responsibilities and objectives to be achieved. The specification outlines the skills, traits and aptitudes necessary for the desired level of performance, and should be written in indicative terms so that the evidence needed for effective assessment can be collected.

When a vacancy is filled there is often temptation to look at the work done by previous post-holders or that needs to be done now. Rarely, is the opportunity taken to look at what the job will be required to contribute to the overall success of the organization. Any organization is only a product of its component parts, and the achievements of its plans depend on the collective efforts of all its members. The way the work is divided and the amount of effort expended by its members contribute directly to the level of performance.

Many organizations make use of business plans to guide their operations, but how many of these include details of human resource requirements, and link the work to be done to the way in which the jobs are defined? Human resource planning is a technique described in personnel textbooks. They describe how the future objectives of the organization can be achieved in terms of the numbers of people required and skills they need to possess. Rarely do these plans, if used at all, contain details of how the work is to be divided between those people.

It can also be seen from advertisements and recruitment literature that very little systematic job design is done. This is a shame, for it is an opportunity missed. How a job is built up not only affects performance levels, it also influences the satisfaction obtained by the post-holder. Well-designed jobs can motivate individuals and accommodate their personal and career development. They can also enable the employing organization to look forward at how its objectives can be achieved.

Poor job design can lead to unfair treatment and discrimination. This can occur, for example, in part-time jobs whose holders are unable to carry out the full range of tasks available to full-timers or have reduced access to developmental opportunities. This can limit career development or impede the promotional prospects of the part-time post-holders.

Good job design starts with an initial analysis of what the organization requires in terms of its business plans. This should be more than a look at past, successful performance. It should be linked closely to the future needs of the organization and its operations in terms of what:

∎ can be reasonably expected of the post-holder;

∎ will be required in the future to maintain success;

∎ needs to be done to achieve new objectives;

∎ will lead to improved individual and organizational performance.

Simple ways of carrying out this analysis will be described later in the chapter.

The first stage of the analysis presents the opportunity for past assumptions and historic models to be challenged. We tend to build up pictures of the type of people we think are best suited to certain jobs and places in the organization. These pictures are limited by our own experiences of people, and images of what will most likely lead to future success. It is certain that these images are flawed, as their foundations are based on incomplete information, prejudices and false assumptions. If new job descriptions and employee specifications are based on the requirements of the job to be done in the future, some of the traditional stereotypes can be eliminated.

When we look at how to create forward-looking and realistic job descriptions and employee specifications, we will consider the implications of equal opportunities legislation. Statutes and case law, which place obligations on employers, tend to be minimalist – they say what should not be done rather than indicate what can be done to correct historic unfairness. Employers are increasingly required to consider their practices, as new legislation is being introduced to combat forms of discrimination other than those caused by gender or racial bias. The removal of the ceilings on damage payments also increases the penalties of getting this aspect of recruitment and selection wrong. There are legal steps that can be taken to remedy previous discrimination. We will therefore look at some of the positive action approaches that can be taken in the early stages of the recruitment and selection process.

DESIGNING THE JOB

Once a vacancy has occurred, it is generally accepted that the first stage in recruiting the person to fill it is to prepare the job description – but really this should be the second step. The first should be the design of the job. A job is more than a collection of tasks. It should have meaning and a purpose. It should be related to the objectives of the organization and the part of the organization in which it is located. It should also be capable of being done by a human being. A job can be made undoable in a number of ways:

▮ Its design can be so poor that the individual occupying it cannot hope to succeed.

▮ The component tasks may be disjointed and unrelated.

▮ If there are too many duties or too few, the job may not make sense.

▮ It can be so unrewarding that most post-holders would be demotivated.

▮ The range of skills required can be too wide to be found in any one individual.

SCIENTIFIC MANAGEMENT

The traditional approach to job design is rooted in Taylorism. Frederick Taylor (1991) was the father of scientific management, and one of the first to set down the general principles used to organize labour. His approach was developed in the late 19th century for the heavy industries of the United States. His goal was to increase the productivity of the labourer, and he believed in the notion of 'economic man' (that an individual seeks to maximize his or her own benefit and so will increase his or her efforts to achieve greater gain). Taylor's ideas laid down the foundations for the division and organization of work, and has been used to develop found in many payments by results schemes.

Taylor's approach was rooted in the belief that there was only one way to do a job – the right way. This led to the study of work, and the establishment of rule books that codified working methods. Taylor went on to recommend that an individual worker's skills should be assessed so that the worker and the job could be matched. Workers would be paid for the results of their skill and effort, and they expected to work alongside others engaged on similar tasks in functional groups. The workers would be under the control of a functional foreman whose legitimate authority would be drawn from expertise in those areas of work.

The idea of functional grouping came from the work of the 18th century economist Adam Smith. He suggested that tight division of labour would have three advantages:

▌ The simplification of routines would improve the dexterity of the worker.

▌ Routinization of operations would reduce time delays. If the worker was deployed on one task he or she would not have to change tools or material.

▌ Specialist machines could be used to aid production.

Ted was a successful entrepreneur. He had a history of buying small companies in difficulty, streamlining their operations and taking them from the brink of bankruptcy back to full viability. He had used the same approach for revitalizing each company he had acquired. He examined the organization as a flow process and broke the systems into their component stages. He then considered ways of simplifying each to enable it to link from the previous stage smoothly into the next.

In most of the companies he had bought, he had found that the staff tended to follow whatever was being processed from start to finish. His experience indicated that this was extremely inefficient. The staff were not good at anything in particular and did not take a pride in their work. Ted believed that it was far better to encourage staff to specialize on a single aspect, develop their skills in that area of work, and get a sense of a job well done.

This approach led to other problems, such as disputes between groups of workers, and there was a tendency for one group to blame another if mistakes were made. However, the improvements to profitability of the operations meant that it was possible to employ good-quality supervisors who were able to put a stop to any silliness.

By the time he retired Ted had created a conglomeration of small and medium-sized companies, was chairman of the local chamber of commerce and had received an OBE.

Evidence of this thinking can still be seen in the way that work is organized in many organizations. The assembly line is still the basis of mass production; the use of precise rules can be found in fast food outlets and call centres to ensure standardization of product and service. Plant and equipment are controlled by computers to reduce the chances of human error and the risk of accident; they also eliminate boring jobs.

Although many work practices are still grounded in 19th-century thinking about people's behaviour at work and the sources of their motivation, the underpinning beliefs has been challenged. The biggest flaw with Taylorism is that in reality people are not economic and rational. Motives other than personal profit drive people to work productively. Taylor's principles were developed in the context of the US steel mills which were staffed largely by immigrant workers. Many of these people were ill-educated, nearly illiterate and at starvation level. Unsurprisingly the need to eat predominated their thinking and their motivation at work. Since then other motivators and drives have been identified, and have been used to inform the less traditional thinking behind job design.

> *The development of the scientific management theories did not take account of the context in which people were employed. They worked harder to earn more money so they and their families could eat; not to become better off.*

HUMAN RELATIONS SCHOOL

Later research indicated that other factors affected levels of performance and motivation. The 'science' of management and its study increasingly became influenced by the related work of psychologists and sociologists. Various investigations into productivity set the foundations for modern approaches to the construction, organization and management of work. The rational economic approach was questioned and replaced by the human relations school. It is beyond the scope of this book to explore the details of the underpinning theories, but the interested reader will find ample coverage in standard textbooks such as Handy (1985) or Child (1984).

Two theories of motivation and job satisfaction are of interest here and have stood the test of time. Despite criticisms and efforts to discredit them, the theories developed by Maslow and Hertzberg continue to have both appeal and practical application. They are simple and understandable, and can be related to reality in ways recognized by managers and other people at work, and later work tends to complement rather than replace their ideas.

Abraham Maslow (1954) was a theoretical psychologist who hypothesized about the factors that motivate individuals. His work was put forward in the early 1950s as an untested idea. Nevertheless it was accepted, and it continues to be cited largely because of its intuitive appeal. Maslow suggested that human motives can be arranged in a hierarchy of priorities (see Figure 1.1). The basic assumption Maslow made to underpin his hypothesis was that as one base need was satisfied, the individual would be motivated to satisfy the next.

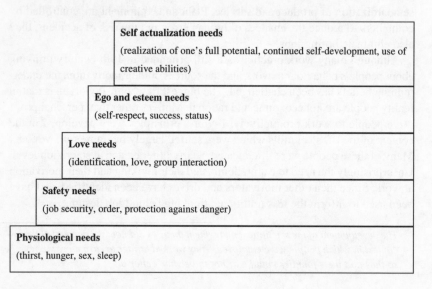

Figure 1.1 *Maslow's hierarchy of needs*

Maslow's work differed considerably from that of Taylor. He recognized that human beings were driven by a number of factors – not just money – and when ultimately the needs in deficit were satisfied, individuals would be motivated by the wish to be themselves.

The image of the 'self-actualized' person is perhaps now tarnished by the stereotype of the free love hippies of the 1960s. Really, the term is used to describe an individual able to focus on developing, realizing and using his or her best abilities. Maslow, in developing his theory, recognized that individuals were motivated by different factors in different circumstances for different

The company was set up by three friends – Ian, Mary and Rhand. They had studied for their professional qualifications together but had drifted apart. A few years later they met again, by accident, at a conference. When they had caught up with each other's histories, it became clear that none of them were happy working for the large organizations that currently employed them. They decided to set up a consultancy that would allow them to be their own bosses and to do the sort of work that really interested them.

Rhand was a little worried. She had recently taken on a large mortgage and was struggling to make ends meet. Giving up her large salary would be a big step for her. Still she was prepared to give it a go.

Ian had similar but different concerns. He had a small family and was concerned about his longer-term security. His current employer had very generous pension and health provisions and had made guarantees against redundancy. He felt that he would have to take out substantial insurance to make sure his family was safeguarded if the consultancy was not successful.

Mary was worried about leaving her current colleagues. She had built up a very close group of friends among the people at work. Leaving them would be sad, but Ian assured her that if they were real friends, they would stay in touch.

Within two years they had established the business as a successful company. Its reputation was spreading, and number of clients were increasing to such an extent that the three friends were considering expanding and taking on extra staff. They all agreed that the risks had been worth taking. The potential now available for them to develop their own talents and achieve was far greater than it would have been if they had stayed with their previous employers. With hindsight, they wondered what had concerned them.

reasons. He was aware that the hierarchy was more than the simple straight-line progression shown in Figure 1.1.

The other often-quoted research was carried out by Frederick Hertzberg and his associates (Hertzberg, Mausner and Snyderman, 1959). Dissatisfied by previous work, Hertzberg and his team set out to question workers about the factors that led to their satisfaction and dissatisfaction at work. On the basis of hundreds of questionnaires and interviews, clusters of factors were isolated. These were separated into those incidents that led to increased satisfaction and those which did not. These two sections were labelled as 'hygiene factors' and 'motivators'. The latter term was used to describe those factors that would lead a worker to increase effort. The former, they found, only served to maintain the level of motivation if they were right. More importantly, if they were wrong they would demotivate a worker.

Table 1.1 *Hertzberg's hygiene factors and motivators*

Hygiene factors (main source of bad feelings when wrong; slight increase in performance when right)	Motivators (increased satisfaction when right; slight decrease in in performance when wrong)
Company policy and administration	Achievement
Supervision	Recognition
Relationship with supervisor	Work itself
Work conditions	Responsibility
Salary	Advancement
Relationship with peers	Growth
Status	
Security	

Thomas was the personnel manager for a production company in the West of England. He was proud of his company's reputation for being a good employer. Whenever a vacancy arose, which was rare, he was flooded with applications. He was devastated when the accounts staff went on strike. The reason for the walk-out was a trivial dispute that had occurred between the office supervisor and Robert. Robert was one of the longest-serving members of staff, and was known as being reliable even if he did not act on his own initiative very much. The cause of the argument was not clear but the supervisor ended it by shouting a verbal warning to him across the office. The union convener seized the opportunity and called on the other members to walk out.

Thomas was faced with a situation where both the convener and the supervisor had broken the rules, and a group of staff was extremely angry with everyone. He called the two combatants together and demanded that they both apologize to each other. The warning was rescinded, and the convener and supervisor both undertook to stay within agreed procedures in future. But still the staff were angry, and Thomas was puzzled why the staff had been so ready to walk out and risk their jobs when their conditions of employment were so good. He decided to investigate, as he was concerned about a similar thing happening again.

He called in a consultant to undertake a confidential staff attitude survey. The results demonstrated that the staff felt that the company, as an employer was all right, but the supervisor was extremely unpopular. In their view the office was overcrowded, their equipment was of poor quality, and training opportunities were denied to them. The supervisor, a number of people said, did not listen to anything they had to say about the running of the office. She was too busy on her own pet projects.

Thomas talked to the supervisor, who had only been with the company for two years. It transpired that she did not know the company's policy on access to training and development. She believed that because she did not have a separate budget she could not fund any staff training, and therefore had been telling staff they could not attend any courses until she had sorted the budget. This had taken low priority as she had been more concerned with the specification for a new system. This was the reason she had told the staff that there was no point in considering any changes to the office layout, only she had not told the staff about her plans for the new system.

It soon became clear to Thomas that the real reason for the walk-out had been the supervisor's failure to communicate properly with her staff. She agreed to introduce a monthly briefing session and to make sure that the staff both knew about developments and had the opportunity to voice their views properly.

Some common themes can be seen in both Maslow's hierarchy and Hertzberg's theory, especially the importance of relationships and the need for achievement and growth. In fact, it was this emphasis on relationships that led to these and associated theories being labelled as the human relations school.

Complementary work in the UK carried out by the Tavistock Institute around the same time demonstrated that the division of work into functional specialisms led to the separation of work groups from each other, increased inter-group conflict and reduction in productivity. Thus the links between the technology of work and social relationships were proven.

Both the quality of working relationships and the nature of the work affect the will to work.

WORK DESIGN

During the 1960s and 1970s most of the experiments in work design concentrated on finding ways to make work more meaningful, as a method of motivating workers to improve their productivity as well as increasing their satisfaction. Initiatives such as quality of working life, quality circles, autonomous work groups, and job enlargement, enrichment and rotation programmes are among those frequently reported. Looking back on the reports of the various initiatives, they seem to be more concerned with describing techniques used than finding an underpinning model for more general application.

Maslow and Hertzberg, even though flawed, provide guidance to a manager on ways of organizing and managing work. The research of Hackman and Oldham (1980) into job satisfaction characteristics is also useful. They identified three critical states – the core job dimensions, critical psychological states, and personal and work outcome – that are likely to affect motivation and job satisfaction. The features of the job are linked (as shown in Figure 1.2) to the likely impact they are thought to have on the individual's state of mind. How individuals experience the job (its component parts and in its entirety) affect the outcomes they obtain from their work, which in turn influence the level of their overall job satisfaction.

Around the same time, management by objectives (MbO) was being developed as a technique to link individual responsibilities into the overall aims of the organization through a process of joint goal setting, monitoring and evaluation of achievement. It was based on principles similar to goal-setting theory: both identify the importance of clear shared objectives, claiming that hard (but achievable) goals result in higher performance. The importance of the specific goals, rather than vague expressions of ambition, and the need for incentives to be linked to specific goals, were essential parts of any MbO/goal-setting process. The line manager, it is argued, plays a critical role in the attainment or non-attainment of goals. Even though MbO was rejected as being prescriptive, and the process of setting and agreeing goals too problematic, its application did have some successes – so much so that similar approaches, perhaps with different names, continue to be used.

The need to achieve was one of the three drivers identified in the 1950s by McClelland (1953). When linked with expectancy theory, there is some theoretic basis to the following assertion – when people know what is expected of them and they know what rewards or punishments achievement or non-achievement will bring, they are likely to direct their efforts accordingly. McClelland's work regained attention in the 1980s when his research was used to aid the search for competent performance. He argued that the needs of individuals are more complex than those previously suggested by Maslow. He proposed that many needs are socially acquired rather than being inherent, and vary according to culture. He defined three types of socially acquired need – achievement, power and affiliation. These were used by the McBer Consultancy teams in their research into the difference between an average and superior performer, and ultimately became the competency statements described by Boyatzis (1982).

Some other interesting work has been done by Alban-Metcalfe and Nicholson (1984) and Nicholson and West (1988), which supports the US findings. They show that the work preferences given below are common to members of both genders and generally affect levels of performance:

1.   Work content – challenging work to do.

2.   The quality of senior management.

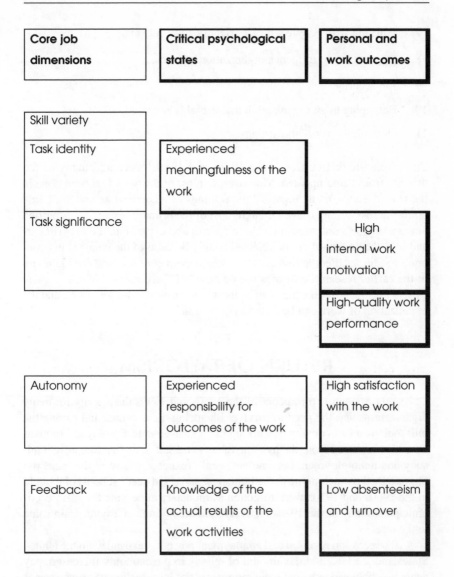

Figure 1.2 *Hackman and Oldham – Job satisfaction characteristics*

3. Work where individual accomplishment is appreciated and recognition given for achievement.

4. Opportunity to improve knowledge and skills.

5. A job where the individual can be creative in doing things their way.

6. Opportunities for advancement.

7. Working with people who are friendly and congenial.

8. Opportunity to influence organizational policies.

9. Job security.

10. Belonging to an organization that is highly regarded.

11. Opportunity for high earnings.

The economic difficulties of the 1970s and 1980s prevented many of the theories from being updated. Moreover, as most of the work had been done in the United States, many regarded the findings as inappropriate and not transferable across cultures. Even though most of the primary research was carried out at a time of continuous economic growth and expansion, the experiments and hypothesis should not be rejected simply because of the changes in economic conditions. People to a certain extent remain constant, and the longevity of the earlier research indicates the potential of these ideas. There are many current examples of how they can be used to improve the design of jobs and the organization of work can be found in operation.

RETURN OF TAYLORISM

During the economic turbulence of the 1980s and 1990s the priority for many organizations was the need to survive. Balancing the accounts and paying the bills took over from quality of working life improvements. Employees' motivation drivers altered from the hygiene factors and self-actualization, as redundancy and unemployment became very real prospects. Many of the ideas put forward by those belonging to the human resource and needs schools of thought in the 1960s and 1970s were forgotten as monetarism became the main economic philosophy of the 1980s recovery, and the notions of Taylor again came to the fore.

As the recession reversed and employment prospects expanded, in the United States and the UK, and the amount of money in the economy increased, pay again was believed to be the main motivator. The introduction of private sector business methods into the public sector demonstrated this thinking. However, many of the approaches copied by public sector managers, believing them to be examples of good practice and the right way to tackle the new problems they were facing, were in fact techniques that had been replaced in the more forward-looking organizations. The most controversial of these was performance-related and merit pay. Dainty (1987) asked, 'Is progress over?' when he summarized the main areas of research. He concluded that little had been done to establish the results of the earlier experiments into motivation and job satisfaction as everyday practices.

This lack of progress, the return to the belief in the 'rational economic man' and functional specialism, can be seen in the way job design was described at the time. For example Armstrong (2001) describes the process as 'deciding on the contents of a job, its duties and responsibilities and the relationships that exist between the job holder and his/her superiors, subordinates and colleagues'. Torrington and Hall (1995) describe it as 'the specification of the contents, methods and relationships of jobs in order to satisfy technological and organizational requirements as well as the social and personal requirements of the job holder'. Both definitions implied a top-down focus based on the division of labour into functional component parts.

Similar thinking informed the approach employed then by the National Council for Vocational Qualifications to identify occupational competency statements. Functional analysis was the method used to identify the key purpose of each occupational role and to break it down into units and component elements. This approach was much criticized for being reductionist and atomistic, and failing to portray the job as a holistic entity. An individual may be seen as competent across all the elements yet be unable to perform the job competently. On the other hand, this approach has helped some organizations to think more carefully about the ways in which tasks are gathered together to make up jobs that have a meaning and provide satisfaction for the post-holder.

Kakabadse, Ludlow and Vinnicombe (1987) said:

> There are two main approaches [to work design]: scientific management and the job characteristics model. Under the principles of scientific management, it is considered that work can be broken down into manageable tasks . . . In the job characteristics model . . . the person needs to have knowledge of his results and the person needs to feel the responsibility for the results of his work, so that he is aware of his accountability for work outcomes . . . By combining the key elements of needs, incentives and expectancy theory, it is possible to develop strategies for increasing the levels of motivation of individuals.

The relationship between these key elements is even more complex than suggested, and rather than simply combining them, the content of the work and the way it is divided between workers should be viewed as being interactive processes, as each affects the other in ways that make it sometimes difficult for the post-holder to separate out which are the most and less important factors.

The design of jobs should take a broad approach so that the tasks to be done can be linked to the person required to perform them.

ALTERNATIVES TO TRADITIONAL JOB DESIGN

The recession of the early 1990s saw the removal of trade unions as buffers against bad employment practices and the return of weak management. Periods of unemployment were not uncommon, even for professionals and managers, and the increased availability of performance-linked rewards meant that people were no longer prepared to be treated as units of production. However, the fragility of the use of money and pay-related benefits alone as motivators was demonstrated when it was found that high salaries did not always result in excellent performance. Since then, many employers have tried to move away from traditional bureaucratic methods and rigid hierarchies based on expertise and longevity. In addition the expectations of the workforce have changed as the levels of unemployment have declined.

The world of work, at the beginning of the 21st century, is a very different place from that of 10 years ago. The trend in organizations is towards flatter structures, decentralization of decision making to the lowest levels in the hierarchy, the increased employment of professional or knowledge workers, and the wish to involve staff in their work. Change is normal. All of these factors require jobs to be designed in different ways.

The economic uncertainty of the 1990s led to a stressful culture of long working hours and the prospect of unemployment. This led workers to accept that any one job would not last for life. There has therefore been a change in the expectations of employees. There are reports of skill shortages, and as a result, job seekers are better able to negotiate a reward package comprising elements additional to salary. These can include the opportunity to develop skills, increase the individual's employability and transferability, and ways of improving job satisfaction. Disjointed career paths are no longer feared – they are sought by some, tired of corporate existence. Charles Handy (1989 and 1994) had accurately predicted the types of job that are now reported. Workers and managers alike now seek the opportunities to apply their intelligence and develop their skills and abilities. The way jobs are designed can facilitate growth or inhibit it.

There are other factors to be considered in addition to the mere design of a job. Work–life balance is of increasing importance as employees tire of the long hours culture and employers, because of well-publicized cases, are held responsible for reducing unnecessary stresses. Labour shortages and low levels of unemployment meant that those with marketable skills are in demand. Recruitment and the retention of experienced and skilled employees are very real concerns for some organizations, and as some employers and sectors report that staff shortages are inhibiting growth, there are some very real economic drivers for the creation of work environments that are attractive, safe and conducive to success.

The traditional approaches to the design of work, as indicated above, were based on assumed factors of motivation and job satisfaction. Because of the different conditions of the 1980s and early 1990s, they were seen as providing normative theories rather than practical guidance. The methods used to encourage higher levels of performance included payment by results, fear of job loss, blame and bullying. High levels of unemployment meant that employers did not have to tempt staff by inducements. A job that paid a wage for many occupations was, in parts of the country, attraction enough. This meant that very little progress was made in finding ways of improving the quality of working conditions or gaining greater insight into what encourages people to work harder and maintain high standards of performance.

Undoubtedly for some, pay is a main source of motivation. The experiences of the last decade have proved that money does work as a motivator in some sectors. Attitudes have altered, and receiving a pay packet is seen as the main reason for going to work. In some parts of the country, where unemployment levels are very low, low-paying jobs remain unfilled. Moreover, low pay levels are seen as a reason that some employers, particularly in the public sector, find it difficult to recruit and retain staff. Nevertheless, there have been reports of the problems created by performance related pay, for example in Bevan and Thompson (1992). These include the damage done to team working, misfocused effort and gender inequalities. As Armstrong (2001) said, 'It is a bad mistake to believe that money by itself will result in sustained motivation . . . People react in widely different ways to any form of motivation. The assumption that money in the form of PRP [performance related pay] will motivate all people equally is untenable. And it is this belief that has led governments, as well as managements, in the direction of making the naive and unjustifiable assumption that PRP by itself can act as a lever for change and can make a major impact on performance.'

Scientific management returned briefly during the 1980s and 1990s, but the economic upturn in the new century brought new insight: other factors as well as money can be motivational. There is now growing interest in finding other ways of motivating staff and dealing with the motivational issues. This can be seen in the way the National Health Service, perhaps the employer most hard-hit by recruitment and retention problems, has placed 'improving working lives' at the heart of its human resource strategy. The source of some of the actions included in the plans can be seen to be rooted in the work of Maslow, Hertzberg, Hackman and Oldham and others. Although these have been the subject of valid criticism, they still offer some ideas for what managers can do practically to create a working environment that motives staff, provides job satisfaction and results in high levels of performance.

The change in thinking is clearly illustrated in Armstrong (2001), which provides a new definition – 'job and role design – deciding on the content and accountabilities of jobs or roles in order to maximize intrinsic motivation and job satisfaction'. This suggests links between:

■   the way the work is divided;

■   what motivates the individual;

■   the sources of job satisfaction;

■   required performance levels;

■   the broader role to be occupied in the organization.

The relationships between these factors cannot be portrayed in simple straight-line terms. People are not rational creatures behaving according to predictions. They differ and behave unpredictably, even when conditions are static. In times of change and turbulence, human behaviour can be either totally predictable or random and irrational. As conditions of constant change are endemic to most people's working lives, the traditional models of work design now need to be refined into more sophisticated models, combining all the elements known to affect people's attitudes to their work and employer.

The relationship between work, motivational factors and the individual is complex.

JOBS OR ROLES

'Jobs' tend to be collections of tasks drawn together for completion by a person employed for that reason. The tasks are fixed and the ways of doing them prescribed. Changes to the list of tasks are only achieved after a formal process. However, for many organizations, this approach is too rigid and inflexible. The world of work is no longer that simple. Change is real and normal. Employers need to be dynamic to survive, and individuals have to be flexible if they are to remain employable.

The word 'role' is increasingly being used in organizations instead of 'job'. A role is different in that it is used to describe the part the individual is expected to play in the organization. It is a more fluid concept as individuals have greater capacity to shape their roles and determine the level of contribution made to the achievement of the organization's goals. This can be more than just the level of performance and standard of competency; it includes the part the individual plays in the wider life of the organization. A role profile (rather than a job description) outlines what the role-holder is expected (or agrees) to achieve. These may evolve with time and change as the needs of the employer alter. Role-holders have greater capacity to influence and scope to develop their interests and skills.

A job is a collection of tasks to be done. A role defines the part an individual plays in achieving the organization's goals.

Regardless of which term is appropriate, the design of both is constrained by a number of factors. Figure 1.3 shows how a more holistic approach to the definition of jobs or outline of roles can be taken. The separate elements of the factors are intertwined and so should not be seen in isolation from each other. Rather they interact and influence each other, contributing iteratively to:

▌ the overall quality of the individual's working life;

▌ the achievability of the job or role's purpose;

▌ the achievement of the individual's expectations;

▌ the contribution to the organization's performance.

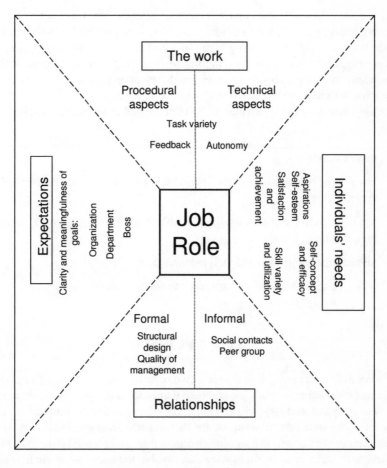

Figure 1.3 *A holistic approach to jobs and roles*

EXPECTATIONS

The clarity and meaningfulness of the goals of the organization, the section in which the post-holder is to be located, the boss's requirements, and the definition of the job are fundamental to effective performance. If the reasons for doing the job are unclear, the chances of the post-holder achieving the desired result, obtaining a sense of a job well done or achieving any personal satisfaction are slim. The first questions to be answered when designing a job are:

■ **why** the job or role is being set up;

■ **what** is it intended to achieve;

■ **how** it contributes to the achievement of the organization's goals.

All too often, in reality the approach taken is different. The tasks to be carried out are bundled together into a 'job'. Someone is appointed to do them with little if any consideration being given to whether these tasks fit together. In larger organizations, it can be tempting to create a hierarchy to control the operations and employees. A more design-driven approach would be to examine what activities are needed to achieve the organization's overall goals, then work out how they can be divided and grouped together so that each individual role:

■ makes sense;

■ has a purpose and makes a contribution that has an obvious meaning to the organization;

■ requires complementary skills to enable it to be occupied by a flawed human being;

■ gives scope for growth and skill enhancement;

■ will give the holder satisfaction and a sense of achievement.

THE WORK

It is possible to break a job or role into two separate but complementary parts. The **technical aspects** of any job are those that concern the tools and techniques used to carry out the tasks, which require knowledge and skills for their effective use. The **procedural aspects** are the internal arrangements used by a particular organization, such as administrative rules and internal processes. For example the task of decision making can involve the use of tools such as the Delphi technique or decision trees. The skills needed to use these would be common regardless of the organization in which the individual was employed. The procedural aspects, however, would require knowledge of the organization's committee structures, and to whom responsibility for making a particular decision was delegated.

The ways in which these two aspects interact and combine affect how the job is carried out, and limit the contribution a role-holder is able to make to the organization. Over-routinized jobs or separation of the tasks from the results obscure the way in which the work can be performed, for it is without any context. Lack of meaning can lead eventually to either misdirection of effort or learnt incapacity.

Learnt incapacity occurs when an employee finds the minimum level of performance that is acceptable. It is often found when the results of effort or lack of effect are not clear, and the employee is able to say, 'Not my responsibility'. This can be avoided by ensuring that each job or role is designed to include areas of work linked to some direct output, and that each employee has a valid and meaningful part to play in its achievement. This is now known as single point responsibility. Accountability clearly attributed also makes the provision of feedback more straightforward.

Feedback is essential if individual employees are to assess the value of their contributions in relation to each other and the achievement of overall goals. It is also a valuable source of information to aid an individual's development. We will discuss the importance of feedback again, as the provision of helpful information at the end of a selection process can be a benefit given back to candidates.

All the components built into a job, or combined in a role, will have a direct effect on the ability and willingness of the individual to perform it to the desired standard. However performance at work is not found in isolation. The context and conditions under which the individual is required to work also have some impact, as do the relationships developed during the working day.

RELATIONSHIPS

As described above, a number of theories on motivation and job satisfaction emphasize the importance of the relationship between the post-holder and other people who are significant. Those who are significant can include peers, managers and subordinates, people in other parts of the organization, and even those who work for other organizations with whom the individual's employer has a relationship. These other people and their expectations can influence the way in which individuals carry out their work. People are also influenced by the culture of the work group, its norms, accepted standards, and the informal groupings and friendships that grow up between group members.

The nature and extent of formal relationships are set out by the structures and reporting lines – up, down and across the organization. The way in which information flows, the systems used and the quality of communication channels affect individuals' perceptions, understanding of organizational goals and availability of feedback, and have direct impact on individual achievement.

Individual needs

Maslow's hierarchy of needs acknowledges the importance of monetary rewards. Hertzberg argued that if the salary was wrong, it would demotivate; if it were right it would maintain performance levels, but not increase them. Expectancy theory confirms this by suggesting the available rewards must be in a 'currency' that the individual values. If this be money, so be it. The increase in consumerism and the advent of performance-related rewards have focused employees' attention more on the value and worth of their pay packet. Even so, pay is known to be only one source of motivation and incentive. The quality of the working environment, how people are treated, and a complex range of benefits are also regarded as being important. People include many interrelated factors when they describe 'a rewarding job'.

The variety of skills needed to perform a job can add to its intrinsic interest. Dividing work into a series of simple routines, as recommended by scientific management, was seen as a way of increasing productivity, not job satisfaction. It soon became clear that as workers became bored, the levels of productive declined and the chances of mistakes increased. Human beings are not robots. Boredom was therefore counteracted on assembly lines by varying tasks, thus enabling the range of skills needed to be extended. The reasoning behind this approach was that an individual wants some variation as well as the opportunity to make use of any existing skills.

If the work to be done requires a limited range of skills, there is a chance of the worker becoming bored.

However, any one individual's range of talents is inevitably limited. Expecting one person to operate across too wide a range of skills is unreasonable. It will likely result in failure in some areas and will be demotivating.

Individuals need to be able to see a link between the amount of effort they are expected to make and the chances of achieving the agreed objectives and outcomes. They also need to believe that the rewards will be distributed equitably between themselves and others in the organization. Most people can tolerate an unequal distribution if they can understand the reasons for it. However, they do not find it easy to accept the situation where those making lower levels of contribution achieve higher rewards. Perceived unfairness has an influence on individuals' perceptions of their own abilities and sense of self-esteem. They will not make an effort or see themselves in a good light if the results of their hard work and application of skills and knowledge are not recognized or recognizable.

The term 'self-efficacy' means the sense of power and influence individuals believe they have over their own destiny. The loss of self-efficacy leads to a sense of hopelessness. Someone suffering from low self-efficacy can appear to be lethargic and low in energy. The quality of work and levels of performance tend also to be low, and the individuals' sense of achievement, or even belief in their own ability to achieve, is absent.

There have been many studies now on the causes of stress at work. One causal factor often identified is the amount of control individuals feel they have over their work. This can include the amount of work, the speed at which they are expected to complete tasks, and their ability to affect the factors that are likely to influence its successful outcome. It is possible to design a job or role in a way that gives an individual control or in a way that removes it – by, for example, requiring too wide a range of skills or breaking up tasks in such a way that no one individual is responsible for achieving a successful outcome.

The individual's aspirations and the reality of the job should also have some harmony. While objectives should be stretching, if they are too high their very inaccessibility can be demotivating. Similarly, if they do not fit with the hopes and desires individuals hold for their future, this mismatch can lead to a loss of interest and drive. Having to work hard at tasks that are not taking you where you want to be hardly encourages you to get out of bed in the morning. But the chance to work in a way that is clearly leading in the direction you want to go, and provides you with opportunities to develop your skills, as well as the rewards you seek, adds up to a dream job.

If all these factors are remembered when a job or role is being set up or redefined, the result will be based on firm foundations, and will lead naturally into the formal description of purpose and responsibilities. The checklist in Table 1.2 is given to help ensure that these have been considered.

JOB DESCRIPTIONS

The Trade Union Reform and Employment Rights Act 1993 requires that every employee shall have, after two months of continuous employment, a statement that includes the title of the job which the employee is employed to do or a brief description of the work for which the employee is employed. The inclusion of a job description with a contract of employment shows that the job description is intended to be a contractual arrangement. What should that description include and what should it look like?

Taylor (2002) says, 'Job descriptions are one of the best-established institutions in the personnel and development field. As a result, a consensus has grown up about what they should include and the level of detail that should be used. They thus vary surprisingly little from one organization to another in terms of style and coverage.' They provide basic information about the job under the

Table 1.2 *Checklist for job or role design*

Purpose	*Examples/comments*
Is the purpose of the job or role clearly and unequivocally expressed?	To be responsible for the efficient organization and the effective operation of a client-centred service.
Is its contribution to the organization's objectives evident?	Key tasks: ▐ to contribute to the organization's management by being a full and active member of the executive team; ▐ to ensure the department's operations and expenditure are in accordance with business plans; ▐ to plan, enable and evaluate the personal and professional development of the department's staff.
Is the job or role's contribution to the work of the department obvious?	Words such as 'liaise, facilitate, provide for' are vague enough to enable the point of responsibility to be obscured.
Is the post-holder responsible for the successful completion of the whole job?	Can all members of the team recognize their individual and unique contributions or do their efforts vanish into the whole?
Do the internal systems help the post-holder perform to the level required?	An administrative systems designed years ago to satisfy a superseded need can prevent the now needed responsive and flexible approach to customer service.
Skill range Is there a reasonable but not too extensive range of tasks?	A job or role that requires highly developed interpersonal skills as well as large amounts of detail and high levels of accuracy needs an extraordinary individual.

Table 1.2 *(Contd.)*

Purpose	*Examples/comments*
Do the opportunities exist for the post-holder to use the knowledge and skills associated with effective performance of the job?	Over-recruiting well-qualified trainees for dead end jobs leads to frustration and high turnover. If the recruits cannot leave, rebellion is likely to brew. Similarly, people without the underpinning knowledge or required skills may underperform because organizational expectations are unrealistically high.
Can individuals make full use of their skills and develop their skill base?	If the best qualified, most experienced applicant was appointed – someone who could hit the ground running – how long will it be before he or she runs off?

Relationships

Are the formal relationships clearly specified and related to the achievement of the objectives?	Normally up-down reporting relationships are outlined in job descriptions. Specifying the relationships with significant others and the nature of the relationship can be helpful. This is especially important in matrix organizations when roles have cross-organizational or departmental responsibilities.
Is there opportunity to develop working relationships within and across the department's boundaries?	Myopia and parochialism are two of the most serious chronic illnesses found in large organizations. Secondments, cross-working and shared projects can be designed into jobs, as can opportunities for involvement in training and development and policy development.
Are colleagues available with whom the post-holder can discuss professional issues?	Professional debate and discussion are valuable ways of developing skills and extending thinking.

Table 1.2 *(Contd.)*

Purpose	*Examples/comments*
	Specialist posts can be isolated and insulated. Building in developmental duties can help ensure that 'professional stagnation' does not creep up on the post-holder.

Job outcomes

Purpose	*Examples/comments*
Can post-holders see the results of their efforts?	Jobs in supporting roles such as an office junior or secretary often have no direct output of their own; most of the employee's efforts contribute to the achievement of others. Everyone likes to have their effort acknowledged.
Can the results of the post-holder's efforts be recognized?	Has the job been divided laterally or horizontally? For example a receptionist may take in customer complaints and pass them on to the 'right' department for a response. Alternatively the receptionist may be responsible for receiving and replying to complaints.
Do post-holders have the opportunity to influence their own levels of performance and achievement of the objectives?	Setting a salesperson taxing targets which result in high levels of pay for the individual and high sales levels for the company is fine for everyone, providing the salesperson can ensure that production, delivery and invoicing deadlines are met.

Rewards

Purpose	*Examples/comments*
Are the rewards appropriate and obtainable?	If the reward for hard work is even more difficult and complex work, is the individual likely to work hard? If the performance-related element of pay is 10% and the individual needs to work 50%

Table 1.2 *(Contd.)*

Purpose	Examples/comments
	harder than his or her colleagues to obtain it, is he or she likely to work harder than the others?
Are the rewards linked directly to the performance of the post-holder?	If it is not clear what needs to be done to gain promotion, how can individuals develop the skills needed, and how motivated will they be to try to get promoted?

headings of the job title, reporting relationships, overall purpose and principal accountabilities, and tasks or duties.

Despite the common coverage, a huge range of possible formats – from a brief paragraph to a lengthy document outlining every possible task a post-holder could be ever be expected to perform – can be found. The latter tends to be most common in larger organizations based on bureaucratic principles. (A bureaucracy is an organization with a tightly structured hierarchy, staffed by trained experts, with clearly defined functions, roles and relationships, and reliant on written records.) Job descriptions of this type have the advantage of being comprehensive. Typically they are to be compiled from the results of a thorough analysis of the job. This is also a source of strength. As they can be highly prescriptive they can have a tendency towards rigidity. They are enduring and so can withstand the passage of time. Therefore, they are better suited to organizations operating in stable conditions. They also can aid other personnel functions in addition to recruitment and selection, such as grading, and can contribute to the assessment of performance.

Their precision can be their weakness. They tend not to accommodate change. Slow evolution can be dealt with – the job description can be modified by subtraction and addition. However rapid, radical change is more difficult. The inflexibility of such job descriptions cannot respond to situations that require responses different from 'more or less than'. The most usual response when different tasks and objectives have to be taken on is the preparation of new job descriptions. This need to produce new job descriptions can create other difficulties, such as conflict with post-holders, and add another load to managers in addition to those already caused by the changing situation.

The use of too prescriptive job descriptions can lead to other problems. These can include demarcation disputes characterized by statements such as, 'It's not in my job description', or It's not my responsibility'. Other common responses to changes to the job description include:

▌   the request for a review of the pay grade;

▌   lengthy disputes about the detailed wording of alterations;

▌   demands for precise indications defining the meaning of the new clauses.

A job description usually provides a statement outlining the key contribution the job will make to the organization's goals. It is also common to find a specification of reporting lines and relationships. This is followed by a summary of main tasks or key objectives. Written in the active case, the tasks or objectives will assess performance and assign accountability. They can also indicate the relative importance of the different areas of work. An example is given in Figure 1.4.

Writing a job description

In the example shown as Figure 1.4, the main duties are not listed; rather the contents are grouped together in clusters. This enables areas of work that are related in practice to be drawn together to demonstrate their relationships. Other methods of ordering the contents can include listing in priority or sequential order, or reflecting the frequency of each task.

Often the post is named before the job description is drawn up. It can be argued that this should be done at the end. Once the purpose and main areas of responsibility have been defined and the relationships made clear, the label attached to the post should be obvious. Giving the job a name too early can tempt the definer to fit the purpose and main duties to the title. Really the title should be a simple indication of what the job is about. Long hierarchies in many-layered organizations can lead to some lovely names that tell the uninitiated absolutely nothing. What does a senior principal assistant do? Who is assisted, who is junior and if there is a principal, are there secondaries?

The purpose of producing a job description is not to catalogue every possible task or routine a post-holder may be required to perform. It is to create a working description of the job the post-holder will occupy. It should be useful for the post-holder and help him or her understand what is expected. It should also help the manager and others in the organization decide whether the post-holder's performance is to the standard agreed. While it should be an accurate representation of the job, it should also be flexible enough to adjust to the most likely changes to be encountered. This does not mean it should be a catch-all. Nor can it be expected to last forever. There will be times when a job description becomes outdated and therefore should be discarded.

At one time it was advised that the phrase 'and any other duties that may be assigned or agreed' be included in a job description. The current thinking is to make sure that the contents realistically represent the job to be done in its entirety, but not to attempt to list every eventuality. Providing the description is accurate (that is, it is produced from analysis and design), realistic and contains

Job title: Works Manager
Responsible to   Managing Director
Responsible for Senior Engineers
                 Works Supervisors

Purpose

To agree and implement an operational plan for the XYZ Works which ensures efficient, effective and safe production and develops working methods and the skills of staff.

Main duties

1. Planning:
   a) Propose and agree operational plans designed to achieve XYZ's business plan.
   b) Monitor the implementation of the plan to ensure that necessary action can be taken and future plans adjusted as necessary.
   c) Assess the reaction of customers and ensure that their feedback is used for planning and modification of current operations.
2. Operations:
   a) Implement the plan as agreed.
   b) Monitor and adjust operations to ensure that working methods remain efficient and effective.
   c) Ensure compliance with Health and Safety legislation and that safety procedures are followed.
   d) Monitor the implementation of the plans and achievement of agreed objectives.
   e) Take remedial action as required to ensure that operations remain effective.
3. Development:
   a) Review working methods and organization continuously.
   b) Instigate changes within the scope of the Operational Plan.
   c) Negotiate other changes as needed.
   b) Facilitate the participation of the workforce in review mechanisms.
4. Staff:
   a) Instigate and operate an appraisal system to review the performance of all staff.
   b) Agree personal objectives and review performance of engineers and supervisors.
   c) Agree, implement and evaluate development plans for all staff.
   d) Establish communication systems which ensure that staff are kept fully up to date and allow them to participate appropriately in decision making.
5. Self-management:
   a) Prioritize and manage own workload.
   b) Engage in personal and professional development.
   c) Review own performance and participate in appraisal activities.
   d) Contribute as part of the senior management team to the overall management of the XYZ Company.

Figure 1.4 *Sample job description*

scope for change, there should be no need to try to be all-inclusive. A job description is just that – not a prescription.

Role outlines

The more modern approach is to use a role outline to specify the purpose of the role and the part the holder will play in the organization. This can be in the form of a brief paragraph which summarizes the purpose of the role and indicates, broadly, the main areas of responsibility. This is an example:

> Works Manager will be responsible for the day to day management of the Engineering Works of XYZ Company, its efficient, effective and safe operation and the management of the staff. The post-holder will be expected to be part of the company's management team and implement the planning, operational and personnel policies and practices, as agreed.

The strength of this approach is the flexibility born from ambiguity. The meaning of the outline can be negotiated and renegotiated when needs be. This can be ongoing, should the circumstances warrant change.

However ambiguity has the potential for dispute. Many senior executives have parted company with their employing organization because of different interpretations of role, and the meaning of degrees of responsibility and account-ability in practice. It is possible to combine the precision of the traditional approach and the thumbnail sketch into a profile of the role that outlines its purpose and states its key areas of responsibility in terms of what is to be achieved.

Role profiles

The middle way between the detailed job description and the brief role outline is the role profile. This approach provides the means of summarizing the purpose of the role, its contribution to the organizational objectives and the main areas of accountability. These accountabilities can take the form of targets, objectives or areas of responsibility. They should focus on what is to be the result of the role-holder's activities. See Figure 1.5.

While these accountabilities are broad, they contain measurable standards and reflect the values of the organization. Increasingly this approach is accom-panied by a specification of the competencies the role-holder will need to possess or develop to be effective and remain so. A competency is defined by Boyzatis (1982) as 'an underlying characteristic of a person which results in effective and superior performance in a job'. More simply, it is a standard of behaviour. A competency framework is therefore a collection of behaviours that, in the context of the organization, are required for effective performance and achievement. The framework can be applied flexibly to a number of roles

---

Role profile: Call Centre Team Leader

Purpose: To ensure that all team members achieve their objectives and provide the highest standard of customer care at all times.

Key accountabilities

1   To agree objectives and regularly review performance with team members.
2   To recruit, develop, motivate and retain competent team members.
3   To deal with causes of concern promptly, within company policy.
4   To work with other team leaders to obtain feedback from customers, monitor their levels of satisfaction and develop ways of improving standards within cost constraints.

Figure 1.5 *Sample role profile*

in the organization, as they will be relevant to many if not all. Thus for the role in Figure 1.5 the following competencies will be needed:

Communication
Able to communicate clearly and concisely orally and in writing, taking account of the needs of the recipient.
Leadership
Agree task objectives, distribute work equitably to members of the team, taking account of their abilities, and help them focus their efforts on the achievement of the team objectives.
Be able to work as a member of a team as well as a team leader.
Service
Initiate contact with customers to explore their needs and adapt the level of service, within agreed limits, to achieve high levels of satisfaction.
Explore trends and patterns to anticipate areas where changes to services will be required to maintain standards of customer satisfaction.
Decision making
Investigate and take steps to resolve problems affecting the work of the team.
Work with other team leaders to propose practical solutions to difficulties impeding the work of the call centre.
Recognize areas of potential or future difficulty and contribute to the development of solutions to avoid problems or secure improvements.

All of the above can be assessed on the basis of evidence, and developed if needed, as they can be used to inform the role-holder of the actions expected of him or her. This approach can be contrasted to the more traditional employee specification often used alongside a job description.

EMPLOYEE SPECIFICATION

Once the job description has been drafted, work can start on the compilation of an employee specification. There are several ways of doing this, each as good as the other. Torrington and Hall (1995) say that an employee (or person) specification is 'a statement, derived from the job analysis process and the job description, of the characteristics that an individual would need to possess in order to fulfil the requirements of a job'. The use of the word 'characteristics' presents the first of many issues encountered during the production of a specification.

Many employers use a common formula such as the Rodger's seven point plan to write a specification. The main attraction of a pro forma is that it provides a checklist to ensure that the features deemed essential for the ideal post-holder are included. This makes it easy to complete, possibly with thought being given to what is meant by each component. It can be very easy to include the characteristics of the last post-holder; describe, as a stereotype, the dream person; or replicate, as a clone, an idealized image of previous successful employees.

Contents

A good specification does what is says – it contains statements specifying what the job- or role-holder will need to do, adequately and competently, to succeed. It should not be a historic document, looking back at past requirements. Drawing up a specification or competency framework presents the chance to look into the future to predict:

▮ what characteristics will be required;

▮ which areas are likely to present difficulty;

▮ what critical work tasks will need to be completed.

This approach will enable the analysis of requirements to be grounded in the real challenges facing the person appointed to the job or role, and take account of the organization's context. It should result in a document that will be flexible enough to allow for change and development.

Various questions can help the compiler think critically about the features needed for the achievement of the job, or the role's purpose. These include:

▮ What will lead me to say, in a year's time, whether the person appointed has been successful or unsuccessful in post?

▮ What will the person be doing to make me think the appointment was the right decision?

▊   Which problems, if resolved, will make the most impact on the organization?

▊   What skills and background will be needed to tackle these problems?

The first two will elicit the critical measures in behavioural terms, and the last two the possible critical incidents and skills required to resolve them.

The specification, while looking forward, needs to be reasonable, for there can be a danger (and this is a particular vulnerability of competency frameworks) of describing a superperson – some one who is perfect in every respect and performs to the utmost of expectations – or even a superhuman – someone having skills and abilities over and above what is normally found in any one person.

For example it would be unrealistic to expect an individual to have a higher degree, substantial work experience and be aged under 30. This can also be seen in descriptions of the types of work experience, range of skills and aptitudes required. For example a person inclined to work alone, on detailed tasks that require close attention and thoroughness, is unlikely to be good at teamwork. Similarly it is not easy for an individual to gain experience in both the public and private sectors, or in manufacturing as well as financial services and retailing. This may be nothing to do with the person's abilities and employability; more to do with opportunities and the prejudices of employers in the different sectors.

Table 1.3 gives some questions that can be used when compiling a specification.

Even when a realistic and reasonable specification has been compiled, finding the person who matches every part perfectly is highly unlikely. The recruitment and selection process can only hope to result in the best fit. The ultimate match may require some adjustments on both sides. Some organizations do this by deciding which features are essential, and so must be matched, and which are desirable. The latter can either be done without, or obtained in other ways, such as the development of the person appointed.

Language

Language is the vehicle used to convey images and encode value systems. We will return to this topic again, for the way in which language is used during the recruitment and selection process can lead to indirect discrimination.

Great care is needed at the outset of the process, particularly with the language used in the specification. This is an outline of behaviours, attainments and aptitudes needed by the person being sought and should not be based on stereotypes. These are examples of characteristics taken to represent all members of a particular group. For example a common stereotype of a manager is of someone who sits at a desk and spends all his or her time making decisions. Stereotypes extend to appearance, behaviour and psychological makeup, and lead to assumptions about background, intelligence and likely responses.

Table 1.3 *Considerations when compiling a specification*

Attainment	What has the individual obtained to evidence his or her cognitive abilities and level of knowledge (or know-how)? What educational requirements and specialist knowledge are *really* needed for successful completion of the task? It can be easy to use educational qualifications as indicators. Doing this can exclude those who did not have the opportunity to sit exams, yet have acquired sufficient levels of know-how in different ways.
Achievement	What roles should have been occupied or tasks completed to indicate the post-holder is adequately prepared for the role or job? These can be gained in and out of work.
Abilities These can be learnt and developed from experience, feedback and practice.	What skills need to be evident (or latent) for the competent performance of the tasks?
Aptitudes A personal inclination or preference such as being a team worker, a self-starter, an innovator or able to pay attention to detail.	Where will the post-holder's strengths lie? What particular talents will he or she need to possess? These can be evidenced from out of work interests but should be relevant to the area of work.

Biases

Some interesting work has been done into how gender and other biases can be built unwittingly into specifications and competency frameworks. These will also be discussed again. Suffice it to say here that the specification and framework should be focused on the behaviours, skills and knowledge required to do the job or occupy the role, rather than on personality traits. If this is remembered, the chance of including unjustifiable features will be reduced.

The use of behavioural language helps to avoid stereotypes, assumptions and unrelated values. Questions such as those in Table 1.3 help to make explicit what could otherwise be waffly, imprecise terms. The specification should indicate what is expected of the successful post-holder in terms of:

∎   attainments;

∎   achievements that can be evidenced;

∎   abilities (skills that can be learnt);

∎   aptitudes (or inclinations) relevant to the job, role and organization.

The specification should not merely describe the individual who will be the best on the day. It should look to the future, and so be the basis for the longer-term development of the person appointed. It should also establish the criteria for assessing subsequent performance.

SUMMARY

This chapter has examined job design and suggests that the principles found in scientific management, the human relations school and needs theories should be combined to take a different and holistic approach more suitable for the expectations of people working in the 21st century. The importance of integrating a number of factors with the demands of the role or job is to ensure that:

∎   the job is constructed in relation to organizational need;

∎   the expectations of the post-holder and the organization are explicit and understood;

∎   the formal and informal working relationships are acknowledged;

∎   the skills needed for effective performance are complementary;

∎   the job or role provides for the needs and growth of the individual.

Only when the design work has been completed should the purpose, main duties, responsibilities or accountabilities required of the occupant be described. The format used should aim at creating a flexible working tool that will endure and guide the occupant and his or her manager, and form the basis for the person specification.

Drawing up the employee specification or competency framework provides the opportunity to challenge stereotypes and historic biases. This will go towards enabling the post to be filled by someone able to develop and meet the challenges of the future as well as perform to the standard required now. The job description (or the role profile and competency framework) contains the information needed to start the recruitment phase of the process. Chapter 2 will describe the various ways these documents can be used to inform the decisions made at the short-listing and later selection stages.

2

Attracting the right person

Displaying an advertisement in a suitable place is generally seen as being the main way to attract applicants for a vacant post. The appropriate place could be a Job Centre, a newspaper or trade journal, a local shop or a board outside the head office building. Recruitment advertising is big business, which is governed by legislation and represents a major source of income to the media. Recruitment agencies are also governed by statute, have a professional code of practice and can be fiercely competitive.

Sometimes the existence of a vacancy is publicized by asking existing staff if they know of anyone, or requesting them to tell their friends and family about it. Even though word of mouth advertising has been strongly condemned as being discriminatory since the Sex Discrimination Act 1974, it is known to continue. The Labour Force Survey carried out quarterly by the government shows that in 2001 more than half of all employees obtained a job by hearing from someone who had worked with the company or replying to an advertisement. A more detailed breakdown is given in Table 2.1.

The different approaches adopted by men and women are interesting, and suggest that women prefer to use more formal channels. Difference due to gender, however, should not be allowed to influence choice of media. Good

Table 2.1 *How individuals obtained their last jobs 2001*

Method	Men (%)	Women (%)
Hearing from someone who worked there	30	25
Replying to advertisement	25	31
Direct application	14	17
Private employment agency or business	10	10
Jobcentre	9	8
Other	12	9

practice, as well as equal opportunities legislation, suggests that open advertisement in as many media as is feasible is the best way to attract a broad range of candidates. Fishing in a small pool may sometimes seem attractive, as it can reduce the number of applicants, but it can also serve to reduce the pool of talent. We will return to this point later.

The recessions and expansions of the last 10 years have fundamentally changed the labour market. Some organizations, fearful of their future, learnt how to hedge their bets by using short-term contracts. This approach is now subject to new regulation, and the flexibility it gave previously has been reduced, as staff employed on fixed-term contracts acquire the same rights as permanent employees.

High levels of unemployment allow some employers to take the 'take it or leave it' attitude to terms and conditions and the quality of employees' working life. Low levels of unemployment mean that this approach will not suffice, as employees soon learn to move to employers who value their contributions.

In addition, changes to the demographic structure of the workforce has affected the labour market. Organizations shed staff through redundancy and early retirement to save money and reduce costs. Come the upturn in the economy they found themselves without the experience and knowledge needed. They also found that competition for the people remaining in the labour market was greater than before. It has been known for a long time that the numbers of people economically active would reduce as the Baby Boomer generation approached retirement and the low birth rates of the decades following the 1960s failed to replace those leaving the labour market. Redundancy and early retirement speeded up their departure.

The economic fortunes of different parts of the country have varied considerably. Some parts, for example the Thames Valley, have blossomed while others, such as the North East, continue to see deprivation and economic slowdown. This means that where they continue to exist, the skills, experience and people sought by employers can be in the wrong place with the wrong profile. Thus there can be groups of workers whose skills used to be highly valued but who are not able to find employers who want them, yet at the same time, there can be employers desperate to find those very same or similar skills, but 200 miles away.

It is well known that British employees spend more time at work than their European counterparts. The long hours culture has become a normal feature of working life in the UK, as has change and stress. The pace of change has increased dramatically, to such an extent to find someone not experiencing reorganizations at work is rare – change is normal. This means that levels of uncertainty are high and in some organizations, even though the skill shortages are well known, there is a level of job insecurity amongst the workforce. All of this leads to stress. The discussions about work–life balance are not just the latest fad. They are about a very real concern as the levels of production, quality of work and the health and safety of employees can be seriously and adversely affected if a sensible balance is not achieved.

All the changes in the labour market are leading to a switch in the balance of power. While employers can offer employment, the people whose skills are in demand are able to say 'No' to offers of employment. They are clearer about their expectations and requirements from a job and an employer, and they are aware that the final step is not the offer of an appointment, but the decision to accept.

Skill shortages have switched the balance of power more towards the employee and away from the employer.

As a result of these changes, the traditional approaches to recruitment need to be reviewed and their effectiveness assessed against different criteria. Increasingly, from the job seekers' point of view, what is being advertised is more than a job with a salary attached. It forms a considerable part of their waking life – they want rewards in addition to money. They seek interesting work, good colleagues, respect from their bosses, career development opportunities and all the other things we discussed in Chapter 1.

The way in which the job (or role) is advertised and where it is placed need to reflect these different expectations. But care is needed to ensure that what is being advertised (or sold) is an accurate representation of the job. In this respect, recruitment advertising is not different from any other form of advertising, and the same general principles apply. For example, a loosely worded newspaper advertisement can generate hundreds of applications from people attracted by what is on offer, but none pay possess the essential skills needed for effective performance. Alternatively an attractive, easy to fill post can attract only a few applications, all from individuals who are appointable. Which is the best advertisement?

If level of response is the only criterion for assessing the quality of the advertisement, the first would have been the success and the second the failure. In reality it is the other way round, for the whole recruitment process is more complex than encouraging large numbers of people. The aim is to attract the attention of the right people, and encourage them to submit an application. The first part of the chapter will examine the separate stages in the recruitment process, using some ideas drawn from marketing. These are relevant if the vacancy to be filled is seen as a product, service or other form of goods and the aim is to:

I   reach the right people at the right time;

I   interest them in what is on offer;

I   tempt them to react in an appropriate fashion (in this case submitting an application).

The second part of the chapter considers the design and operation of various recruitment methods, and gives examples of how they may be best used. The traditional approaches will be mentioned, but since these can easily be referenced in the textbooks, more attention will be given to 'other' methods such as radio, mail shots, recruitment events, targeting and the Internet.

MARKETING THE JOB

A fresh view of the employment contract is needed if the approaches commonly used in marketing are to be useful for recruitment. Employment is no longer a binding, life-long agreement in which the employer holds all the cards. When skilled and experienced employees are scarce and their talents are in demand by other employers, the master–servant relationship is an invalid concept. When employees feel able to market their skills and know that other employers will value what they are able to offer, employers are at risk of losing staff to competitors if they feel exploited and undervalued. Increasingly, too, skilled people can find other ways of earning in addition to working for someone else. Self-employment has increased, albeit gradually, and the greater provision of training and education opportunities makes career change a real option. Therefore the wise employer, especially in areas where skills are in high demand, is seeing the employment contract as a contract between two equal partners:

> I have work that needs doing and you want employment. I will pay you a reasonable amount and provide other relevant benefits. I will treat you with respect and provide opportunities for training and development and job satisfaction.
>
> You will do a fair day's work, use your skills and behave in a reasonable manner to my other employees and customers.

The applicants you want to attract

Continuing the analogy, the employee specification or competency framework can become a profile of the target audience or segment of the labour market, for these documents will need to contain descriptions of the required attainment, achievement, abilities and aptitudes, set out so they can be recognized and evidenced. Drawing up these documents needs care if the temptation of generalization is to be avoided. Generalities tend to lead to stereotypes, and unreasonable boundaries being placed around the definition of the ideal applicant. A way to avoid this danger is to consider what the person will need to be able to do or know (inputs) to achieve the desired results or standard of performance (outputs). The job description or role profile will outline the outputs. The following questions may be helpful:

■ What will the person appointed need to know to do the work satisfactorily?

∎   What skills will be used?

∎   How will that knowledge and those skills have been gained?

∎   What type of experiences will the successful applicant have had?

∎   Could these have been gained in ways other than paid employment, such as
     . . . ?

∎   What sort of work would the applicants need to prefer (such as predictable
     work that changes frequently, clearly defined tasks or ones that are ambigu-
     ous and require initiative)?

∎   What sort of working arrangements would they prefer (for example alone,
     with others, in positions of responsibility, operating routine systems,
     development opportunities)?

∎   What would they expect from a job?

∎   What sort of organization would they want to work for?

∎   Where are they and what are they doing now?

Once a profile of the desired applicant has been developed, we can start thinking about where the people in the target market segment are likely to be. This
thinking explains why some organizations advertise in parts of the country other
than where they are based. For example, a company in Leicester wanting people
with heavy engineering skills might be advised to search in South Yorkshire or
Wales. Manchester would be a good location to seek people with electronic
component experience. It is worth remembering, though, that the very people
being sought may not be looking for a job. The consequences of this will be
discussed later.

Labour market data

There are various sources of information that help a recruiter explore the labour
market more thoroughly. Most local councils carry out labour market research,
and the Department for Work and Pensions, through *Labour Market Trends* and
other sources of statistics such as those provided by NOMIS, gives information
about skills shortages and employment patterns in various regions and sectors.
The local authorities below county council level may carry out further analysis
in their own areas, and the careers services (now Connexions) will have information to help young job seekers. Job Centres or Jobcentre Plus provide a range
of services for employers. Some areas have active Chambers of Commerce
which provide support services to their members. Other areas have Business
Link offices whose staff may also be able to help with local intelligence and
knowledge.

The information gathered about the relevant labour market, like any market research information, will help the recruiter make critical decisions about how best to target the people being sought. The information, if at all possible, should be gathered from two sources and have as broad a base as is feasible. But quality of information, not quantity, should be the watchword. The aim of carrying out labour market research is to gather an accurate and up to date snapshot of the area or occupation. It is not to obtain a detailed and statistically valid analysis. The purpose of labour market information is to support the recruiter in:

█ deciding how and where to contact the people with the knowledge, skills and experience required;

█ finding out if they are available locally or whether a wider geographic boundary needs to be drawn;

█ deciding what will be needed to attract those people.

It will also inform judgements on how best to promote the employing organization. The following questions will also guide these decisions.

What do potential employees already know about the organization?

Its existing image constrains what can be said as part of a recruitment campaign. While the Fair Trading legislation does not cover recruitment advertising, only a foolish organization would try to falsify its reality to prospective employees. All that would be achieved in the long run would be high turnover and recruitment costs. Newly appointed employees find out the reality fairly quickly. If they cannot leave, they can easily become disillusioned, having a negative impact on the moral and productivity of their colleagues.

Often organizations are not aware of their real image, so they spend time and money telling the outside world what is already known. Other organizations take for granted that they and their employment benefits (such as pensions, sickness schemes, and policies such as dependent care leave) are common knowledge, and neglect to sell themselves to potential employees. We often fail to follow Robbie Burns' advice and become blind to how others see us. It may be worth finding out what the organization's public face looks like to those on the outside. Market research can help to test out how much information there is in the public domain. This will allow the recruiter to decide how much more or less information needs to be given, and what action is required to create the sort of image the organization wishes to portray.

Market research used to explore what the market already knows about the organization will help to determine what needs to be communicated. Obviously once the initial research has been done, carrying out a comprehensive investigation every time a post requires filling is unnecessary. It would be expensive and probably add only detail to the existing picture. Once a sound base of information has been established, certain assumptions can safely be made, then only simple checks need to be made to confirm their accuracy.

The scope and size of any research project also depends on the scale and size of the organization. A small local estate agency wishing to appoint a receptionist will know its reputation from existing data showing the level of responses to its normal business of placing 'house for sale' advertising. On the other hand, a large multinational holding company may be almost unknown to the general public, and so will need to augment recruitment advertising with some information describing the organization.

What do you want potential applicants to know?

Depending on the results of the market research and the existing information about the organization's public profile, the recruiter can decide how much more information will be needed to attract potential applicants. The point of sending out information at the first stage of recruitment is to encourage suitably qualified and experienced individuals to express their interest in the vacancy. In other words, its purpose is to sell the vacancy. However, there is little point in overdoing it. The message being sent out should be appealing but accurate. If it paints a false image, the potential applicants will quickly find out the truth.

Getting the desired message to the desired group is only one part of the process. We often think of marketing in terms of promotion and publicity. Another aspect is making sure that the 'product' is delivered to its consumer. But this is more than 'getting the pig to market'. The potential consumer has to be in the same place, want the product, be attracted by the presentation and promotion, and be prepared to pay the price being asked. We will look at how these four Ps can be used to consider ways in which a vacancy (the product) can be sold to potential applicants (the consumers).

The choice of medium (place)

A message can be placed in many different locations that can contribute or detract from its ability to be received in the way in which the sender intended. Often in recruitment, the message was seen as an advertisement and the main decisions concerned which newspaper to use. In reality, as we saw in Table 2.1, job seekers make use of a number of different sources of information in their hunt for employment. But the simple table conceals the way in which different segments of the labour market make use of different media. Each medium has its own particular strengths, but if one is used without consideration being given to the audience that will be receiving the message, the effort expended in sending it out could be wasted. Some of the channels frequently used for recruitment advertising are discussed below, with an indication of the profile of their likely audience, to illustrate the options available to a recruiter.

Newspapers

Different dailies and Sunday papers are aimed at specific market segments, each with its own distinct characteristics. Some carry more job advertisements than others. The *Guardian* claims to carry most advertisements, and is reputed to be read mainly by the liberal to leftish intelligentsia. The *Sun* contains very few vacancy advertisements and is bought mostly by members of the working class. Trade and professional journals are bought (or received) by those belonging to a particular occupational area, or are members of a professional body. Some women's journals have started to carry vacancy advertisements, as employers have strived to find ways of accessing 'non-traditional' audiences.

The Internet

The use of the Internet as a medium for recruitment activity has blossomed in line with its general use. It provides very clear benefits for both the employer and potential employees. The two biggest advantages are speed and breadth of coverage, particularly for those recruiting on a worldwide basis. There are some downsides, some of which will be discussed below. Some of the biggest factors that need to be considered at the outset are whether members of the target group have access to the Internet, whether the ability to use it is a requirement of the job, and how the advertisement can be worded so that responses from hundreds of hopefuls from across the world are not received, unless of course that is what is intended.

Job Centres

The main use of Job Centres is by those out of employment and required to attend for Jobseekers' interviews, or those in work seeking typically lower-waged, lower-skilled jobs.

Radio

This is a growing medium and need not be as expensive as is sometimes assumed. Clearly national radio sells advertisement slots at a premium, but many local stations run campaigns which, when compared to the cost of a display advertisement in a national newspaper, can be very competitively priced. Sometimes local television stations publicize vacancies.

Recruitment agencies

Agencies exist to make a profit. Advertising is therefore carried out with two purposes – to promote the agency as well as the vacancies they are filling on behalf of their clients. They will make use of a number of media including:

■ windows, notice and sandwich boards outside their offices;

■ press adverts;

■ locating their offices in high street positions;

■ adverts in the media such as trade handbooks;

■ sponsorships;

■ direct approaches to employers to 'introduce' people registered on their databases.

People seeking work can approach the agency personally, or they may be invited to consider a particular job the agency has been asked to fill. Some agencies specialize in certain types of occupational group, level of jobs or industrial sectors; some are small local companies and others are national generalists. A professional body, the Recruitment and Employment Confederation, provides professional training and education, and has a code of conduct. Membership of the REC gives some indication of an individual agency's standards.

Recruitment in some ways is a very traditional activity, with distinct stages and parameters within which those stages are designed and executed. The choice of medium for the message is influenced by a large but finite number of other factors, which have nothing to do with the organization or its vacancy. These traditions can limit the scope for innovation, as the aim is to ensure that the message gets into the right marketplace, and the expectations of that market will constrain what is possible. For example, there is little point in advertising for a domestic worker for a local residential home in *The Times,* nor is there any reason for expecting a good response to an advertisement for a financial analyst in *Construction News.* People looking for jobs will hunt in the outlets known to carry vacancy advertisements relevant to them. Those looking for applicants will advertise in outlets known to be used by job seekers.

The job (product)

The way the vacancy is packaged and presented to its potential consumers will influence the way in which they perceive it. Research has been conducted into the elements of job advertisements that attracted job seekers' attention. Job seekers look first for a job title (or heading), then location, then the salary, to see if these match their requirements. If these details catch the reader's attention, the job seeker is more likely to read the rest of the copy.

Designing and writing newspaper advertisements has become such a skilled task that in-house efforts can look extremely amateurish. As the cost of placing press adverts, particularly in regional and national newspapers, can be very high, many small employers are obliged to find other ways of recruiting staff. However, between 25 and 30 per cent of people obtaining a new job did so by responding to an advertisement. It is therefore one of the most effective ways of finding suitable applicants quickly.

As recruitment advertisements also contribute to the general promotion of the employing organization, the following general principles can help to maximize the use of an advertisement.

Image

The job seeker first sees the whole advert. This may be a flier, a sandwich board, a poster, a letter, or a newspaper advertisement. In the case of the latter, the advert is competing with many others on the page. (Advert designers know how important white space – that surrounding the text – is to the eye.) Figure 2.1, based on an advert in a national newspaper, is an example of how striking nothing can be.

> If you can fill this space, ring 0345 9876

Figure 2.1 *An imaginative use of white space*

This appeared alongside other more traditional advertisements for creative and media posts, so it had a context. But can you imagine the impact it made on a page full of text? Most job vacancies cannot get away with this minimalist approach, and need to use other ways to attract attention. The border style and use of logo, the typeface and layout all contribute to the image being painted, and need to be complementary. Otherwise, the end product can look a mess.

Presentation

The content of the advertisement is also important. The importance of post title, location and salary has already been mentioned, but it is surprising the number of advertisements that do not give those basic details. Salary, especially, is often a big secret, reserved for the initiated few only. For the rest, we are told 'salary negotiable'. If we are lucky we may be told to 'expect c£35K'.

Some advertisements, particularly those that try to attract attention by using snappy slogans, hide the job title in the text. Figure 2.2 shows how enthusiasm can get in the way of selling the job.

WE ARE LOOKING FOR THE VERY BEST
IN THE WORLD

ARE YOU THAT PERSON?

We have a REALLY exciting opportunity for a skilled and able **special person**. If you have had *managed* a busy shop, provided a high standard of *quality service* and *trained* new staff you will have had the experience we want. We want a **strong personality**, a **good communicator** and an **energetic leader**. If you are ready go places and looking for some new challenges with a **successful** and **adventurous** company ring me **NOW**.
Peter Smith on 0133 23 67 58 99

Figure 2.2 *Which job is being advertised?*

Location

This can also be used to advantage. For example an advert for graduate management trainees was placed by a large national organization. Its main base is just outside a small market town, midway between two cities. One of the cities is a popular tourist venue and is generally regarded as being a very pleasant place to live. The other, the nearest to the organization's base, is an industrial centre, generally seen as a dump. Guess which city was given in the address?

Increasingly though, the use of e-mail addresses and 0800 phone numbers mean that employers can conceal their location. It is to be seen whether this is advantageous. The huge differences in the costs of living, particularly housing, have made location a real consideration for many job seekers, especially for those mid-career who are likely to have families to move with them.

Some advertisements try to get everything into one space. Basic information about the employer, the job and the qualities sought needs to be included, but how much is to be made available is a value judgement. Market research can help you to decide what and how much to include. It also depends on the medium to be used, and in part on how much is already known about the organization and the type of job. A scan of advertisements suggests that these decisions are not often made on an informed basis.

Many are overloaded with information that could be provided in other ways, at other times. The indiscriminate use of words leads to dense, small print. This overkill does not tempt people to read on, and can achieve the reverse of what was intended. The purpose of the advertisement of a job vacancy is to interest possible candidates. They should have enough information on which to base their initial decision – find out more. This first stage is critical. It is the occasion when many potentially good applicants might choose not to go further, because the initial advertisement does not appeal to them. Contrast the two advertisements in Figures 2.3 and 2.4 to see how the same job can be portrayed in totally different ways.

TUTORS TO DEVELOP JOB-SEEKING SKILLS
c £18,000
South Yorkshire, the Midlands and South Wales
Experienced trainers are needed by one the country's largest providers of programmes for the unemployed. You will need good presentation skills and experience of working on government funded projects. You will also need to understand the difficulties facing those looking for jobs in areas of high unemployment. Interviews will be held in various locations around the country. For more information telephone A.J. Smethurst to whom applications should be sent.
HELPING THE UNEMPLOYED
115, WESTLEY ROAD,
KINGSVILLE
KG3 5JP
0345 9876

Figure 2.3 *Trainer advertisement, version one*

These could easily take the form of a flier, poster, enclosure with a letter, or an advertisement in a newspaper or journal. They illustrate how phraseology, tone and layout can influence the picture of the job. This naturally will influence the readers' decisions, their immediate view of the job and the employing organization, and will condition their approach to the latter stages of the application (if their decision is to proceed). Research has shown that we all form our impressions early, on a limited amount of information. The information obtained is

---

Could you help others find their future?

A leading provider of training opportunities aimed at the unemployed seeks to appoint experienced trainers. Those appointed will be expected to deliver programmes aimed at the development of job search skills. To do this effectively those appointed will already possess well-developed presentational and communication skills and have considerable experience of working on government funded initiatives. The ability to relate well to individuals who have experienced the disadvantages caused by high levels of prolonged unemployment is also essential.

The appointed person will be based in South Yorkshire, the Midlands or South Wales, depending on personal preference and circumstances. Interviews will be conducted locally. The salary paid will be in the region of £18,000 and will be accompanied by attractive benefits.

Applications should be sent to A.J. Smethurst at Helping the Unemployed, 115 Westley Road Kingsville KG3 5JP. Mr Smethurst will be pleased to discuss the post and may be contacted on 0345 9876.

Figure 2.4 *Trainer advertisement, version two*

used to confirm that impression; disproving information is discounted. It is therefore important to the long-term success in the post that the initial impression given by the advertisement is attractive and accurate.

Language

The tone and phrasing used in the advertisement is also important. The examples given above illustrate differences in tone. The following examples show how different words and expressions can be used to build gender-specific stereotypes that may be viewed as discriminatory. It is well known that the use of gender labels (man, woman) is not permitted in press advertisements except under certain circumstances. The legislation was enacted in 1974, but it is still possible to see advertisements looking for 'foremen' or 'managers who have experience of hands-on man management'.

Discrimination can occur in less obvious, often unconscious ways. Some research was conducted to find out if people could identify the characteristics of the candidates most likely to succeed when applying for five jobs. The jobs were exactly the same except that the descriptions of the desired applicants were written in gender-laden ways. The two extreme advertisements were those in Figures 2.5 and 2.6.

The research discovered that potential applicants could detect bias, intended or otherwise, in the advertisements and could predict whether a man or a

---

**TRAINEE MANAGERS WANTED
BY LEADING RETAILER**
We want to appoint trainee managers to be based in our stores located across the country. We are looking for self-starting individuals who have the confidence to set the pace of change. We are dynamic and thrusting and take an aggressive stance to the competition in our market. We want people who are prepared to work hard to keep up with us and who are determined to forge ahead in their careers.
If you have these talents and wish to join our challenging training scheme, please call 081 234 5678.

Figure 2.5 *Gender stereotyping, version one*

**TRAINEE MANAGERS WANTED
BY LEADING RETAILER**
We want to appoint trainee managers to join our team of staff located in stores across the country. We are looking for capable individuals who are able to guide and enable staff through the changes we are facing. We are an energetic organization, enthusiastic to take on challenges and meet competition. We want people who are committed to enhancing the quality of our services to our customers and staff.
If you are interested in using your talents and wish to develop along with us, please call 081 234 5678.

Figure 2.6 *Gender stereotyping, version two*

woman would be appointed. What happens is that the image portrayed is compared by individuals to their own self-image and their images of others. If the self-image matches, individuals will assess their chances of success as good. They are therefore more likely to apply for the job in question. If the images do not match, the individual will be unlikely to apply. Other research has suggested that women are less likely than men to apply for jobs with high salaries, as they tend to undervalue themselves.

Similarly, members of ethnic or other minority groups are not likely to seek employment in organizations that evidently only want applications from one particular ethnic group. The evidence used to form this judgement may be anecdotal or impressionistic. Nevertheless, it may be strong enough to dissuade well-qualified applicants from responding to the advertisement. While legislation concerns itself with blatant discrimination and exclusion, the above examples demonstrate how stereotypical images can be reinforced and communicated.

The cost of applying (price)

Applying for jobs does not cost an applicant a great deal of money. Or does it? One of the major difficulties facing those out of paid employment is the amount of money it takes to submit large numbers of applications. Obtaining information about vacancies (in newspapers and trade journals) is expensive. Producing letters of application, CVs and making telephone calls also incur costs. Some of the programmes aimed at helping the unemployed back to work provide these facilities to reduce the burden. What they cannot do is provide time, for submitting a good quality application does require some time to be spent on it. Those who work in organizations with a long hours culture, with long journeys to and from work, are time-poor.

One way of reducing the amount of time needed to create an application is to draw up standard CVs that can be used time and again, but is this approach really cost-effective? Employers are arrogant and can detect the all-purpose letter of application and general CV. A typical response is, 'If applicants can't be bothered to think about my job and customize their application, they cannot want it that much.' While this is an understandable reaction to standardized applications, it also demonstrates a failure to understand the reality of applying for jobs.

Typically when an applicant is asked to send in a CV, the employer expects applicants to tailor their submission to suit the requirements of the job or role and the organization. Application forms are also widely used. These are primarily designed to meet the needs of the selectors, and while some employers consider the ease of completion, the main purpose is to ensure that all applicants give the information asked for in the same order. However filling in an application form takes time, thought and effort.

Some employers ask applicants to do other things to augment their submission. These can include completing a supplementary questionnaire, providing multiple copies of their application, preparing a presentation, submitting an 'essay' or compiling a portfolio of evidence. These all expect applicants to invest energy, time and commitment, very early in the recruitment process.

Hidden costs

Organizations also expect applicants to invest in other ways. The effort needed to get additional information, obtain application forms and meet deadlines can exact a high price from potential candidates, with little likelihood of their efforts realizing any return or even response. Letters acknowledging the receipt of an application are rare; the chances of being given feedback on the application even less common. Those designing recruitment activities generally give little attention to the 'price' they are asking applicants to pay.

Another hidden cost is the time and effort an applicant is expected to spend in working out what the employing organization is looking for. Additional information packs may be very attractive, well produced and packaged, but how often are the needs of the potential applicant considered? Some are dense, written in idiosyncratic jargon, and give huge quantities of information about the organization, its location and internal structures. While they contain a lot of information about the culture of the employer, they do little to help applicants structure their submission.

Obtaining additional information can also cost in different ways. How many of us have rung to speak to the named person, only to find that he or she is not available? How many times has it not been possible to make contact because the phone line has been continually engaged? This, of course, assumes that the applicant is able to make private phone calls during the working day. The latest trend is to give only an e-mail address. This assumes the individual has access to a computer with an Internet connection.

Why people look for a new job

What makes someone apply for a job? What is in it for them? Many different assumptions are held about why people do and do not go to work. We discussed some of the more commonly held views in Chapter 1. Some of these are based on research findings; other views are based on general beliefs about people and what they seek from life. Having a job brings rewards other than money, such as companionship, social esteem and useful ways of passing the time. Maslow's (1954) hierarchy of needs give some insight into the factors that drive people, and expectancy theory suggests that these needs can be very different for different people.

Once they are in work, what motivates people to move on? At one time, at the end of formal education young people were encouraged to identify which trade or profession they would enter. Once they had chosen, the expectation was that they would remain in that occupation, often with the same employer, for the whole of their working life. Advancement was achieved by upward progression with that employer. This pattern of employment has been eroded over the last 30 years, though sometimes it seems that young people are still encouraged to choose in their later teens or early twenties what they are going to do for the next 40 years. There is some evidence of people remaining in the same occupational group for the bulk of their working lives, and there is anecdotal evidence of people having portfolios of income-generating activities, rather than one job.

Research carried out by the Department for Education and Employment in 1998 found that in general men held more jobs than women. However both men and women aged between 45 and 59 had had on average seven jobs during their working lifetime. Those over 60 had an average of six. Younger generations had

had proportionally more jobs at any given age. This can be explained by the high levels of youth unemployment in the early 1980s. People may have worked in one or perhaps two different occupations, but in around three different industries. This suggests that younger people have greater experience than previous generations, but this still tends to be in similar areas of work.

Nicholson and West (1988) found that managers who look to move have three broad types of motivation: circumstantial, avoidance and future orientation. Most gave the latter reason, but further analysis showed mixed motives concerning avoidance (reasons for escaping current circumstances) and the wish to improve career prospects or standards of living. (More men than women wanted to move to earn more and improve their living standards.)

Generally people who are happy in their jobs do not scan the situations vacant columns as a matter of course, yet the people with the knowledge, skills and experience being sought may be in this group. If they are not thinking about changing employers, why would they want to put a lot of time and energy into submitting an application? Running a newspaper advertisement that appears in one outlet on one day may be missed by the 'best' person for the job. And if that person is not looking anyway, other ways are needed to attract his or her attention and stimulate interest in the job.

If employers want to attract a strong field of applicants they must make it as easy as possible for potential applicants to make contact, obtain information and express their interest. It helps if the recruiter sees the process through the eyes of the potential applicant.

▮ The advertisement is the first place where potential applicants are told what the organization is looking for and what skills, abilities or experiences they should evidence. This should be done in an unambiguous fashion.

▮ Some organizations find it helpful to provide guidance notes to applicants on how to submit their application.

▮ Applicants should be told clearly how to express their interest in the vacancy. They need to know what should be included with their CV or application. Application forms, if used, should be designed to be easy to complete.

▮ There is no reason why applicants cannot supply information in stages. Initially only enough is needed for initial screening. Is it really necessary for them all to provide initially copacious detail about their complete career history? This can be obtained later from those meeting the minimum criteria who go forward to the later stages.

▮ Those who reach the second stage can be asked to submit extra material to support their application if they wish it to be carried on. Extra information about the organization can also be given to applicants to help them at this stage and subsequent stages.

Promoting the vacancy

For any communication to be effective, the audience to whom it is aimed should be defined. In the context of recruitment, this is 'suitably qualified, experienced individuals who are able and willing to perform the job to the agreed standard for the organization in question' (Torrington and Hall, 1995).

The content of the message should be designed to portray the image the sender desires to communicate. This should be an accurate representation of the organization and the work to be done. There should also be some mechanisms for checking whether the message has been received as intended.

The vehicle used for the transmission of the message is also an important factor. The medium should aim to get to the majority of the target audience. How best to do this is very dependent on:

■ how many people have the required knowledge and skills;

■ how difficult will it be to attract them;

■ where are they located in the labour market;

■ which media will reach them;

■ how long will it take for them to receive the message;

■ how much the chosen medium will cost (money, time, imagination, effort);

■ whether the chosen media comply with equal opportunities legislation;

■ whether the chosen media help to promote the organization as well as the job.

The concept of marketing may introduce some additional considerations that help the preparation of an advertisement. The application of the four Ps (people, price, promotion and place) can offer some suggestions on ways to improve targeting, and so the success rate of recruitment activity. An effective recruitment campaign has been defined as one that attracts suitably qualified and experienced candidates who are appointable. The size of the response should be big enough to provide choice and comparison. Too many applicants can defeat the purpose, as decision making can be paralysed by having too large a choice.

How the marketing approach can help

A marketing approach can contribute to the effectiveness of the campaign by focusing the message and concentrating resources. It forces the recruiter to consider what the contents of the message should be and at whom it should be aimed. Once the broad parameters of the message have been decided, the contents can be drafted in detail. The copy for the advertisement comes primarily from the job description or role profile, and the specification or competency framework. The advertisement is the first, and in some cases the only, chance to persuade the 'best' applicants to express their interest. The image created and language used should say to potential employees, 'This is the job for you in an organization you will want to work for.'

Before the advertisement content is finalized, consideration should be given to what the target audience knows already and what the organization wants the market to know. This will enable each individual advertisement to make a contribution to the more general promotion of the employer's image.

Once the message is drafted in broad shape and detail, it is possible to decide how best to transmit it. The medium is part of the message. It too says something about the job and the organization, and can influence the success or failure of the campaign.

When the huge range of media available for the advertisement of a vacancy is considered, the use of the market concept as a framework can produce some radical solutions to the problem of how best to get the message to the right people. Some ideas are discussed below. Obviously the most appropriate method for the purpose should be chosen, and some care needs to be exercised, especially in relation to equal opportunities legislation. We discussed how tradition can limit options and often thought is only given to which newspaper or agency to use. The other possibilities are numerous. Some will be described briefly below, with examples of how they may be used. Reference to Fyock (1993) is suggested for some interesting US ideas.

RECRUITMENT METHODS

The second part of this chapter will put to use of the concepts outlined previously. Most personnel textbooks give brief indications of how to place advertisements in newspapers, and outline the services offered by recruitment agencies and search consultants. These descriptions will be taken further, and the practicalities of these and other methods described. Some ideas of alternative approaches will also be offered. Some of them may seem a little bizarre. The labour market is changing rapidly, and therefore sometimes it is appropriate to try out different ways of attracting the attention of people who may not be looking for another job. The contribution recruitment can make to promoting the organization must not be neglected. Combining both the need to fill a particular post and the wish to contribute to the employer's overall image can produce some innovate and effective approaches. What are the real reasons for not experimenting in a controlled way?

Advertisements

Press advertisements

Press advertisements are those placed in both newspapers and trade journals. Three factors influence the choice of media – cost, profile of the readership and circulation. The first depends on the size of advertisement, its nature and the newspaper or journal. An advertisement in a national daily or Sunday paper can cost thousands of pounds, in a local paper a few hundred pounds. Against this must be balanced with the profile of the paper's readership, its size and market share. (This information can be found in *British Rate and Data* (*BRAD*), a monthly publication providing such information for the advertising business.)

Readership profile is another important factor, particularly when choosing trade journals, including those aimed at occupational or professional groupings (such as the *Architects' Journal* and *Catering and Hotel Keeper*) or those engaged in a particular area of work (for example *Construction News*).

The price charged by the publisher can vary considerably, as does the frequency of publication. This needs to be built into the time allowed for filling the vacancy and setting closing dates. Most professional journals appear at least monthly, but allowance should be made for the time required for the preparation of the advertisement, and the journal's lead time for receipt of copy. In addition it is necessary to ensure that the majority of likely applicants have long enough to receive the journal, obtain additional information, and prepare and submit their application, so the closing date may need to be as much as six weeks after publication. It should also be remembered that monthly professional journals are often kept for one or two weeks before being read. Newspaper advertisements usually have less than a week's lead time, but tend to be thrown away after one or two days.

As with most other aspects of life, recruitment advertising has fashions, and there are other people with vested interests in addition to employers and job seekers. While recruitment agencies work for their clients, they also have their own needs to satisfy, and competition between agencies can be fierce. Filling vacancies is only one of several measures of success used by the agencies. Client profiles, profit and continued existence are others. The annual advertising awards are also used as indicators, and the aim of winning can influence an agency's thinking. The employing organization is very much in the hands of its agent when commissioning an advertisement, and unless it provides a tight brief, can be prey to fashions and the agency's priorities.

Newspapers and journals receive substantial income from selling advertising space, and situations vacant columns can sell papers. For many professionals the only direct service they receive for their annual subscription is the body's journal, and the main value of this is the jobs pages.

Table 2.2 lists some of the main factors to be considered when deciding whether to use press advertising. Decisions about these will determine the size, style, wording and use of graphics and colour.

Table 2.2 *Factors affecting the design of advertisements*

The image of the organization	The advertisement should reflect and enhance the organization's public image. For example, a traditional firm of solicitors would not do itself justice by using avant-garde, full page coloured spreads, nor would it recruit staff who would fit easily into its culture.
The nature of the job	The advertisement for a chief executive demands very different treatment from that for a working chargehand, and this can be influenced by how potential applicants would respond if an inappropriate advertisement was placed.
The chosen media	Different media have distinctive styles that affect the 'fit' of an individual advertisement. It is well worth looking at a few back issues of the preferred newspaper or journal to see what works on its pages and what does not. A frivolous advertisement placed in a serious paper is not likely to work as well as it might if it were placed in a more suitable medium.
The predilection of the target market	An advertisement for a chartered accountant to work in a large, long-established, traditional organization would hardly attract the 'right' sort of candidate if it were headed, 'Do you have a creative way with figures?' Sometimes it is worth flouting normal conventions, but this needs to be done with a certain degree of circumspection.

Many personnel textbooks contain guidance on how best to use newspaper and trade journal advertisements, but they tend to omit some of the basic essentials followed by the advertising industry. Attention is generally given to content and media choice rather than design considerations.

Each advertisement is competing for the reader's eye on the page. Most readers do not engage in a systematic search of the paper for a particular vacancy. They are more likely to be scanning the pages to see if there is anything of interest. They will be looking for a word or image that attracts their attention. Only then will they read on to see if the advertisement contains anything that is of interest.

The design and layout of the advertisement influences initial eye appeal more than the copy. Thus the overall 'picture' on the page is of primary importance, followed by attractiveness, balance and readability. Getting this right takes the skilled work of a graphic designer, particularly if the advertisement is to appear in the national press. Some argue that the attractiveness of an advertisement's style depends largely on personal taste. This is not always true. Some variables have a known effect on eye appeal.

The size of type, the length of lines and clarity of typeface affect readability. The border style, use of colour and inclusion of graphics are also factors that can make an advertisement stand out from the rest. Their use often depends on how much the employer is prepared to spend and the level of competition for suitable candidates. It is interesting to contrast the nature and style of adverts when the levels of unemployment are high with those seen when they are low. Assuming the employer wishes to keep advertising costs to a minimum, research has shown that one factor that makes the difference between an attractive and an unattractive advertisement is the black to white ratio. Consider the two following layouts for the same post. Both take the same amount of space on the page.

SYSTEMS DEVELOPMENT MANAGER

ABC, an advanced integrated graphic reproduction and design group, specializing in magazine production on paper and multi media seek a Systems Development Manager. He/she will be responsible for staff training and development using a variety of Mac, PC and Scitex equipment. The successful candidate will be capable of producing full colour design and multi media work on the system and will have a strong track record in both staff development and client contact. Send CV to Mickie Smith, ABC, 3rd Floor, Luker House, 3/5 Baker Street, Luton.

Figure 2.7 *The black and white ratio, version one*

Newspaper advertising is something most employers will have to use at some time, but not all will be able to afford the services of an agency, copywriter or graphic designer. However, the difference between an attractive press advert and one which passes without notice is not always cost. Yes, the use of a professional can help, but thought, careful wording and use of space can make a big difference, as Figures 2.7 and 2.8 show.

Internet

In 2000 the Chartered Institute of Personnel and Department estimated 47 per cent of all employers were making use of the Internet. However, it is viewed as being more appropriate for some occupations than others. The main advantage

---

Systems Development Manager
WANTED to work with Mac, PC and Scitex equipment and be responsible for:
- training and development
- client contact
- full colour design
- multimedia work

You should have a strong track record in these areas. We are a design group specializing in advanced integrated graphic design and reproduction for paper and multimedia magazine production.

Please send your CV to ABC, 3rd Floor, Luker House, 3/5 Baker Street, Luton

---

Figure 2.8 *The black and white ratio, version two*

is that the Internet is not really just one medium; it gives access to other media as well as enabling advertisements to be displayed on free-standing Web pages. Other media found on the Internet include:

▮ Newspapers and journals. Some newspapers and journals such as the *Guardian, New Scientist* and *Sunday Times* display vacancy advertisements on their own Web pages. Regional and local newspapers tend to make use of an intermediary, such as Fish4Jobs. This gathers all adverts placed in the participating newspapers and provides a single point of access for the job seeker.

▮ Employers, particularly large organizations including those in the public sector, display information about current vacancies and the organization. This has many benefits for the organization, for information about working for the organization can be displayed at the same time and in the same place as the vacancy advertisement. Some employers also have online application facilities, so that interested candidates can submit their application immediately. Alternatively application forms can be downloaded, for later completion. There are considerable advantages for multinational companies or those recruiting in the global labour market, for the advert needs to be placed only once.

▮ Recruitment agencies. Some, particularly the larger ones, have their own Web sites. Others subscribe to services such as Monster. This type of service provides a service to recruitment agencies, often the smaller, local ones. These service providers can also offer facilities directly to employers, and can be set up in the form of a consortium such as Jobs.ac.uk, which lists vacancies in universities, or Ability, created for employers wanting to recruit people with disabilities.

I Online screening. Some Web sites enable candidates to apply directly to the employer. This can include the completion of online psychometric and other forms of testing. There are lots of questions about the validity of this, for it can be very difficult to prove that the person purporting to apply for the job is the same person as the one completing the test.

I CVs. The Internet allows individual job seekers to advertise themselves widely at low cost. It also enables them to specify the type of job they are looking for, and facilitates a match.

Even though the use of the Internet is growing exponentially, not everyone has access or is able to use the Internet. It is often used for professional and technical occupations, rather than semi-skilled or unskilled types of job. It is also worldwide, so unless the advertisement is carefully worded, applications from the other side of the globe could come flooding in. The organization also has to decide how to respond to the replies, in advance to avoid its computer system becoming jammed.

Radio and television advertising

Radio and television occasionally broadcast job advertisements. Most local stations run community services and like to demonstrate their commitment to the local area, especially if it earns them income and audience share. However radio and television advertising can be expensive, especially the latter. Air time costs, and so does the time and expertise required for professional production. Most viewers and listeners are experienced and sophisticated, so expect to receive high quality messages.

Television and radio have extremely good market research data, and know who is tuned in when. This knowledge can help advertisers to decide when to broadcast their message. It is also in their best interests to make sure that the messages broadcast fit in with the general standards they are seeking to achieve. For those organizations wishing to make use of these media for the first time, the station may be willing to provide initial guidance and suggest how the employer might proceed.

Despite the drawbacks caused by the expense and planning needed to ensure a professional end product, radio and television are worth considering, particularly if the organization needs to recruit a large number of people, or when the employer wants to get to a hard to reach group.

Ross Services is a supplier of office equipment and stationery. Recently it diversified to provide secretarial and clerical services in response to demands from its customers. The modest pilot proved to be an overwhelming success, so Ross has decided to expand and extend this part of the business. Part of the expansion plan is to offer services at the edges of 'the normal business day'. Some valued customers have said how much they would welcome early morning and early evening support to help prepare for rush meetings and to tidy up after hectic days.

The town in which Ross is based, however, has suffered from a long recession, and most experienced office staff are in well-paid jobs. Those registered unemployed tend to be lacking in experience, but market research has indicated that there is a large number of potentially suitably qualified people (mainly women) not registered as seeking work. Ross realized that the Job Centre and advertising in the local newspaper would not necessarily reach people wanting to work only a few number of hours at unsocial times of the day, when their domestic commitments could be covered by others, but daytime local radio has a large audience amongst this group.

Fliers

The use of fliers (leaflets or small posters) is mainly found in targeted recruitment campaigns. The target audience is defined by the requirements of the specification. Market research identifies potential candidates and helps devise ways of reaching that group. In times of high employment, this approach tends to be used for local advertising for occupations where skill shortages exist and there are not many people actively seeking alternative jobs.

The fliers can be distributed by hand, for example in the middle of a busy city centre at lunchtime, or by post. Some organizations, such as professional bodies, allow others to access their membership, for example by providing fliers for insertion into the professional journal for a fee. However, this form of advertising can have very low response rates: maybe one out of every 1,000 leaflets.

Fliers can also be used alongside small newspaper advertisements. This dual approach was tried by one organization trying to increase the participation of members of groups under-represented in its workforce, and found to be effective. The approach generated more enquiries than was expected and the general standard of the applications was higher than those previously attracted. Individuals wrote to the organization expressing support for its action and thanking the organization for contacting them. Thus, the approach succeeded in encouraging suitably qualified applicants; it also contributed to the organization's public image.

Some organizations, especially large employers, send out internal vacancy bulletins. These can be distributed on paper, or increasingly on internal Web sites (an intranet) or generally on Internet pages. It is highly likely that existing employees will pass the bulletin on to family and friends looking for jobs. Hence, as we saw in Table 2.1, there is a high proportion finding their new job through someone already working for the employer.

However, the Race Relations and Equal Opportunities Commissions advise against advertising solely within closed groups. To avoid this happening, employers can make their internal bulletin more widely available by sending it to the local Job Centre and to community groups. Others send the bulletin to similar nearby employers. It should be made clear if any of the jobs are restricted to existing employers (for example, as is needed at times of organizational change). This avoids raised expectations and the generation of unacceptable applications.

Another way to use a flier is to send copies to organizations and locations where potential applicants may be found. Sometimes, one employer, particularly in the same (often public) sector, will approach others to ask them to circulate vacancy advertisements. The likelihood of the advertisement being passed on depends on the level of competition for staff.

Another way of making the existence of a vacancy known to a wider audience is to distribute the notice to venues such as libraries, post offices, doctors' surgeries and the meeting places of community groups. This can be a useful way of contacting people not in paid employment, such as the self-employed, the disabled or those caring for dependants. An attractive flier need not be expensive to produce, as modern word processors and printers can achieve a high standard. The main cost of using this approach is likely to be distribution.

OFFICE STAFF
Wanted for
Manor Community Forum
To work Monday, Wednesday and Friday
10.00 am to 2.00 pm

Duties will include:	Skills needed:
● Filing	● Word processing
● Typing	(using Easiword)
● Reception duties	● Telephone skills
● Book keeping	● Elementary book keeping

If you would like to apply, please call into the Forum Office,
236 Princess Way, or telephone Robin on 345987

Figure 2.9 *Sample flier*

Mail shots

Fliers can be the basis for mail shots either with or without a covering letter. This approach is most effective when a large number of people, spread over a large geographic area, are to be contacted. However, care is required – we all know how irritating it is to receive junk mail.

The postal service can distribute the mail shot along with the regular post, or a distribution agency can be employed to leaflet a town or area. Increasingly mail shots are sent out on the e-mail system, but again, unsolicited messages can receive low levels of response or irritate the recipients. Potentially this can give a negative image and reflect badly on the organization.

On the other hand, well-designed and accurately targeted mail shots can be very effective. Their primary purpose is to attract the attention of potential applicants who do not read the vacant adverts in newspapers or the professional press. These may be people out of employment or those not seeking to leave their present jobs. They may be people with skills not normally associated with a particular job, who would probably not respond to an ordinary advertisement.

Like fliers, this type of advertising can have a very low response rate, so a careful cost–benefit analysis should be carried out. Nevertheless, careful mailing can achieve some startling results, as the example shows.

Newfit Engineering was trying to attract more female applicants into a traditionally male occupation. The women in the professional body were sent a letter, and a copy of the advertisement due to appear in the professional journal. The women were told of the vacancy and the company's wish to increase the number of women in a group in which they were currently under-represented. The approach and wording had been checked, and on the advice of the Equal Opportunities Commission, it was stressed that any appointment would only be made on the grounds of merit. The number of well-qualified women applicant increased considerably.

The most surprising pay-off, however, was the number of people who wrote – not complaining but saying they had never considered that particular area of work before, and even though they did not wish to apply for the particular vacancy, they would consider the area of work in future. The approach achieved its objective and made a significant contribution to the company's image as a progressive employer.

Brochures

Additional information packs, or material aimed at a particular category of recruits, such as graduate trainees, are frequently packaged as brochures. These are distributed through outlets such as careers offices, during 'milk round' events, job centres or training centres. Traditionally they are glossy and high cost, and in the past they have been used mainly by large organizations. Modern reproduction methods have placed the use of brochures within the price range of most employing organizations. Their main values are their ability to promote the organization as well as the job, and their use in reaching people who do not read newspapers or visit the normal venues used by job seekers.

Recruitment brochures can fall into two categories. The first is high-cost, mass-produced glossies. These are most commonly used for bulk recruitment in areas of work where skills are short, or competition for staff is high. They are most economical when it is possible to get to large numbers of potential applicants quickly. Exhibitions, displays or recruitment fairs are usually supported by such quality publicity material. The use of brochures can enhance the image of the employer, but the content should convey an accurate message. Exaggeration raises expectations which, if not met, eventually lead to disillusioned staff or high turnover rates.

Second, information brochures are used to support the use of other means to attract applicants. Some employers find it helpful to send potential application enquirers additional information about the organization and the job. Research has revealed that the amount of information available during the recruitment and selection process can influence the long-term success of the appointment. If applicants have sufficient information early on, they can decide whether the job and the organization are likely to be right for them. It also helps them to provide the information for the selectors in a format that will make short-listing and other selection activities easier.

These brochures need not be high cost. Modern computers and printers make the compilation of publications to a good and acceptable standard accessible to most organizations. The brochure should provide information about:

- the organization;
- its business and values;
- the terms and conditions of employment;
- the job or role and where it is based in the organization;
- the key features of the job or role;
- what will be offered to the successful applicant as part of the reward package and the other benefits, such as development opportunities or other facilities.

If the applicants will have to relocate, additional information about the area, housing, schools and general environs may be helpful.

Recruitment fairs

Recruitment fairs can vary from general events organized on behalf of a number of organizations, with a large range of career opportunities on display, to events hosted by one employer. The former are frequently organized by the careers services, now called Connexions, or newspapers, and are aimed at school leavers and other job seekers. The latter can be held when the organization is seeking to employ a number of staff at once, for example to support a planned increase in business, or when a new branch or outlet is being opened.

Recently XYZ Ltd needed nearly 100 temporary office staff to help with a major promotional campaign. The personnel manager decided to hold a recruitment fair, and publicized it through the local press and radio, and posters. Potential applicants were invited to take some work-related tests (such as a typing test, a clerical aptitude test and writing a simple letter). They also had the chance to talk to existing staff about the work before deciding whether to submit a formal application. These activities meant that there was no need to short-list. Those who had completed the tests satisfactorily and had decided, after talking to the staff, to submit an application were invited for interview. This meant that the recruiters could concentrate on checking experience, understanding of the role and social fit.

The recruitment fair also opened XYZ's doors to people who had previously had no contact with it. The professional organization of the event and the friendly approach taken by the staff did a lot to build the company's local reputation. The whole project proved to be economic and effective and eventually some of the staff were engaged as permanent employees.

Similar events are organized by caterers and other employers who need to employ large numbers of staff for one-off events or functions. It allows the skills of the applicants to be seen, and some initial training is given to those selected.

A slightly different approach is the open day. This type of event would be suitable, for example, when a company was opening a new store, branch, office or unit. Inviting interested people to visit the location, meet existing staff or representatives and talk about the work could appear time-consuming but can be a low-cost way of attracting and meeting potential employees, as well as telling the local population about the company's plans. It enables information to be transmitted, questions answered and potential applications to be assessed initially.

Sometimes such events are held in hotels or public venues. The disadvantage of this is that potential employees do not have the chance to see the working environment. Regardless of the venue, recruitment fairs and open days need to be publicized effectively and well prepared to ensure that the flow of visitors is controllable, and that staff running the event are adequately prepared and briefed. All work samples and tests have to be planned, and well set up with enough copies of paperwork, documents and supporting leaflets for the antici-pated level of response.

The milk round

The 'milk round' is the term used for the annual events during which employers recruit graduates. The events are organized on the universities' campuses and are attended by mainly large organizations. The process is very much like the traditional hiring fairs. The main difference is that the initial meeting between prospective employer and employee tends to be followed by further discussions to ensure that the match will produce the 'best' fit for both parties.

Other people's meetings

The main weakness of newspaper and journal advertisements is that they depend totally on the potential candidates obtaining the paper or journal in the first place, then seeing the advertisement. The chances of any one advertisement being seen are very small. It is a 'flag that is flown' on only one day, with limited exposure. Some people do not buy newspapers; others do not join professional bodies or read trade journals. Nevertheless they may have the very qualities being sought by the employer.

Head-hunting, or search, is often used by employers as a means of making contact with potentially suitable individuals. Typically the approach is made by an intermediary who will find appropriate ways of making contact. Many professional bodies and trade associations hold annual conferences and exhibi-tions. They are intended to be places where all kinds of business is done, and so provide the opportunities for informal meetings and exploratory conversations.

Vehicle displays

The idea of mounting job adverts on the side of buses or lorries may seem a little extreme for most employers. However, high levels of employment and skill shortages have resulted in the increased use of this method, particularly by public sector organizations seeking employees for the police service, teaching and nursing. It may also be cost-effective for those organizations that own their own fleet of vehicles and need to recruit large numbers at a particular time.

On the wall approaches

Vacancy boards used to be one of the most common recruitment methods used by employers. Notice boards or posters in windows were displayed, listing the vacancies and inviting applicants into the employment office. The approach was rarely seen during the 1980s and 1990s but interestingly, it is creeping back. Organizations, particularly those employing staff at the lower end of the wage range, with high staff turnover and low recruitment budgets, are resorting to the 'notice in the window' approach. Posters or cards can also be placed the windows of post offices or local shops. The type of job advertised is often part-time, temporary or casual in nature, and many of the employers are small companies. They believe this method is a low-cost and effective method. However, the Commission for Race Equality and the Equal Opportunities Commission caution against recruiting from closed communities. The danger is that the profile of the current workforce is replicated, and opportunities are denied to members of other groups.

Agencies

Job Centres have broadened their role in recent years, from just matching vacancies and jobseekers, to providing a range of services to employers. These include short-listing services, pre-interview screening and search. Jobcentre Plus is also the base for the Disability Service, which works with people with disabilities and aims to help them remain at work, or find suitable work within their range of ability. The service can also guide people towards retraining courses and the New Deal and other programmes.

Employment agencies have a popular image as the supplier of temporary office staff and factory workers. They too have developed their services in line with the changes in the labour market. Their services can include the recruitment of suitably qualified applicants, initial screening, profiling and assessment of skills. They can help the employer with the creation of short-lists and interview arrangements for temporary, interim and permanent staff. The better agencies also provide support during the induction stage, and can help train placed and existing staff. Some have extended their services to take on areas of work employers wish to outsource. Examples include telephone switchboards, office services, data processing and call centres.

The way in which fees are charged for staff recruited by an agency varies, from fees related to the salary of the post to a fixed consultancy fee. The broad principles governing the operation of employment agencies and businesses are laid down in statute. The 1973 Employment Agencies Act specifies the records that need to be kept, the level of confidentiality to be maintained, the legality of the worker's employment status, and the way in which fees are charged. Agencies are forbidden from charging the job seeker, and the fees levied on employers must be set out in a clear and written statement of terms of business. The better agencies belong to the Recruitment and Employment Confederation, which trains staff and sets out standards for agencies.

The major value of using an agency is its ability to provide a total, professional service. For employers with little experience of recruiting staff or when anonymity is needed, the benefits may be worth the price.

Recruitment consultants

Consultants provide very similar services to employment agencies. There are two major differences. One is that consultancies tend to work on more senior, professional and management posts, whereas agencies tend to concentrate more on lower-paid jobs such as catering, office, stores, manual and junior management. Consultancies also engage in search. The advantage of engaging a recruitment consultancy is that they can provide expertise and labour.

Using an agency also enables the employing organization to remain anonymous if it so wishes. The consultancy can carry out checks on candidates which it would not be so easy for a potential employer to do. Search consultancies (or head-hunters) have networks that allow them to make discreet enquiries about past records, reputations of individuals and their current activities. They can also approach individuals and explore their possible interest in a position in a way that an employing organization could not.

The search technique has attracted much criticism from equal opportunities activists who see it as a means of ensuring that the status quo is preserved and clones are appointed. The use of established networks and 'old boys clubs' can limit the pool of potential applicants and deny those not in the network access to opportunities. Search consultants have a professional body and have developed a code of ethics. The better ones are very conscious of the equal opportunities requirements, and are ready to engage in proper positive action.

Their role as intermediaries and advisors can enable them to make a positive contribution by questioning the status quo while taking the initial brief. They can broaden the horizons of the employing organization by exploring assumptions, suggesting alternatives and searching previously unconsidered sources. They can also add value to difference as they present applicants for consideration. Moreover, they can encourage reticent individuals to put themselves forward. Research has indicated that members of minority groups devalue their skills and themselves to such an extent that they will not apply for some posts they are well able to fill, believing that their chances of success will be low.

A search consultant can help promote equality of opportunity by challenging the employer's assumptions and searching for the required skills in places normally not explored.

The first step in the process often used by recruitment consultants is the brief. This is translated, via the job description, role profile, specification and competency framework, into an outline of the type of person being sought.

The likely location of suitably qualified people is considered, and a search strategy developed. This could include desk research: looking for people in similar areas of work who, for example, have published or spoken on a relevant topic publicly. A search of recent applicants for similar posts adds names to the list of possibles. Information about these individuals is obtained directly from the individual, from colleagues, peers, employers or informed others.

Sometimes known 'experts' are asked to make nominations, or newspaper advertisements (either confidential or publicizing the name of the employing organization) are run. The individual can be approached directly and asked to submit a letter of interest or a CV.

From this initial data, the search consultant checks for basic requirements against the job or role requirements, and if these are met, arranges to meet the individual. The individuals and consultants have discussions about the job or role and the organization. Their expectations and understanding, and their suitability against the job requirements, are all explored. Checks will be carried out, and from all the information obtained about the candidates, a long-list will be submitted to the client organization.

The selected individuals will be invited to meet the prospective employer. More discussions may take place, other checks be made and formal references be taken up. This degree of pre-selection screening means that only a very few candidates take part in the final stages of selection.

While the use of search consultants is comparatively common, particularly for senior management and executive positions, little research seems to have been carried out to assess the predictive validity or effectiveness of their contribution. In fact Cook (2001), perhaps one of the main authorities on the topic, makes no mention of recruitment agencies. Most other common forms of recruiting employees have been subjected to scrutiny, and rich evidence exists to enable the comparative benefit of each to be assessed. The whole process of search and its reliance on data obtained from others, discussions with an agent of the employing organization rather than a member, and face to face interviews would benefit from examination.

The process of search contains several distinct steps, each of which is prone to its own particular errors and bias:

Initial briefing

A busy manager may be forgiven for thinking that having engaged a recruitment consultant, he or she has handed over responsibility for filling the vacancy. If this is not the case, why use one? However, this can be tantamount to avoidance – the manager can avoid thinking deeply and critically about the detail of the work to be done, what will be required of the post-holder, what skills, knowledge and experience will be needed, and how the selection decisions will be made. Unless the consultant is very competent and adept at questioning, the manager's abdication can lead to the painting of a superficial image, full of assumptions and caricatures. And unless care is taken to check understanding, the use of words in common parlance can result in misunderstandings, as the following example illustrates:

I want a good communicator who can lead the team through a period of rapid change.

Intended meaning: *I want someone who can write really sharp, concise reports and is able to steer good people gently through a short period of externally imposed turbulence.*

Heard message: *I want a good public speaker who can sell a convincing story to a group of people who are resisting the need to change their working practices.*

Search strategy

Again, handing over total responsibility for the recruitment phase to the consultant is easy. In practice, however, it is better if this is planned jointly. The consultant is given professional advice, fronts the process and provides labour. The manager ensures the organization's requirements and values are embodied in the process.

If search is to be used, the manager and other staff may be able to suggest appropriate individuals or likely sources of suitable applicants. Confidential advertising is often used to give a degree of anonymity to the employer at the start of the process. However if the organization's name is to be used, the opportunity should be exploited to the full, as it can contribute to its overall public image.

Search process

The way in which potential applicants' names are gathered is a critical part of the strategy. One of the criteria used to select a consultancy is the size of its database. This is a list of the people who have contacted the consultancy and people it knows about. These may be gathered as a result of previous recruitment activities, contacts made with individuals in other organizations from other business transactions, meetings attended and so on. Getting the consultant to reveal information about this database may be difficult, as some could see it as being commercially sensitive, but if the consultant is well known and well regarded, giving some indication should not be a problem. To the employer, it is important to know how wide the net is being cast, and to ensure that members from all groups in society are not being unjustifiably excluded.

In addition to using their own databases, consultancies have access to other sources of information about potentially suitable candidates. The size of the consultant's networks is another indicator. Each sector has its own circles and knows how to access these. Being able to tap into these is a measure of the consultant's ability. However, there is a danger of concentrating on the easy circles – the ones that are very well known and public, but accessing them may not be that easy for some. The 'club', conference circuit or professional meetings are examples of the sort of networks open to many. They are also examples of networks that are difficult for some to gain access to. In addition, there are many competent and potentially suitable people who may choose not to be active in such groups. They too need to be sourced if the employing organization is to be presented with a balanced selection from which to form a short-list.

Preliminary meetings

The nature of biases and errors in the ways in which we form initial impressions will be described at some length in Chapter 3. Suffice to say here that the process is flawed. Most recruiters are aware that initial impressions are formed within 30 seconds of meeting a person for the first time. However, it is rare that a recruiter faces an applicant with no previous information about the person. This will form an image that will be combined with the recruiter's personal assumptions, stereotypes and prejudices (prejudgements). Subsequent interactions are used subconsciously to confirm that initial impression, while similar efforts will be made to discount any contradictory information.

An initial meeting between the consultant, acting as an agent of the employer, and the prospective candidate is often used to screen and select people perceived to be suitable. The consultant may consciously make use of the briefing given by the employer, but inevitably this will be underpinned by the individual's existing beliefs and value patterns. The better consultants are well aware of how their personal views may influence their perceptions, and are able to control their effect.

One to one interviews have long been reported as a poor predictor of subsequent performance. Smith, Gregg and Andrews (1989) say, 'Many researchers over the last 30 years have confirmed that interviews are very bad predictors of job performance. In other words they are not a valid selection method.' Yet they continue to be used extensively as the main method of gathering information about candidates, and are the basis for decision making. It is possible to improve interviews, for example by using competency frameworks and detailed examination of the candidate's contribution to significant events. Interviews are conducted mostly by managers who are employed by the recruiting organization and well versed in its culture and requirements. If a consultant is to interview on behalf of the organization, care needs to be taken in the briefing to ensure the consultant has a good insight into the nuances and values. This should be more than half an hour's chat about the job. At the very least, the consultant should have an appreciation of the organization's values and some insight into its culture.

The consultant is also acting as an agent of the organization, and therefore its ambassador. Prospective candidates will make judgements about the organization from the behaviour of the people they meet, whether they are direct employees or agents. There are reports of consultants acting in less than professional ways. Examples include holding interviews in hotel bedrooms, motorway service stations and pubs, and being dismissive of applicants very early in the interview. This sort of behaviour does not reflect well on either search consultants or employing organizations.

References

Checks are carried out and the opinions of others about the applicant are sought to inform the compilation of the long-list. Usually the names of people willing to give references are supplied by the applicant. These people are then approached with the applicant's agreement. This agreement frees referees and enables them to supply information without contravening data protection legislation. Sometimes other people are contacted, without the applicant's knowledge. These may be people who worked with applicants in the past (such as managers, colleagues or subordinates) or perhaps did business with them. These less formal approaches should only be sanctioned if they add value to the selection process, for they may constitute an invasion of privacy. Moreover, comments gathered in an unstructured way may be impressionistic, not based on relevant evidence.

We tend to place great weight on the views of others. However, we do not necessarily know the basis or reason for their opinions, their abilities or expertise in forming judgements, or whether they have any 'axes to grind'. The halo effect – a success in one area of work or good comment is regarded as being representative of the whole of the individual's ability – and the Satan effect – a lack of skill or negative comment is taken to reflect low competence – influence our judgements about other people. Finally, how competent is another person to assess a candidate's future performance in a new job working for another employer? People change and develop, and their performance varies in different surroundings with different people with different pressures.

House of Lords rulings have a bearing, particularly in the Spring v Guardian Royal case concerning the use of references. A previous employer has a duty of care to be honest and informative to safeguard an individual's future employment prospects, while providing the future employer with as accurate a portrayal of the individual's abilities as possible. The provider of the reference also should not slander or defame another person. These restrictions have been given as reasons against the provision of written references.

The alternative is to obtain verbal comments of which there is no record. Reliance on comments obtained in this way is fraught with danger, even though some employers still believe these 'off the top' comments are more revealing. If these comments are obtained by a third party and then conveyed to a potential employer, there is always a chance of the information being distorted or misreported.

Human rights legislation now gives individuals the right to privacy. Obtaining views of others about an individual, without that person's agreement, may be a breach of this right. Research has indicated that references have a low predictive validity, yet most employers continue to give them a value in the process, take the trouble to obtain them, and make use of their contents when making selection decisions.

We will return to the issue of references later, when ways of improving their value whilst safeguarding the rights of the individual will be discussed.

Presentation of the long-list

Once the consultant has drawn up the long-list, it is presented, perhaps in written form, to the employers. The consultant may supplement the documents with a verbal explanation. This is when the employer needs to check that the assumptions used by the consultant coincide with the organization's values and requirements, and that the selection criteria have been applied consistently. The relevancy of the references and processes by which they were obtained should also be made explicit. The employer should also be aware of the extent of the search, and be provided with information about the applicants who have not been long-listed. This is not to doubt the consultant; rather to safeguard against Type II errors.

Type I errors, in selection terms, are made when the wrong person is appointed. Type II errors occur when the best person is rejected. There is also the need to monitor the backgrounds of those being put forward in the long-list against the profile of the applicants, to ensure that minority groups have not been excluded unfairly. A reputable consultant should have no difficulty with any of these quality checks.

The employer, on the basis of the information presented and possibly with some guidance from the consultant, will decide who to call for the next stage of the selection process. It is unwise for the decision to be made by one person alone. We will discuss at greater length below why more than one decision maker is advisable.

Feedback to unsuccessful applicants

Normally this is provided by the consultant. Most often this is done in the form of a letter thanking the applicants. The tone of this letter can have a lasting impact, so care and consideration should be taken in its drafting. Even though the letter is written by the consultant, it will reflect on the organization, so there is no reason why the employer should not have sight of this important document before it is sent out.

Some applicants, particularly those on the long-list, may request verbal feedback. This will probably be addressed to the consultant, as they will have been in direct contact with each other. However, the content of the feedback should be considered by both the consultant and the employer during the long-listing meeting.

Allowing the consultant to provide the feedback should not be seen as a chance for the employer to avoid the responsibility of carrying out what is seen by some as an unpleasant task. As the consultant will have developed some form of relationship with the applicant, it is not unreasonable for him or her to discuss why the individual's application is not being taken forward. The employer has a responsibility for ensuring that applicants are treated well and are given good quality feedback (that is, information they are able to use to learn from and develop their skills) if they request it. It is important that they leave the process with positive feelings, for applicants will associate their treatment with the employing organization as much as the consultant.

Selection events

Normally the employer organizes the selection events in accordance with its internal procedures. Consultants can help and advise as needed, but deciding what to do and how to do it must be the responsibility of the employer. Asking an external agent to be involved is not reasonable. The employer will live with the consequences of the decision, so ultimate responsibility cannot be shared or passed on.

Once the decision has been made and an offer put to an applicant, the consultants can also help with the negotiations that follow. These ongoing discussions have increased, especially at senior levels, as the use of individual and complex reward packages has become more widespread and contracts become more involved. Making sure the end agreement is clear and mutually beneficial is critical; getting out of such contracts is becoming more difficult and costly. Therefore it is advisable that the preliminary stages of the negotiations are conducted with care and professional advice.

For the smaller employer this type of arrangement is not an everyday occurrence. It can be very easy to make a mistake and find that the contract is vague or contains unintentional clauses. Employment law is complex, and not all solicitors are well versed in its intricacies or up to date. However employment is the core business of recruitment consultants, and they have developed their expertise so they can offer this service at the closing stages of the recruitment and selection process.

Once the decision to appoint has been made, it is easy to forget the unsuccessful candidates. However, they deserve to be debriefed, and many organizations have recognized this. With the arrogance of the powerful, debriefing is taken to mean the provision of feedback to candidates on their performance and inadequacies against the specification. How often are candidates asked to provide feedback to employers about the recruitment and selection process?

Candidates who are not appointed deserve consideration at a time of 'rejection'. The opportunity of a debriefing and provision of helpful feedback is often welcomed. In addition, the follow-up discussion can provide insight into how the candidates perceived the process and how they felt they had been treated. This exchange can be a way of discharging negative emotion about the process, and possibly head off the potential of complaint. It can also provide the employer and consultant with useful information about how to improve practice. How else do we learn, if we do not obtain feedback from the recipients of our services?

Selecting consultants

Word of mouth is regarded as the best form of publicity, and recommendation is often used to decide which consultant to use. Specialist directories produced by the professional body and *The Personnel Manager's Handbook* list the largest, and provide information that helps with the selection. The local telephone or business directory is another source, as are the vacancy advertisements in the press. Some employers invite a small number of consultancies to make presentations outlining their services and facilities, and make their choice on that basis. The following checklist may guide the selection:

I   How long has the consultancy been in business?

I   What experience has it had of recruiting employees in your area and type of operation?

I   How large is its database, and what access does it have to sources of information about potential applicants?

I   Can examples of previous assignments, for example advertisements placed, literature produced or an anonymous report on a candidate, be produced?

I   How extensive and up to date is the consultant's knowledge of employment law and equal opportunities issues?

I   Is the consultancy able and willing to provide names of previous clients, and can references be obtained from them?

I   Which consultant will be handling the assignment?

I   What degree of experience has that person had of recruitment in general, at the level of the post in question and in your specific sector?

I   What support will be available to the individual consultant?

I   What are the terms of business? Consultancies have their own idiosyncratic methods of charging which can make direct comparison difficult. If it is not clear, get the consultant to work through an example.

Managing consultants

Even though a consultant has been engaged, the employer cannot hand over the whole process and wait for a few plum candidates to appear for interview. The managers responsible for the appointment have two responsibilities: first, the partnership with the consultant for the duration of the assignment, and second, the management of the consultant.

The aim of the latter is to ensure that the assignment is conducted in line with the employer's requirements, according to the terms of business and in the spirit of the employer's values. How the assignment is to be managed should be discussed when the business terms are being agreed. The responsibility of the manager will include:

▌ Confirming that the initial brief has been thorough and understood. This enables early remedial action to be taken if there is any doubt about the clarity of understanding. It will save time later, avoid wasting effort and misleading applicants.

▌ Checking advertising copy and recruitment literature to ensure that the messages are those the employer wants to convey.

▌ Agreeing any extra charges. Sometimes unquoted costs can be loaded on top of the agreed fees. These can include 'extras' for advertising, such as premium space payments, production costs, redrafting costs, and the consultant's expenses incurred in visiting applicants. All of this should be clarified when the initial contract is agreed, but can get forgotten.

▌ Agreeing which techniques will used to compile long-lists. Consultants have their own preferred methods, which may differ from the employing organization. These can include tests, questionnaires and different forms of interviewing. The consultant should be asked about working methods and appropriate registrations checked.

▌ Checking to ensure that the consultant is treating the applicants in the way in which the employing organization wishes. In the past, there is anecdotal evidence to suggest that some consultants have treated women applicants inappropriately by bullying and haranguing them to see if they are able to withstand pressure. Whilst this reflects on the consultant, it also has a negative impact on the organization using that consultant and the use of search consultants in general.

▌ Making sure that the criteria has been used as the basis for the long-list. Simple reiteration of the specification and requirements is not enough. The manager should check on how they have been applied. This helps to confirm that the consultant has understood the brief and the culture of the organization. It also helps to ensure that Type II errors (the best candidate being rejected) have been avoided.

If the working relationship with the consultant has been developed as a partnership, this discussion should flow as part of the continuing dialogue. If the consultant has been working with a 'magic box of tricks', using assumptions and personal prejudices, it will be more difficult for the decision-making criteria to be made explicit if challenged. The employer will be jointly responsible for any unjustifiable and unfair decisions or processes.

The ultimate objectives of the employer and consultant are different. The consultant's main measure of success is filling of the post and retaining the employer as a client, while the employer wants someone in post who will be effective for some time. These differences can be seen in fee structures. For example, some consultants request the first payment within two weeks of taking the brief, the second on the production of the long-list, and the final one when an offer of appointment is made. The consultant will be looking for an appointment to be made, preferably quickly, so that another assignment can be started. However, the employer may decide that not to appoint is the best decision. This possibility should be considered initially when the assignment is agreed.

Search committees

Using a committee (comprised usually of existing managers or others whose opinion is valued by the employer) to find suitably qualified candidates is a traditional technique most commonly used in professional organizations such as universities. Members of the committee contact individuals known to them, and others who may know of potentially suitable people. Inevitably the process relies on networks and relationships.

This method can favour the status quo and result in cloning unless a deliberate effort is made to avoid replicating the known, safe and predictable. Alternatively, if the committee is set up to do so, it can be used to broaden the base of the search. Committee members can positively encourage people from under-represented groups, who would not necessarily reply to a public advertisement, to put themselves forward.

The chair of the committee has responsibilities in addition to managing the search process. The committee will naturally be prone to the influences of group dynamics that can detract from the search for the best candidate. Power plays and positioning by the members and other people involved in the search can take over. The danger of this is a compromise appointment that suits no one, and a post-holder who cannot do the job.

Despite the pitfalls, this method has been used satisfactorily and is known to have advantages in very small communities of specialists where social fit with existing teams is as important as skills, knowledge and understanding. Search committees can also be used to challenge assumptions, introduce different criteria and provide alternative ways of encouraging diversity into an organization.

Positive action

Under the provisions of the current equal opportunities legislation, positive action can only be taken if it can be demonstrated that members of one group are significantly under-represented in relation to other groups. The purpose of this form of action is to enable members of the under-represented groups to reach a position in which they can compete on the same grounds as members of the majority groups. Some employers, committed to increasing opportunities to disabled people, offer them the opportunity of an immediate interview. Training schemes, confidence-building activities and practical support are other examples of methods that can legally be used. The most obvious example of positive approaches are encouraging statements included in public advertisements. The following is an example of how such a statement can be worded.

Women are under-represented at this level in the company. Applications from them will be particularly welcomed. The appointment will be made on the grounds of merit.

Phrasing of this nature can also be used in fliers, letters informing potential applications about the existence of the job, mail outs and other proactive methods of publicizing a vacancy. Not only need the tactic be confined to attracting applications from individual members of particular population groups, it can also be used to find particular skills or experience needed to balance the staff profile.

ZANIZBAR CAFE WANTS CHEFS

Qualified to C & G 770, with several years' experience of fast food outlets, you will be required to work 7 hour shifts between 10.00 and 12.00 on 5 out of 7 days and should have a good public manner. We particularly seek applications from those experienced in vegetarian cooking to help us expand in this area. Ring 789345 if you meet the bill.

Figure 2.10 *Example of a positive action advert*

Speculative letters and files of past, suitable applicants

Job seekers are often advised to contact possible employers on a speculative basis, asking for help to find suitable employment or offering themselves for work. Most often, these letters receive no response. Sometimes a letter of regret is sent, or one directing the author to press advertisements. Occasionally the letter will attract a positive response and a meeting.

When levels of unemployment are high, an employer can be flooded with such letters from a large number of inexperienced, unqualified people desperately seeking work. Times have changed, and the labour market has a different profile, including mature workers, women and people with disabilities seeking to return to work. They are being more adventurous in their job-seeking strategies, as Table 2.1 on page 48 indicates. Employers ignore these approaches at their cost, as they are a source of information about possible suitable candidates.

It is also advisable to keep past applications in case candidates complain about their treatment and the fairness of the procedures. If these records are being maintained for one purpose, there is no reason why these should not be re-examined if another similar post falls vacant. Possible candidates may have been overlooked, especially if a large number of applications were received. Even if the application had been rejected the first time round, the second job could be just different enough to make the person sufficiently close to the new specification to merit reconsideration.

Training schemes and work placements

These are used by many colleges and training providers as an integral part of the training programme or course of study. Placements can vary from a few weeks to a full year, depending on the course and its level. Combining work with formal study can have benefits for the placement provider just as much as for the trainee. While the primary purpose of the placement is to give practical and relevant experience to support theoretical input, it can have other benefits. These schemes bring the trainees into direct contact with potential employers, and employers into contact with potential employees.

Cook (2001) argues that work sampling is one of the best predictors of performance. Therefore, getting to know trainees and their standard of work while they are on a training placement is a good way of assessing whether the individuals are capable of doing the job. Actual experience will also demonstrate whether they are able to work with other members of the team. For the trainee, having direct experience of the area of work before entering into a contract is a good way of testing out whether reality matches expectations.

HOW TO KNOW YOU HAVE SUCCEEDED

As with any operation, the success of recruitment activities should be reviewed and evaluated. The review will examine each stage in the process and provide feedback so that changes can be made, based on evidence and experience. Information should be gathered systematically and combined with the views of all those involved in the process. It is not unusual to debrief managers and other staff involved after an appointment is made, but how often are the views of those being processed sought? Useful information can be obtained from the people who took part. Their opinions and descriptions of their experiences can provide a different perspective, which will be invaluable in helping the employer improve the quality of its recruitment processes.

Evaluation is different from review. While the latter looks at the detail, evaluation is concerned with the assessment of the overall effectiveness of the whole recruitment campaign. Evaluation will include the evidence provided by the review. In addition, it will question whether the process and its component stages have done the job they were intended to do.

▌ What was the full cost of recruitment process in terms of:

- – effort, expertise and time;
- – actual expenditure (in relation to the salary or value of the post)?

▌ How many enquiries were generated:

- – number of applications;
- – number of lost enquiries and the reasons why they did not convert into applications;
- – number of applications from suitably qualified applicants;
- – profile of applicants and level of applications from groups under-represented in the organization?

▌ Did applicants receive the information they needed for their decisions?

▌ Did the information provide applicants with an attractive impression of the organization?

▌ Did the information portray an accurate picture of the organization such that the newly appointed individual's expectations were met?

▌ How long did it take to get the person in post?

▌ Has the employee's performance matched the level predicted?

▌ Did the recruitment process contribute to overall image of the employer?

We will discuss evaluation again in more detail, as it is important to view recruitment in the same way as the marketing function, and the same degree of rigour should be used in carrying out the assessment. It is also important to ensure that recruitment and selection contribute to the employer's human resource strategy and the achievement of its overall objectives.

SUMMARY

The marketing concept has been used to demonstrate how recruitment can, and should, be more than deciding where to place an advertisement. The four Ps help the recruiter think through and make systematic decisions about how best to bring the vacancy to the attention of likely and suitable applicants.

Traditional methods such as newspapers and Job Centres are widely used to communicate with applicants but, as the labour market changes so should the media and the message. Skill shortages and mismatches mean that sometimes potential applicants need to be wooed, and the competition between employers can be fierce for those with talents and experience in short supply. The wish to promote equal opportunity policies has led some employers to take positive action to encourage members of under-represented groups to apply. Alternative ways of attracting candidates are being used. The increased availability of the Internet has introduced a totally new medium, and the use of recruitment consultants has become more widespread.

Because of the cost of recruitment consultants and the implications for the equality of opportunity, their selection and management has been discussed at some length. If used properly, they can add great value to the process, particularly if the employer has limited experience of recruiting employees. However, if the briefing is poor and the consultant left to recruit in isolation, the chances of error are increased.

Recruitment practices are aimed at attracting attention, creating impressions and matching perceptions. These tend to be based on assumptions, and can be influenced by cultural differences and values. The argument for challenging these assumptions is powerful – if organizations are to cater for all potential customers, they need to understand their requirements. Evidence demonstrates that the best way to do this is to ensure that the profile of the workforce is broad-based. Moreover, long-term survival requires the organization to draw from and develop a wide range of diverse talents. Positive action, taken as part of normal recruitment practice, is the way in which people from different backgrounds are brought to an employer's attention, and the existence of the opportunity to theirs.

The perceptions of the potential employer and potential employee are formed from the information both provide before a formal application is made and a short-list compiled. This information builds the foundations from which decisions are made. As with any other human decision-making process, these decisions are prone to flaws and are based on personal bias. How these errors are made and ways in which the influence of bias can be reduced so that decision making is as robust as is humanly possible will be discussed next.

3

Making decisions

Having successfully attracted expressions of interest in a vacancy, we will need to start making judgements which will lead to the ultimate identification of the most suitable person. Decisions are made at various points throughout the process; some will be free-standing, others determined by previously taken actions. All should be based on information and evidence.

As part of the recruitment process both the employer and potential employee will have deliberately supplied information. Other information will probably be given unwittingly. (For example the announcement of poor half-year profits at the same time as an advertisement for the director of marketing will affect the response rate.) The information thus given will go before us and be used to create images. These are combined with the existing views and beliefs that we all hold and that inform our perceptions of others. These perceptions, added to existing views, are used to make pre-judgements, which influence subsequent decisions.

The decision processes used by human beings to make judgements about other people, particularly when the outcome is uncertain and information is missing, are known to be flawed and can lead to error. Fortunately, it is possible to minimize negative effects by improving the flow and quality of the information on which the decisions are based, and taking steps to reduce the unhelpful influence of bias and the potential for errors. This chapter will be used to explore the decisions commonly made during the recruitment and selection process, how human factors influence these, and what measures can be taken to ensure that judgements are made effectively and fairly.

INFORMATION FLOW

Recruitment and selection can be seen as a funnel during which information is fed systematically by both parties. They supply and obtain increasing amounts of detail about each other, as recruitment leads to application and on to short-listing. The flow has two factors that influence its effectiveness. The first is the contents, which should be planned, written and presented in a way that complements the message and suits the audience. The second is the medium, which should be chosen to transmit the message in ways that are effective and also complementary.

Roe (1989) identifies four commonly found functions:

▌ **information gathering:** obtaining information about job openings, job content, job requirements and so on, and on physical, behavioural and biographical characteristics of applicants;

▌ **prediction:** transforming information on past or present applicant characteristics into predictions about their future behaviour and the resulting contribution to organizational goals;

▌ **decision making:** transforming predictive information on applicants into a preferred action;

▌ **information supply:** producing information on applicant characteristics, predicted behaviours, plans for action (decisions), and so on.

The changes in the labour market mean that traditional ways of providing information about the job or role are no longer good enough. Those seeking employment expect and demand to know more about what they are going to be doing and about the employer. They want to know about the nature of the organization, so they can decide if the opportunity is likely to offer what they are seeking. Especially in occupations where skills are in short supply, applicants are increasingly seeing themselves in control, and they are, if the organization is dependent on their skills for its ultimate success.

Some employers respond to this situation by jacking up salaries and introducing other pay-related perks, and often this approach does place the employer in a strong competitive position. However, as we discussed in Chapter 1, people are looking for other benefits from their work in addition to their take-home pay packet. They expect to be told about other aspects of the job, and have the opportunity to discuss options with the potential employer. This should affect the ways in which information is exchanged, and mean that decisions are based on more systematic and considered approaches.

Improving both decision making and information exchange can have benefits for the employer as well as the applicant.

Good quality information provided via the effective use of appropriate media helps everyone make better, more considered decisions:

■ It helps applicants decide if the job is for them and if they are qualified to satisfy the selection criteria.

■ Initial self-selection reduces the number of spurious applications.

■ Applicants are guided towards presenting their applications in ways which are easier for the employing organization to consider and short-list.

However, the effective exchange of information can have a cost implication. The production of high quality information takes time and thought, and the physical design costs money. Consequently, the proposed methods of supplying information to and obtaining information from applicants must take into account constraints and practicalities facing the employing organization.

WHAT INFORMATION IS NEEDED TO MAKE DECISIONS

There has been some interesting research into how the exchange of information during the early days of an employment contract can effect its subsequent success. Herriot (1989a) considered many aspects of the recruitment and selection process over a number of years, and described the nature of the psychological contract formed at the beginning of an employment as critical. He also argues that, unless organizations recruit and retain the quality of staff they need to conduct their own unique business, they will not stay in existence very long. Therefore the efforts expended during the design of the recruitment process and thereafter to ensure that expectations and requirements are matched will pay off. Similarly, if misunderstandings (even though they may be about the most simple issue) are not clarified and discontent is allowed to develop, the ultimate cost could be considerable.

Employing a high quality workforce does not necessarily mean having only the highest qualified, most experienced on the payroll. It does mean, however, that staff at all levels are equipped and competent to do their current job or hold their present role, and are able to learn and adapt to meet the needs of the future. Experience is important, but when the problems of tomorrow are totally different from those of yesterday, staff can not rely on previously used solutions. They need to be creative and forward-looking. Moreover, if staff are to feel genuinely involved and part of their employer's business, they need to have some idea what the future might hold. Thus when appointing employees, or transferring or promoting existing staff, employers need to develop ways of conveying a realistic assessment of the future and the context of the business.

The nature of information

Handy (1985) describes the employment contract as 'essentially a set of expect-ations. Individuals have sets of results that they expect from the organization, results that will satisfy certain of their (different) needs and in return for which they will expend some of their energies and talents. Similarly the organization has its set of expectations of the individuals and its list of payments or outcomes that it will give to them.'

Makin (1989), in describing the selection of professional staff, says that the current practices need to change to enable employers and individuals to engage in a process of matching. This, he argues, will allow parties to determine whether the other will satisfy their expectations and needs. They need informa-tion about each other's future expectations, possibilities and opportunities. Particularly, potential employees will be asking possible employers questions such as:

▌ Where is this job going to take me?

▌ What will I learn?

▌ How will I be treated during the selection process and as an employee?

▌ What will be expected of me?

▌ Will I be able to deliver?

▌ What will I receive in return for my efforts?

Guest and co-workers (1996) identified these expectations as components of the 'psychological' contract. This is developed over time and altered as conditions change. It is also likely to be unwritten and only partly understood by the other party. Misunderstandings and misinterpretations can lead to role confusion over standards, level of input expected, availability of opportunities and provisions of rewards. Many breakdowns in the employer–employee relationship can be attributed to mismatches in the components of the psychological contract. This is why it is important that as much as possible is made explicit, as early as possible, while the relationship is being developed and both parties are able to influence the content.

Relevant and accurate information given to applicants in advertisements and additional information packs are the foundations used during the negotiation of the employment contract. They can also be used for the creation of initial induction and training material. (This is described more in Chapter 8.) This information creates an image in future employees' minds about the organization and their role in it. If this picture is accurate, the employees will find that matching their expectations with reality is no problem. The chances of the understandings of both the employer and employee about key objectives, performance standards and working methods being in harmony will be increased if they are built up from discussions and the exchange of information that are held over a period of time. The new employee's fit into the organization's culture will be eased, as the underpinning assumptions will have been explored and values made explicit.

Information flow

The information given builds an image of the job in the mind of an individual. When applying we all consider what we want from a job and an employer against the images being presented. We decide whether or not to submit an application from the evidence we are given and that we obtain from other sources. If the picture does not match our requirements we do not submit an application. The exchange and flow of information during the recruitment process is shown in Figure 3.1. How this flow of information can be controlled and facilitated is shown in the boxed example.

Driving Forward Ltd, a producer of gears, needed a new sales manager. Peter had announced that he was going to retire after 20 years with the company. The MD called in Peter and the personnel manager to discuss how to appoint a successor. The MD decided that the new person would continue Peter's work but new ways were also needed. Between them they created an outline of the job to be done and a statement of the competencies that would be required by the post-holder. The three of them agreed that no one inside the company met the specification; a new set of skills and experience was needed.

As the company's products were highly specialist and technical expertise would be needed by the manager, they decided that the pool of qualified applicants would be quite small, so they felt that advertising the post would not necessarily be the best way to find potential candidates. They also thought that a public advert would not help their customers' confidence in the company's stability. Instead, they decided to put together a list of likely candidates they knew in the industry. The personnel manager contacted other personnel managers to ask if they knew of anyone who met the specification and might be interested; the MD contacted the employers' association, which agreed to circulate an anonymous request for expressions of interest; and Peter made use of his own networks.

When the MD, Peter and the personnel manager were satisfied they had searched far enough, they compared lists. Twelve names appeared on each list. These individuals were invited to meet Peter and the personnel manager to discuss the job, see the location of the company and its environs, and most importantly, to meet potential colleagues. After these initial meetings four of the visitors said they were still interested in the job.

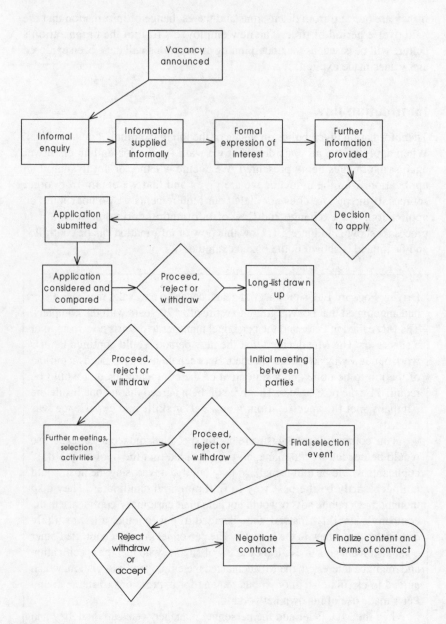

Figure 3.1 *Information flow*

At this stage a formal selection process was started. These individuals were sent information about the company's products, its annual report, and an edited copy of the business plan. They were also given the names of the company's major customers and were encouraged to seek as much information about the organization as they wanted. Their CVs were checked against the specification, and suitable activities run to explore what each candidate was able to do in practice. Reference checks were made and an appointments panel constituted. This included the MD, the personnel and production managers and an adviser from the employers' association.

The final interviewing process was seen by all the parties as a negotiation. The candidates were supplying skills and the organization was purchasing them. The candidates knew they were competing for the 'contract' and the company knew it would have to give out sensitive information if it wanted the candidates to give a good 'pitch'. After all, the job was for a sales manager – if the candidates could not sell themselves, would they be able to sell the company's products?

If clear messages are not transmitted early in the selection process, the damage done by the mismatch can be costly to both parties.

For the employee

Being in the wrong job can damage:

- job satisfaction;
- self-esteem;
- career progression;
- family life;
- future prospects.

For the organization

A poor appointment decision can lead to:

- Appointing someone unable to do the job. This can result in:
  - mistakes;
  - loss of productivity;
  - low quality customer service;

- – shoddy goods;
- – poor work relations;
- – lowering other staff's morale. This can be worse than a high turnover.
▊ Appointing someone too well qualified for a job. This can result in:
- – boredom;
- – frustration;
- – rebellion;
- – disgruntlement;
- – arrogance;
- – poor treatment of colleagues.
▊ The loss of the best candidate.

Another recruitment mistake is made when the right person for the job, from the employer's point of view, decides not to proceed. This is particularly serious if this decision is made because of inaccurate information. Often, it is difficult to prove that this type of error has happened. If an enquiry about the vacancy has been made but no application results, it is possible to investigate what deterred the enquirer. And if applications are withdrawn, it is possible to ask the applicants why. But if the interest generated by the advertisement does not result in even an enquiry, it is very difficult to discover what has happened.

THE DIFFICULTIES IN MAKING DECISIONS

Human decisions are never perfect. Judgements are inevitably made on limited information and under uncertain conditions. We all make errors of judgement and are biased because we are human. It is possible to reduce the negative impact of these normal characteristics and improve our decision making by understanding how common flaws occur. Some simple actions, such as enhancing the quality and flow of information and making explicit the decision-making criteria, can made a considerable difference. These actions, however, should be based on some understanding of normal human decision-making processes, and be designed to achieve a particular purpose. Those wishing to explore these issues at greater length are referred to Bazerman (1994), which is a useful guide to individual and group management decision making. The errors most likely to occur in recruitment and selection are described below.

Escalating the commitment to a course of action

The more we invest in a course of action or a decision, the more we become committed to it. This escalation of commitment results from a typical chain of events:

1. The original decision is made on a limited amount of information. Nevertheless, making the decision will have been costly in terms of time, effort and expenditure. For example even a modest recruitment campaign can cost several thousands of pounds in time, paper and advertising.

2. Early indicators suggest that the decision is not achieving the desired results. For example the advertisement does not attract the size of response expected, or at first glance the calibre of applicants does not seem high.

3. The size of the initial commitment is seen as being too great to waste. Expressions such 'We can't go back now', 'We need someone in post quickly' or 'Our customers know we have a vacancy and are getting anxious about our ability to deliver' can be heard.

4. More is invested to try to remedy the situation and save the face of the decision maker. Further action is taken, such as 'We had better re-run the advertisement' or 'Let's start asking around.'

5. The situation gets progressively worse and further decisions are made. 'We had better interview the people who have applied.'

Can you think of occasions when this sort of situation has developed? Nine times out of ten, the end result is that the 'wrong' person is appointed. Even if the candidate works very hard, the confidence of the key people involved in making the appointment will have been eroded by the known weakness of the process, and they will have lost their confidence in the outcome.

The response to the big advertisement has been disappointing. It had been very well planned and designed, and a plum position in a leading Sunday paper had been obtained. The cost of the advert was more than expected, but the chief executive was pleased with it. The personnel manager forecast 30 or more applicants, but only six applications were received, and they were not inspiring. Nevertheless a short-list was drawn up and the candidates interviewed. After the final interview the employer was relieved. Two candidates were appointable. One was definite, the other marginal, but the interviewers though he might 'do at a pinch'. An offer was made to the best candidate, who the next day said, 'Thank you, but I have had a better offer from another organization.' Rather than go back to the drawing board, the

> employer decided to offer the job to the second choice, who accepted the position.
>
> Nine months later the chief executive called a meeting to work out what to do with the new appointment, who clearly was not up to the job. Simultaneously, the individual had been to see the personnel manager to discuss how to get out of the situation.

Rather than face the real problem directly, the parties involved tend to try ways of making the decision work. Actions such as providing additional training, adding extra resources to fill the gaps, making excuses and giving extra time to allow the new person chance to settle in, are frequently heard examples of how employers escalate the commitment to the original decision.

Over-confidence in the quality of the decision

Another common error found in decision making concerns the confidence levels of those involved. Individuals have unwarranted faith in their judgements and abilities to predict uncertain outcomes. There is an adage that advises you not to criticize another person's ability to drive a car or conduct an interview. 'Good' interviewers, who over-assess their abilities to select the right person, are more likely to make a decision based on scant evidence than those who have less faith in themselves, prefer to make decisions using criteria and checklists, and take time to question their own thought processes. All too few interviewers seek feedback on:

▌ their abilities to ask questions to find evidence against the criteria;

▌ their use of questions appropriate to the situation;

▌ how they develop a rapport with candidates;

▌ their skills of encouraging candidates to open up and discuss freely their aspirations and concerns about the job;

▌ their use of the criteria to inform their judgement.

When a poor appointment is made, it is rare that the reason for it is attributed to the poor decision-making abilities of those involved. Generally, other reasons are found. These can include:

▌ The advertisement was not as good as was thought.

▌ The selection event was poorly designed.

▌ The applicants were weak.

■ The appointed person failed to deliver.

Rarely is it the fault of those making the decision.

The same type of error is made by applicants. The reasons given by unsuccessful candidates for not being appointed include:

■ poor decision making by those making the appointment;

■ not being given a fair chance to demonstrate their abilities;

■ the decision having been made beforehand.

Applicants rarely meet each other, so they have limited opportunities to compare their skill levels, and to obtain good quality feedback about their performance in an interview can be difficult. This makes it hard for them to assess accurately their abilities and suitability for a particular type or level of job:

■ How often do we show our CV or application to a colleague for critical appraisal?

■ How many employers are prepared to spend time with unsuccessful applicants, especially those who were rejected at the long- and short-listing stages?

■ How many of us actively seek feedback after an unsuccessful application for a job we really wanted?

Availability of information

The rational model of decision making suggests that, during recruitment and selection, information about all available options is gathered systematically. Once a sufficient quantity and quality of information has been obtained, the alternatives are weighed against each other and the 'best' decision made. The 'best' decision is the one that satisfies the predetermined requirements and obtains the maximum results.

This model is recommended for strategic and large investment decisions. Surely the decision to appointment a member of staff is both strategic and a substantial investment? Yet the normal approach to recruitment and selection is to limit the amount of information supplied and obtained.

■ The advertisement publicizing the vacancy is often the only information given out.

■ Applicants are frequently asked to submit brief letters of application and short CVs.

▌ Applicants are kept at arms' length. If they enquire, the information given
    is superficial and the people supplying it are guarded.

▌ Reference checks are made at the end of the process, and tend to be obtained
    from representatives of previous employers rather than colleagues or
    customers of the individuals concerned. (We will discuss this further in
    Chapter 5, as the motives of those providing the reference and the quality
    of its contents are rarely questioned.)

Research into bias in decision making shows that we strive to fill the vacuum
if sufficient information is not available. We do not exactly make up information to fill the gaps; rather we make use of our previous experiences to explain,
interpret and predict. We all have our own idiosyncratic rules of thumb and use
them when we make decisions, try to predict the future and form judgements
about people.

If information is easily accessed, readily available or can be remembered, it
will be given more value than if the information has to be hunted out. Thus, if
the required information is presented in a way that makes it stand out on an
application form, or the applicant says or does something that is very noticeable,
a strong and lasting impression will be formed.

We also tend to make connections between previous events and experiences
and the situation currently facing us. If the memories of the previous event or
place evoke good feelings, we tend to transfer those feelings on to other things
or people linked in some way to the event or place. This is known as the 'halo'
effect: for example, 'The best manager I ever worked for had studied at Durham
University. Anyone who has a degree from Durham is therefore likely to be
good.'

This tendency applies to the way we form impressions about other people. If
one aspect of an individual's performance is seen as being good, it is generally
believed that this standard will be found in all other areas of performance. Thus
if a candidate makes a good presentation during a selection event, those in the
audience may reason that he or she will also be a good team player and be able
to produce high quality reports.

Applicants make similar judgements about employers, sometimes on the
scantiest of information. For example, an organization with a good pension
scheme is likely to have generous sickness payments and will be committed to
equality of opportunity. These sometimes baseless associations are often the
basis for unreasonable expectations.

Confirmation of initial impressions

Another cause of unreasonable and unrealistic expectations can be found in the
way we seek confirmatory evidence for our initial impressions. We like to
believe that we are good judges of character and hate to be proven wrong. It is

common knowledge that our initial impressions are formed within a very short timescale. (Some research suggests that may be less than 30 seconds.) The way we form our first impressions is not just confined to meeting people. The phenomenon also occurs when we open the envelope containing additional information about a vacancy, or look at an application.

The factors we use to form our initial impressions are the products of our own biases, prejudices (or prejudgements) and stereotypes. Unless the person making the decision is very self-aware and knows how to limit their effect, these biases will influence that person's judgement without being checked or balanced.

The way we view handwriting is an interesting example of how initial impressions are formed on the basis of dubious evidence. Graphology is the study of handwriting. Generally speaking, most British employers say they do not use it to aid to recruitment and selection decisions, though it is used extensively in Europe. Writing with a far-forward slant is taken to indicate an extremely emotional individual, and a backward slant represents someone who is emotionally constrained. The strokes on letters are indicators of personality traits, and the rounding of letters indicates mental processes.

While graphologists undergo training and are members of a professional body, the rest of us interpret handwriting in a less systematic way. Most of us think that people who produce small, neat script with uniformed letters are quiet, almost introverted, with precise habits. On the other hand someone with large, untidy handwriting is bound to be an extrovert and disorganized. Backward-facing letters indicate a pessimist, while someone who writes with a forward slant is adventurous. Rounded ascenders and descenders indicate a mature personality, but spiky, stubby ones are produced by a short-tempered individual.

These truisms affect the way we view the person who has produced the application or written the covering letter. Whether these assumptions are accurate is immaterial – they are made. Exposing them to scrutiny helps us understand the sort of prejudgements we make, and how they create images of the applicant in our minds.

We make other errors as we unconsciously seek to confirm our initial impressions and prove them to be correct. Simultaneously, any evidence that disproves these impressions is discounted.

The advertisement appeared to offer the very opportunity Nicky had been waiting for. He was ready for a move, and the small amount of information contained in the simple newspaper advert was enough to inspire him. He invested a considerable amount of time and energy in carrying out research and preparing his application. He accepted the invitation to visit the employer's premises, and spoke to existing employees about what working for the organization would be like. He was very excited by the prospect and worked hard on preparing for the interview. This went very well, and he was delighted when the job was offered to him. He handed in his resignation to his current employer and looked forward to his new career. He had not even read the newspaper article sent to him by his best friend warning of the company's devastatingly poor year-end results and forecasting massive job losses.

Unless the evidence disproving our initial impressions and preferred conclusion is very strong and undeniable, we are likely to avoid recognizing indicators that suggest the job or organization may be less than ideal. Unfortunately the time when we can no longer deny our errors of judgement comes when it is too late to do anything to prevent a poor decision being made, as in the case of Nicky (see box).

Predictions of success

Selecting the right person and the right job involves an assessment of risk by both parties. The employer assesses the comparative features of each applicant, hopefully using the specification and the job or role requirements, to predict which applicant has the greatest chance of being successful in the long term. Each applicant will assess the chance of the job and of the employer providing the outcome he or she wants from employment. Research into how well various recruitment and selection activities predict future performance tends to focus on the later stages of the process, and takes each activity as a separate episode. As we saw in Figure 3.1, recruitment and selection is a whole process, made up of stages that build on the previous ones. These stages enable the employer and potential employee to gather and supply information about each other so they can assess their goodness of fit, and predict the likelihood of them each obtaining their desired outcome.

> *To err is human. Perfection is the state of angels.*

The recruitment and selection process is made up of a series of decisions made on the basis of limited information, and we are all prone to mistakes when making decisions in uncertain conditions. However, our decision making can be improved if we make sure that we gather relevant and accurate information systematically. This will help to reduce the degree of uncertainty and convert some of the speculations and assumptions into known facts. The following measures can also be taken to reduce the negative impact of the flaws commonly found in decision making:

▮ **Explore expectations and take action to match them.** The whole process can be seen as an exchange between two parties (the seeker of employment and the provider) who want to do business with each other. This contrasts with the traditional approach, in which the employer 'sells' a job and then chooses who will be allowed to have it.

■ **Provide accurate information.** The purpose of giving out information about the job and employing organization is to help the decision-making process. If the employer exaggerates the work and prospects, and the applicants over-sell themselves, one outcome is guaranteed. The other party will eventually find out the truth, and this will lead to disappointment and dissatisfaction.

■ **See the process as a negotiation between two equal parties.** Each possesses equal amounts of power, with rights and responsibilities to the other. Honesty and provision of helpful information can balance the power between the applicant and employer, and contribute to positive exchanges.

■ **The social fit is important to both the parties.** Obtaining a good fit requires different types of information from that traditionally provided. Applicants will want to know more about the job or role than simply its title and a brief outline of duties. They will, at the very least, expect information about the competencies required of the ideal post-holder, and some indication of the priorities and key targets to be achieved. Details of the conditions of employment, a description of the organization and its business, a summary of its priorities and key policies are basic essentials. On the other side, a skeleton CV does not tell a prospective employer whether the potential employee's values and aspirations match those of the organization.

■ **Treat the recruitment and selection process as a flow of information.** Information is gathered and exchanged at each stage. This is to allow the parties to build a picture of each other. If the process is seen in this way, it is possible for both parties to check information supplied for consistency, validate it against information obtained from other sources, and ensure that initial impressions are correct by actively searching for disproving evidence.

■ **Key decision makers can became more aware of their normal biases and the limiting effect of their rules of thumb.** Increased awareness will help to reduce the negative impact of normal errors and flaws in decision making. Decision makers can learn how to check for false assumptions and be conscious of their own preconceived stereotypes. A technique that helps to check for biases is to explore the decision from the alternative point of view. Consider why not rather than why.

■ **The amount of information supplied should be adequate and sufficient.** Supplying too much can be as bad as not giving enough. Over-supply can be off-putting; under-supply encourages the other party to fill in the gaps to confirm the initial impression, which may or may not be accurate.

▌ **Be aware of first impressions.** The natural and subconscious tendency is to give first impressions more value than information gathered later. In reality, all information should have equal weight and be given its full place when the decision is made. As well as giving undue weight to first impressions, we tend to give more value to final impressions and distinctive features or factors which may in fact be irrelevant. These are known as the biases of primacy, recency and saliency.

▌ **Avoid making judgements too soon.** If decisions are suspended, the importance of first impressions will be limited. Waiting until all the evidence has been accumulated enables the pros and cons to be weighed against each other on the basis of all available information.

▌ **Expect to make mistakes.** No one is a perfect judge of other people. If we accept this, we can make sure we gather data from a number of sources to balance our perceptions and reduce the impact of our personal preferences and biases. This also serves to check the information we are being given for inaccuracies. If we are prepared to seek the opinion of others, we will also reduce the chances of assumptions and initial impressions being given undue weight. Checking the decision with other people and comparing the logic each has used to form his or her judgement will help to validate the decision and the process used to make it.

▌ **Seekers of employment and seekers of employees are all 'selling' to each other.** Employers and employees strive to create the best possible impression in the mind of the other. Therefore, do not expect the whole truth and nothing but the truth to be given by either party. Approach the decision in the same way as you would a major investment decision – gather information and check it. If there is no evidence available, accept that this does not confirm or disprove anything at all, it simply means that there is no evidence. Don't make information up if it doesn't exist!

▌ **Take positive steps to check assumptions and interpretations at each stage.** Be sure that impressions are founded on evidence and that the factors that have been discounted are really irrelevant to the decision.

PROVIDING ADDITIONAL INFORMATION

'Employers are competing in a war for talent . . . It goes without saying that the more attractive the recruiting organization, the more likely potential employees are to apply to work there. The most attractive employers will not even need to advertise to receive job applications' (Grout and Perrin, 2002).

Some well-regarded organizations can receive thousands of applications each year from people seeking employment. These tend to be major companies, but it is not unknown for even a small employer to receive hundreds of responses to an advert, particularly if the job on offer is well paid and attractive, and based in an area with high levels of unemployment. However, receiving large numbers of enquiries and speculative applications does not guarantee they are being made by people the organization might want to employ.

The cost of providing additional information may be seen as excessive to some employers, particularly those receiving large numbers of enquiries about vacancies. However, if an appointment is seen as a substantial capital invest-ment, it follows that all parties should base their decision on good quality information. In any case the costs should be seen comparatively. Average earnings stand at about £25,000 per annum and a typical appointment is likely to last five years. When 20 per cent for national insurance contributions and other employer's costs is added, and an allowance of 3 per cent per annum made for inflation, the total cost of the employment over the five-year period would be nearly £200,000.

How much does it cost to produce and send out 1,000 booklets containing additional information about the job and organization – £2,000? The cost of holding an open day is likely to be even less.

Most of the research into the effectiveness of recruitment and selection concentrates on selection techniques used in the final stages of the process. De Witte (1989) said:

> When searching through the literature on personnel policy there are almost no publications on personnel advertising. Notwithstanding the enormous total budget spent on personnel advertisements, no systematic research has been done. A lot of research about interviewing and psychological testing is available. Theories about how persons choose an organization have been developed. These theories assume the existence of the applicant. The question remains how the organization can influence the potential employee. In many cases the first contact is through a personnel advertisement. The effectiveness of this, therefore, is very important.

Cook (2001) makes no mention of how the recruitment process can affect the eventual outcome, focusing instead on selection activities. Taylor (2002) explores the evaluation of recruitment from the employer's perspective by asking three questions: were sufficient numbers of applications received, could the same result be achieved in less expensive ways, and did the methods used fulfil equal opportunities requirements? He goes on to suggest different ways in which the effectiveness of recruitment activities can be evaluated in terms of achieving the employer's desired outcomes, but quotes no comparative research describing how the exchange of information during the recruitment process can affect ultimate performance in post.

We do know from empirical and anecdotal evidence that if the employer's and potential employees' expectations are not in tune, the chances of the employee being effective in post are reduced. Good quality information can also help to encourage those with little chance of being appointed to select them-selves out early in the process. It can also help those who are suitably qualified and interested in applying, to provide information aimed directly at the employer and the job in question. This will aid the selectors' decisions, as the information submitted will be relevant and more likely to be presented in a form that enables comparison to the specification. Moreover, the applicants will be gaining information about what the employer will expect from the successful candidate.

Information packs

Some organizations, mainly those in the publicly funded sector or those engaged in the mass recruitment, for example of graduates, produce packs giving additional information about the job. These packs vary from one or two pages to a large booklet. They also range in quality. Some appear to be a random collection of documents produced for other purposes; some are as carefully constructed as any product sales leaflet. The contents and the style of the pack reflect the culture of the employer, and contribute to prospective employees' impressions.

What does a poorly constructed pack containing long, waffly documents with no obvious connection with the job in question tell the applicants about the job and the employer? Will it encourage them to apply? Another example of a poor pack is the glossy brochure. These are often produced when the size of the recruitment exercise is large enough to justify the cost of employing copy-writers and graphic artists. These sorts of information pack are often seen when the competition for employees is fierce, and they can be very imaginative and attractive. However, many experienced job seekers will see them for what they are – promotional literature whose aim is to paint an attractive image of an organization with a bright future, offering potential employees careers with prospects. The real purpose of this sort of pack is to sell the organization. Providing candidates with the information they need may be secondary.

A good pack is concise, attractive and contains the information relevant from the applicant's perspective, including:

▮ outline of the job or role's key tasks and competencies required;

▮ outline of the management structure, showing the position of the job or role;

▮ description of the department in which the role or job is based, outlining its key targets and relevant statistics;

▮ the employer's mission, priorities and the context in which it is operating;

▮ summary of major policies relating to employment, and the area of work in which the future post-holder will be engaged;

▮ description of what it is like to work for the organization, indicating major facilities, non-pay benefits and values;

▮ information on how to apply and a description of the selection process.

Web-based information

The Internet provides a superb outlet for additional information. The easiest way to use this medium is to make the printed information pack available for download. However, this just transfers the printing cost on to the applicant, and can cause technical and compatability problems for those trying to print out the document. Reading such documents on a screen is not necessarily the easiest and most advisable thing to do. A more accessible approach is to see the Internet as a medium in its own right, with its own distinct advantages. This requires the employer to do more than simply make an existing document available.

Using the Internet to best effect means thinking about how the user will want to access the information, and how to break the information up into single pages. This gives a degree of flexibility that enables the user to move through the pages as questions occur, providing links are given. The list above suggests some ways of dividing up the contents.

It is also advisable to look at how other employers provide additional information to prospective recruits. The police, NHS and armed forces, having experienced recruitment problems, have done a lot of work to promote themselves and make information available. Other employers in the private sector, particularly the very large companies, have also created excellent Web sites that illustrate what is possible.

Recruitment fairs

Some employers invite people who are interested in obtaining employment with them to attend pre-selection meetings, known as recruitment fairs. These events have a dual purpose. First, they aim to provide information, as they enable prospective employees to meet existing staff and see what it will be like to work there without influencing the final decision makers. Second, they enable some sort of screening or initial selection exercises to be conducted. Fairs and similar events typically are organized when an employer is planning to open a new outlet, when large numbers of additional staff need to be recruited, for example to a training programme, or when a peak in demand requires additional staff.

A holiday tour operator launched a new series of holidays with an innovative promotions campaign. This immediately captured the public's imagination, and the number of enquiries and bookings exceeded those anticipated. Consequently a large number of temporary data processing staff were needed urgently to process the enquiries and bookings. Time was of the essence, and the tour operator knew there would be difficulty finding the staff, for computer-literate and office-skilled staff were in short supply in the town.

The computer program was simple to use, yet the staff had to be accurate and able to work at speed.

The company decided to repeat the approach that had been so successful in launching its new products. A radio advertisement was broadcast for three days, inviting interested individuals to meet the tour operator at the local college one afternoon and evening the following week.

With the college's help, the tour operator's data processing suite was replicated in one of the computer studies classrooms. A photographic display was mounted containing pictures of the tour operator's offices, and existing staff were on hand to talk about the holiday tours and the reasons for the unusual recruitment drive. The nature of the work was explained, and the computer program demonstrated. The 'guests' were offered refreshments, and were given the chance to try their hand at data processing. Even if they had not used computers before, they were encouraged to have a go so they could assess their own potential and preference for this type of work. Those seriously interested in working for the company were given written information about the pay, hours and conditions, and were able to discuss the job with the staff. The operator managed to appoint adequate numbers of staff – and sold some more holidays.

Informal visits

Informal visits and meetings can be held on a less ambitious scale. They can be held in response to a speculative letter sent in by someone who appears at first sight to be of interest to the employer, or before a vacancy is advertised, for example, when a member of staff has given several months' notice of leaving. Meetings of this nature enable less formal discussions to be held in advance of the more formal exchanges. In addition to the assessment of suitability against the job requirements and competencies, there is the issue of social fit. This aspect can be particularly important in small organizations that depend on high social cohesion between team members, or those employing staff, such as academics, doctors or lawyers, who have to be able to form close, productive working relationships.

The initial, informal meeting is intended to enable information giving and gathering to take place in a setting where the power between potential employee and employer is more equally balanced. Meetings such as this should not be allowed to have any weight in the final decision, as they can be very prone to influences from the personal preferences, errors and biases discussed above. Nevertheless such a meeting, conducted without prejudice, can be an effective way of exploring the degree of the fit before either party makes a formal commitment. If on the basis of discussions it looks unlikely that a mutually satisfactory arrangement will be possible, either party is able to withdraw without the loss of face that occurs with the more normal recruitment process.

Informal discussions

Some employers offer potential applicants the opportunity of having an informal discussion with someone who knows about the job and organization, but is not necessarily involved in the selection process. This type of discussion may be conducted face to face, but more often it takes place over the telephone. E-mail also provides the chance for this type of 'dialogue' to take place before the formal application is made.

The purpose of the informal discussion is to provide additional information to supplement that contained in the advertisement, and to provide additional insight into the job and the culture of the organization. It also enables any questions the applicants may have to be answered. Being able to discuss the vacancy in this way enables potential applicants to probe areas that may be sensitive without jeopardizing their chances of success, and helps them decide whether to submit an application.

Some employers use the informal discussion as another level of screening. As well as helping potential applicants decide whether the post is likely to offer what they are looking for and if they meet the specification, an informal discussion can also provide indicators of behaviour to help the employer assess the competencies of the candidates. A record of the exchange can be used to assist with short-listing. However, if this is to be done, the person conducting the informal interview should be trained and understand the criteria. Potential applicants should also be made aware that they are being assessed during the conversation.

Finding a new director was proving more difficult than had been anticipated. The job itself was challenging – the customer liaison division was not without its problems – and the pay was not outstanding. Nevertheless Lucy Graham, the chief executive, had not expected it to be this hard to replace Simon. Advertising twice in the leading newspapers had been expensive, and had produced a lot of applications from people with no real understanding of the meaning of quality customer service. The search consultants had produced names with track records, but none of them had been able to demonstrate that they had the imagination to take the service forward while tackling the deep-seated problems that had grown up in the 20 years of Simon's 'reign'.

Then a conversation happened by chance. Lucy was talking to an old friend one weekend about the difficulties she was facing, including appointing the new director. The friend said he knew just the person, and promised to fix a meeting the following week.

The 'person' indeed seemed ideal, having most of the qualities outlined in the specification. Saleem had been abroad for several years and had only just returned home to Britain. In fact he was not really looking for a job just yet. Nevertheless, he said the post seemed to present an interesting challenge. He agreed to submit a formal application and meet other members of the board later that week.

Following several exploratory discussions with board members and staff in the division, Saleem became enthusiastic about the job. Lucy satisfied herself that he matched the specification, and made the necessary checks. A recommendation was made to the chair of the board, and Saleem was appointed within a month of the weekend conversation.

Visits, open days and social events

Inviting potential applicants to visit before making a formal expression of interest in a post is not a traditional way of encouraging applications and exchanging information. However, when an employer has special requirements, for example when experiencing skill shortages or competing for staff, other ways in addition to traditional methods have to be found to attract interest. One way to do this is to invite potential applicants for a pre-application discussion, with an opportunity to see what is entailed in the work.

This approach is used, for example, to encourage young people to join the armed forces, or to tempt ex-employees to return to their former area of work. The health service has been using this approach, together with financial incentives, to remedy the shortages of nurses, doctors and other professionals.

Structured visits and open events tend to be used more commonly when a large number of new employees are to be appointed, for example when selecting for a training scheme, seeking to employ a number of graduates, needing staff for a new venture or temporary staff to cover a short-term peak. Interested individuals are invited to visit the employer, for example through newspaper advertisements, fliers, radio announcements, billboards or similar media. The purpose of the event is to tell potential applicants about the nature and content of the job, outline the needs of the employer and answer any questions. The event may also be designed to allow the comparison of the individual's abilities and fit against the employer's requirements. This may involve some initial selection assessments.

This type of event means that a lot of information can be exchanged without the high cost of paper, postage and the time needed to send out material. It also reduces the load on the individual, and gives both parties first hand experience of each other. The visit can also enable expectations to be matched, as they will be based on actual information rather than on interpretations of written material.

The Bouquet House was planning to open a new store. The new manager had been appointed to finalize the plans and appoint the staff needed to run the outlet. In total 60 people would need to be ready to start work for the opening, two months hence. The town in which the new store was to be located was known to have a ready supply of clerical, retail-experienced and stores staff, as a large supermarket had recently been closed. Even though the Bouquet House's business and merchandise were different from the food retailer's, the personnel directorate believed that if staff of the right calibre were appointed, they could quickly be retrained.

Consequently the manager arranged for the office suite to be ready four weeks before the store's opening date. A radio announcement and an advertisement in the town's weekly newspaper informed the local population that the offices would be open, and staff available to meet anyone interested in working for the Bouquet House the following weekend. Publicity material was prepared and distributed to libraries, surgeries, hairdressers and community centres.

The local population responded enthusiastically. Everyone was curious about the new store, as it was promising a 'new experience in leisure shopping', and not surprisingly those now without jobs were anxious to find new employment. Hundreds of people arrived to see a video display showing film of the company's other stores and explaining the nature of the business. Examples of the company's stock were available for inspection, and demonstrations were made of various pieces of equipment, both those used in the store's operations and those being sold.

Individuals who expressed genuine interest in working for the company were asked to complete, with the help of a member of staff, a simple form which requested biographical data. They were also asked to take some aptitude tests. These examined, among other essential abilities, trainability, customer orientation, numeracy and computer literacy. Those matching the person specifications were asked to return for a final discussion with the store manager the following week.

The result of the exercise was 55 appointments within 10 days, a huge amount of pre-opening publicity and public goodwill. The cost in comparison with traditional recruitment practices and the payback was minimal.

Preliminary interviews

More normally, search consultants hold preliminary interviews for screening purposes, and it is not uncommon for potential applicants for professional positions to be invited to make several visits to the employing organization to meet future colleagues and significant others in a semi-formal setting. This is not canvassing; it is more a way of ensuring the people who will have to work very closely with each other believe they will be able to form working relationships. However this technique does contain dangers, and is open to accusations of personal preference being allowed to take precedence, rather than selection decisions being made on the basis of assessment against the criteria required for effective performance of the role.

Makin (1989) describes some of these problems, especially when the number of people involved in the decision is high. He argues that the process is prone to a number of errors. Nevertheless he supports Herriot (1989a) who 'suggests that the selection process should be a "matching" process between the individual's occupational self-concept and the organization's purpose'. It can be argued that the abilities to form effective working relationships with a range of individuals and influence them are critical requirements in this sort of role. Therefore the process of meeting key individuals has some validity, providing the assessment of competency is made consistently by those involved, using criteria statements that are well understood. Using individual impressions is guaranteed to lead to the use of prejudgements and personal preferences.

To ensure that pre-selection visits and meetings are made in a way that would not unfairly discriminate against any applicant, the following steps are advised:

1. Develop techniques that are acceptable to potential applicants, and that accurately assess a candidate's 'track record' and abilities.

2. These techniques need to be equally acceptable to, and appear valid to, the decision makers.

3. It is made clear to all concerned that a crucial criterion for selection is an adequate match between the individual and the role required by the organization.

The techniques can be designed to take account of normal biases. We will explore these at greater length in later chapters, for they can take account of the normal behaviour and needs of humans when forming new groups or changing the membership of an existing groups. When a group (or tribe) needs to find someone else to join it, it is normal behaviour for existing members to seek others who are like them in some ways and to reject people who are dissimilar. Seeking a new member who has shared values and common experiences is understandable, but this tendency is the basis for cloning and unfair discrimination.

The systematic techniques available for use in recruitment and selection are intended to avoid this. The key is to separate the criteria that describe the job or role requirements from those relating to social fit. Another key to avoiding unjustified discrimination is to ensure that the methods used to attract the applicants are open and accessible to all suitably qualified individuals. Many of these methods were described in Chapter 2.

Using others' opinions and reputation

Sometimes working relationships develop between individuals working for one employer and colleagues in other organizations, for example in the supplier–customer chain. Possibly the individuals could have worked together for a previous employer. These new and renewed relationships grow over time as the individuals have contact with each other, meet and talk. Sometimes this form of working relationship can develop between individuals working for competitive organizations. They will meet at conferences and social events, and their common interests will bring them together.

These relationships can be used as a means of identifying potentially suitable applicants for vacant posts. We have already discussed how recruitment consultants draw up their lists of people to approach, and poaching staff is not unknown. There is a difference between the two activities – the former is explicit and makes use of clear selection criteria, the latter tends to be covert and based on the strength of the relationship. Some employers have tried to impose clauses into employment contracts to prevent valued employees gaining employment with competitors. These are mostly found in the contracts of senior executives and highly skilled specialists. The reason obviously concerns confidentiality, the disclosure of sensitive information and competitive advantage. In this context the individual employee is a business asset. However, employees do have the right to change employers. Preventing this form of recruitment is difficult, especially if the move is initiated by the employee. Even though some employers try to discourage this form of movement by the use of restrictive clauses, they are difficult to enforce.

Most marketers know that the best publicity is what other people say about an organization, its products and services. Public perception is formed over a long period; a single advertising campaign, unless of an enormous scale, will have only a small impact. Attracting a strong field of applicants for a vacant post requires more than simply placing a well-designed advert in a leading newspaper. As we have already discussed we are selling an opportunity; this demands more than a good quality advertisement. The reputation of the employer also has an impact, but building an image as a good employer takes time, thought and a strategic approach.

The use of marketing techniques, as described in Chapter 2, can contribute, but unless that image is based on reality, it will be founded on sand and will fall quickly if people find out that the recruitment activity is merely gloss. Even though word of mouth recruitment is contrary to the spirit of equality of opportunity and is strongly discouraged by both the Commission for Racial Equality and the Equal Opportunities Commission, it must be recognized that the image of an organization is built largely by the tales told by one person to another.

If the employer invests in treating its staff well and provides benefits over and above those generally found, there is no reason why these should not be used to attract applicants. Perversely, many employers do not fully recognize the good things they provide for their employees; some make them available as an expression of philosophy and goodwill rather than seeing them as part of a reward strategy. This blindness is often seen in the public sector, where employment practices have been developed over a long time and are taken for granted. It can be hard to identify what is seen as of value to existing staff and potentially attractive to new employees. Therefore, it might be useful to do some market research before the start of a major recruitment effort. There are also other means of benchmarking practice: for example the Work Foundation (formerly the Industrial Society) 'Best Practice' guides, and *100 Best Companies*. Once they are identified, these features can be used as a means of attracting staff and selling the organization as an employer.

In the same way as an employer's reputation goes before it, the reputation of an individual, especially in the professions, and small and close communities, can precede consideration of his or her application. Using information based on the opinions of others can lead to some very successful appointments. Cook (1988) says that: 'research dating back to the 1920s finds that people are surprisingly good at predicting who among their peers will succeed, and surprisingly honest too. Even when they know their opinions will help determine who gets selected or promoted, people say (fairly) willingly what they think of each other and are (relatively) uninfluenced by who they like and dislike.'

However, making appointments in this way is becoming increasingly controversial. Traditionally judges and senior advisers are appointed following the taking of 'soundings'. This involves those making the appointment testing the reactions of others to each potential applicant. Reputation of individuals as leaders in their field can result in the halo effect (discussed in Chapter 1); or past achievements, rather than current abilities, can lead to the individual's name being added to a short-list. Reference checks are based partly on this premise, but as they are widely used and have additional considerations, their use will be discussed at length later.

Many recruitment consultants rely on reputation during their initial search for candidates. This approach does work, for a reputation is hard to develop and needs to be based on some achievement. Search consultants would not be increasing in number, and their use would be declining rather than expanding, if their services were not useful. However, reputations live on after the reason for their growth has been forgotten, and possibly the talent will have eroded with time and lack of use. Sometimes the context in which individuals were operating at a particular point in their development enabled them to achieve and acquire their reputation. This situation may have been specific, and possibly will not translate to a new organization and the current time. This situation is frequently seen in football managers, and a recent headline, 'Is Memory Lane a route to ruin?' captures the danger of using reputation as a basis for appointment. There is also evidence of very bad appointments being made as a result of assuming that achievement in one industrial sector can translate into another.

Past performance is a valid predictor for future behaviour, but reputation provides weak evidence of current ability.

There have been some famous cases involving the creation of false references, made-up qualifications and obtaining testimonies from people purporting to be who they are not. These included the pathologist at the centre of the furore about the retention of children's organs at the Alder Hey hospital. In July 2001 the *Guardian* reported that 'the independent inquiry concluded that Professor Van Velzen "must never be allowed to practise again" after finding that he lied when applying for the job of senior pathologist at Alder Hey and falsified records and post-mortem examination reports.' Using reputation as the main source of information can invite accusations of unfairness and favouritism. The Law Society and others have challenged the use of soundings for judicial appointments. Although the Peach Report confirmed the practice, the sheer fact that it had been exposed and challenged to such an extent by august bodies suggests that there may be better ways of making good quality appointments, using approaches that are transparent and apparently fair.

However, as Cook suggests, reputation and previous performance can be effective predictors of subsequent behaviour; therefore rather than this option being rejected, ways are needed to reduce the potential for bias and error, and to ensure that assessment is made on actual evidence of achievement and attainment. Information can be obtained from those who were actually involved with the individual, rather than relying entirely on what individuals say about themselves, and what their friends and colleagues say and do not say.

This is not to say that all individuals are dishonest, but it must be said that some are! People's memories naturally distort the past, and alter their perception of their involvement in and responsibility for events. Self-perception can be inaccurate. Some of us form favourable images of ourselves, and others hold quite negative opinions of their abilities. The memories of individuals providing information about the applicants can distort and over-emphasize their own contribution. Friends and colleagues often would rather say nothing than create a poor impression, and in any case, how is their assessment valid in relation to the post for which the person is applying? The values and cultural norms of organizations can be quite distinct, so care is needed to make sure that terms such as an 'excellent performer' and 'first class manager of people' have the same meaning to the potential employer as to the person expressing the view.

Nevertheless, obtaining additional and reliable evidence can help to ascertain a fuller picture of an individual's past achievement and identify that person's unique contribution. The more information is obtained from as many valid and reliable sources as possible, the more it will help to improve the quality of decision making. Matching skills and knowledge can be a comparatively straightforward process if it is based on clear criteria, and canvassing factual evidence about an individual's attainment and expertise should be uncontroversial.

Describing how a job is done or a role filled, as opposed to identifying what *has* been done, is less straightforward. Sometimes the differences are intangible, and employers are not explicitly aware of the unique distinctiveness of their ways of doing things. The terms used to describe the performance of the individual in a reference are assumed to have the same meaning for the new employer. In fact they can have subtle but different interpretations. If the opinion of the referee is given undue weight and is allowed to influence the selection decision, the results of this type of mismatch can lead to a poor outcome – for both parties.

This can be seen in the images of the role of a manager and the qualities required for effective performance. There is a general belief that 'a manager is a manager is a manager' and the skills are transferable between organizations and sectors. The debate about the need for private business skills in the public sector rages, particularly when there are skill and staffing shortages. It is assumed that it is possible and easy to exchange managers and other staff, and expect them immediately to change working practices, thinking and cultural values, without any preparatory work.

> *An effective leader in one context can be seen as a bully in another. Make sure that general terms are avoided or explained.*

One way of avoiding this form of mistake is to ensure that the values and cultural features of the employer are expressed clearly in all documents, including the request to previous employers and others for information about the applicant's previous performance. Additionally, when seeking others' opinions about the applicant's reputation and history, questions aimed at exploring the context in which previous achievements were attained will allow comparisons to be made with the current situation, the requirements of the post and the needs of the new employer.

OBTAINING INFORMATION

The flow of information during recruitment and selection is two-way. However this is not a free exchange. Just as applicants are cautious about the information they supply to prospective employers, so employers are guarded about what they say to potential employees. Both wish to portray themselves in the best light, but this is not always the true light. This can be seen in the ways in which employers are careful about whom applicants are allowed to meet during visits and open days, and what they are permitted to see. Similarly, applicants carefully decide who to name as a referee. There are examples of both applicants and employers being 'generous' in self-presentation, particularly when competition for jobs and skills is fierce.

The best way of overcoming this is for the parties to find out for themselves and not to take information on face value. Just as employers seek references and seek the opinion of others about applicants, there is no reason why potential employees should not seek supplementary information about the organization. In any case having done one's homework can be taken as evidence of being enthusiastic and keen about the job. This goes down well at interview, as it demonstrates the applicant is serious about the job and is interested in working for the employer. Another purpose, though, is to prepare the applicant to ask searching questions about what it is really like to work for the organization.

All the applicants were invited to attend a series of informal meetings before the final selection process. During the morning they were given the opportunity to discuss the job and organization with key individuals in a round of one to one meetings. These were all very amiable and low key. The applicants were told they were free to choose between the buffet lunch provided for them in the restaurant, or availing themselves of the staff facilities, before the final interviews to be held in the afternoon.

Only one applicant declined the formal lunch. Instead he 'went walkabout' and ended up in the staffroom, where he found two members of staff discussing the managing director's behaviour during a recent staff meeting. The applicant had the wisdom to recognize staffroom gossip for what it was, but had some concerns about the tone of the conversation: he had the impression of a dictatorial style, which took questions as indications of disagreement and discussion as open rebellion.

During the final interview the applicant asked the panel about the frequency and conduct of staff meetings. The panel indicated that these were well-ordered, information-giving meetings at which debate, albeit limited, was encouraged. He also questioned the level of morale in the organization. The answer was vague and confirmed the impression given by the staff room conversation. Even though the applicant was offered the job he decided to decline.

SUMMARY

This chapter has explored how recruitment and selection decisions are made under conditions of high uncertainty and risk, and how the exchange of information can facilitate the processes. To be effective, however, the provision of information needs to be equal and a two-way flow. The mechanisms used should recognize that biases and errors occur naturally in human perception. They can be designed to take these into account, thus reducing their impact by making explicit the factors used to form prejudgements. The benefit of having mechanisms that are of good quality (that is, fit for purpose) is the reduction in the risk of making the wrong appointment or losing the right applicant.

For enquirers to become applicants, they need to know from the employer:

■   what is the job to be done;

■   what is the role to be filled;

■   what is to be achieved;

■   what standards are expected;

■   what skills, knowledge and expertise are required;

■   what challenges and problems are to be faced;

■   what rewards are to be obtained;

■   what forms of satisfaction will be offered;

■   what opportunities for growth, development and enhancement will exist.

These will enable the individual to answer the crunch questions:

■   Will I be able to do the job?

■   Will it give me what I want?

■   Will I enjoy working for that organization?

■   Will I be able to work with the people already there?

■   Is there a future for me there?

If the applicants are to be converted into candidates, the employer will need to know if:

■   they have the skills, expertise and knowledge required;

■   they have worked for employers or been involved in situations that would have provided the necessary sort of experience;

■   they have the required level of education and training;

■   the way they present themselves and describe their interests complement the values of the organization.

These lists demonstrate the many opportunities for bias, assumptions and discriminatory prejudice that could influence decision making. This chapter has explored ways of supplying information to applicants to help them make their decisions and submit their applications. It has also touched on methods of gathering information about applicants. The next chapter will take this further, to explore how collecting information from applicants can aid the assessment of risk, predict successful performance, reduce uncertainty and facilitate negotiation between the two parties. There is ample evidence of how redressing the balance of power between the employer and the potential employee can contribute to the development of a positive working relationship, based on matched expectations and shared understanding. The provision and gathering of good quality information can only enhance the major capital investment that is the reality of recruitment and selection.

4

Applications

Once potential applicants have been attracted, information exchanged and firm expressions of interest made by both the prospective employee and the employer, an assessment of the quality of the applications is made. How this is done is shrouded in haziness. There has been little research into the decisions to include an application in a long- or short-list. Similarly, the text books on personnel practice, while describing other parts of the recruitment and selection process at length, only give passing reference (if that) to the sifting, screening and short-listing stages.

As these are critical decisions, we will consider next the nature of initial sifting and what happens in practice. We will then explore the mechanisms needed to ensure that the best candidate is carried through the subsequent phases. These mechanisms should also ensure that the candidates rejected are those who do not match the requirements and specification. The question of discrimination will be explored at some length. Usually the word is used pejoratively and taken to mean the unjustifiable differentiation of individuals. Actually, the word means to make or see a distinction. The whole of decision making in recruitment and selection is to draw out the differences between individuals and compare their fit against the criteria.

Initial screening is the first occasion when the person seeking employment and the potential employer 'meet' and make comparisons about each other. The employer has a job to be done and a specification to be met. The individual has wants and needs to be satisfied. Thus, the whole purpose of recruitment and selection is to enable the parties to discriminate, when they decide whether one will satisfy the requirements of the other.

The deliberate intent of the employer is to reject applications from those who do not meet the specification. The process, theoretically, should be one of rational decision making. It is rarely so. The equal opportunities legislation and good practice guidelines attempt to eliminate unfair practices. However, the advice given tends to be normative. The very fact that there is little reported research into what happens in practice during these initial stages suggests that the way these early decisions are made is not fully understood. Bearing in mind this lack of knowledge, this chapter will suggest how the decisions to exclude some applications and carry forward others can be made more explicit.

There is little point in pretending that human beings are not biased. So when making these suggestions, the existence of prejudgements and assumptions will be taken fully into account. This is to help those faced with making selection decisions understand how these factors can influence their judgement. We will look at how personal decision frames are developed, and what can be done to minimize the negative impact of these normal processes of human perception.

Torrington and Hall (1995) say, 'Care with short-listing increases the chances of being fair to all applicants and lessens the likelihood of calling inappropriate people for interview.' Moreover, care and systems designed to minimize inappropriate discrimination increase the chances of making the right decisions and getting the best person for the job.

HOW TO SHORT-LIST

Short-listing is the transition between recruitment and selection, when the number of applications attracted is reduced by the employer to those chosen to be carried into the selection phase. Even though short-listing has not been subjected to the same degree of research as some of the other aspects of recruitment and selection, Cook (1998) cites some work that demonstrates the 'people who wrote a lot were considered further, as were people who wrote neatly and people who use "certain keywords" – unspecified. People from certain parts of Britain – also unspecified – were more likely to be rejected.' He also quotes 'American research that finds women widely discriminated against at shortlisting stage. Women are also "stereotyped" as being more suitable for some jobs, or for working with other women. Both men and women shortlisters were equally biased against women.' There is a need, therefore, to understand better how short-listing occurs, and ways in which biases and prejudgements distort the fairness and quality of the decision. Once an insight has been gained from this examination, methods can be designed which improve the decision making and reduce the chances of rejecting the 'best' applicant.

Short-listing may comprise several stages depending on the number of applications received, the complexity of the requirements, and the sophistication of the selection processes used by the organization. For example:

▮ initial screening using biodata or reference checks;

▮ comparison against criteria;

▮ pre-interview testing;

▮ pre-meetings with key individuals.

Any of these methods can make use of CVs, application forms or online applications in a number of different forms. Other techniques, such as psychometric tests, are more often used after a short-list has been compiled. They will be described in Chapter 5 as techniques for selection. Some organizations carry out tests using online technology, but there are huge difficulties of ensuring that the person (or persons) completing the test is the individual applying for employment.

It is possible to make use of computing technology to screen CVs or application forms using optical character readers. These look for the occurrence of key words, phrases or terms. There are grave concerns about this methodology. It is very possible that good applicants are rejected simply because the individual has used a slightly different term for the same concept. It also means that decision making is given over to a computer rather than a responsible human being. This is contrary to the principles of natural justice, and may make the employer fall foul of various pieces of legislation relating to data protection and human rights.

Taylor (2002) argues the merits of systematic short-listing and suggests that more than one person be involved. This can be achieved by bringing a group together to go through all the applications and decide collectively. Alternatively, members of the group can examine the applications individually and then meet to compare assessments and decide which applications to include in the short-list and which to reject. There are arguments in favour of both approaches, and likewise some difficulties. Regardless of which method is selected, those involved should be trained and well aware of the criteria being used for the assessment of the applications. They should also follow a systematic process, which involves the thorough examination of each application and the application of some decision criteria to construct the short-list. The nature of decision criteria and how they are used will be discussed below. However, short-listing is rarely the simple, rational process described in textbooks, and seldom are all the criteria made explicit. Ensuring personal preference and bias are eliminated can be asking a lot. An aid such as the checklist in Table 4.1 can help to reduce the influence of these factors by drawing attention to decision criteria to be used explicit.

This appears to be a rational and perfectly logical process. However, it is probable that its use will be flawed, because in practice it is likely that other factors arising from the applications, or the opinions of those involved, will have an effect. It is only reasonable that these matters are discussed and considered. However, they should not be allowed to over-ride the predetermined criteria unless everyone involved agrees the factor has a critical effect. An example of this sort of incident includes none of the applicants having the essential qualification.

We need to remember that judgements made by one person or a group of people about others are prone to distortion, bias and error. Even when standard criteria are used, it is possible that they are applied inconsistently. The same

Table 4.1 *The short-listing process*

Steps	Comments
Decide who is going to short-list.	This could be the line manager, a member of the personnel staff, a recruitment consultant or a team of selectors. Involving several people, preferably those who will make the final decision, is important as it can help to reduce the negative impact of personal preference.
Design the process to be used. Consider the difficulties presented by each and how these could be dealt with:	
▮ *Short-listing by an individual.* If this is unavoidable, a system is needed to ensure that the use of the criteria is consistent and personal bias reduced.	The checklist below can help a manager to examine a lot of applications and be reasonably confident that the same judgements are being made, as they will all make use of the predetermined selection criteria contained in the description of responsibilities and the specification of competencies.
▮ *Group short-listing* – some processes and systems are: – reduce the negative effects of group dynamics; – avoid the introduction of side issues; – ensure the individuals involved use explicit criteria.	Methods such as nominal group technique help to reduce the effects of peer group pressure, while enabling each individual to make an equal contribution. A matrix or checklist will help to obtain consistency.
▮ *Short-listing by several individuals separately.* Again some mechanism is needed to ensure consistency, but this approach can reduce the effects of group pressure.	Integrating the opinions of short-listers can be done in a group setting or by one individual from the completed matrices, using, for example, the principles of the Delphi technique.

Table 4.1 *(Contd.)*

The specification of requirements can form a matrix or decision checklist.	Only those criteria that can be evidenced from the application or other specified sources of information should be used. The essential criteria are used for the first sift (eg qualifications or certain types of experience deemed necessary for adequate performance.
Decide which requirements are essential and which are desirable. Ideally, this is done before the recruitment stage starts.	The desirable criteria are those that are supplementary to those essential for adequate performance in post, provide an added extra, or an area that could developed or acquired through additional training.
Weight the criteria according to their priority.	For example, the most important criterion is deemed to be worth 10 points, the next most important 8 and the least important 1. The others are ranked accordingly, in between. Keeping records of decisions at this stage is important in case decisions are challenged.
Sort the applications against the criteria. The reasons for the selection and rejection of each application should be noted against the relevant criteria until all the criteria have been covered. The applications remaining form the long-list. If a further reduction in numbers is needed, decide how to carry out a further sift.	This is where the weighting of the criteria can be useful. The applications can be assessed against each criterion using a simple scoring mechanism to indicate the strength of match. For example, criteria fully met results in a score of 3. A near match is scored 2 and a weak match 1. No match or lack of evidence receives no score. The score for each criterion is multiplied by its weight, and they are all added to produce a total score. This can be used to select which of the applications should be carried forward.

Table 4.1 *(Contd.)*

The remaining applications can then be sorted into possible and probable candidates. These applicants form the short-list.	The possible are kept on hold in case anything prevents the probable applicants participating in the selection activities.

piece of evidence can be interpreted by each short-lister in a different way. This is because each human being makes decisions from a unique and individual perspective based on his or her own experiences, assumptions, beliefs and values. The best way of overcoming this tendency is to ensure those involved develop a shared understanding of all the criteria.

DECISION FRAMES

Decision frames are the mental constructions that help an individual chose whether to act, not act or ignore the situation. We are constantly faced with choices that require us to make judgements about ourselves, other people and the situations in which we find ourselves if we are to function effectively in the world. Without the ability to make these decisions, we would act in totally random fashions and be unable to make sense of our world. Everyone around us would act in similar unpredictable ways, and as we are not very good at coping with having little control over our own destinies and high levels of uncertainty, our lives would be highly stressful.

Kelly (1955) developed a theory of individuals as natural scientists, struggling to make sense of the world and the people in it. He suggested that we each build our own template that is used to interpret the situation we are in, simplify it and form a basis for predicting what might happen next. This template is constructed from our previous learning: our experiences and the messages and images conveyed to us by influential others (such as parents and teachers) – hence the use of the term 'construct'. We are also conditioned by the mores of the society in which we live. These build our value systems, preferences, and form our construction. We do not seek to have our constructs disproved; rather we seek to validate them even in the face of contradictory evidence. If there is no evidence to support a particular belief, the evidence is fabricated or the situation manipulated so that events, our behaviour and that of others are made to fit.

Our personal constructs inevitably sway our judgements, and mean that dispassionate decisions are virtually impossible. When this theory is combined with the our use of rules of thumb and the biases and errors that occur in decision making, as described in Chapter 3, the possibility of anyone being able to make objective and impartial decisions about other people is minimal. The reality is that we all make judgements on the basis of our own internal constructions, prejudices and assumptions about others. In other words, we all decide subjectively.

Research has demonstrated that training interviewers to improve their decision making in fact did little to change their behaviour. The actual result was that they became more aware of their prejudices. Even though this outcome may not have been the one intended, some improvements to interviewing practice must have resulted. Other research shows that increasing levels of self-awareness are part of learning and can lead to changes in behaviour. There are four basic levels:

I   **Unconscious incompetence:** this is the way I have always conducted an interview. I am good at asking probing questions.

I   **Conscious incompetence:** I should not have asked that question in that way.

I   **Conscious competence:** I had better prepare more carefully and think carefully about the questions I will ask every candidate.

I   **Unconscious competence:** this is the normal way I conduct interviews now. How did I previously do it?

Thus training to increase awareness of the flaws in human decision making can lead to some measures being taken to reduce the effect of the errors, biases and prejudices, and ultimately improve performance. One of the most practical and effective ways of minimizing the impact of the flaws in decision making is the use of high-quality, predetermined and explicit criteria. These make it possible to construct and use mechanisms that force decision makers to make explicit the grounds on which they make their judgements.

The law and the threat of employment tribunals also influence the use of systematic methods to aid decision making. Since the upper limit on the amount of damages that can be ordered in discrimination cases was removed, the threat has more force. The creation of records that demonstrate that decisions were made on the basis of criteria relevant to the job is now advisable, as well as being good practice.

Equally importantly, if employers want to ensure that the best person is appointed, they must be satisfied that the criteria used to make the decision to select or deselect are correct, and reflect the factors actually required for effective performance and fulfilment of the role. There is little consolation in knowing after the event that the strongest applicant chose to work for a major competitor because, for example, the manager responsible for the decision did not approve of the person's hobbies.

Decision matrices or checklists record the reasons applicants were carried through the selection procedure or rejected. They can also help comparisons to be made between applicants, even if their qualifications, experiences and attributes are dissimilar. Evidence can be collected, or areas in need of further checking identified. The use of such aids enables decisions to be validated. The main measures of validity are:

▮ **face and content validity:** the method and its contents appear plausible to those being assessed and to 'experts' in the area;

▮ **construct validity:** the method measures meaningful, relevant criteria;

▮ **criterion validity**: the criteria predict who will be best applicants as determined by relevant modes of assessment;

▮ **reliability:** a manager can check if the same decision would be made about the same applicant at a later time;

▮ **consistency:** other managers can be involved to check if they too would make the same decision.

The decision matrix in Table 4.2 shows how the specification criteria can be used for the compilation of a short-list. It provides a fair process for elimination, using the information supplied by the applicants as evidence.

Each application can be assessed against the matrix, and judgements made about which applicant best fits the criteria. Anyone should be able to take a batch of applications and check them for the factual evidence needed to make the assessment. Missing pieces of information can be obtained at other stages. However, failure to meet the essential criteria would mean that the application was not carried on to the later stages. The matrix can be used to make comparisons between candidates and ensure that the priority requirements are satisfied.

A checklist containing a series of questions may prove useful. This will ensure that the necessary areas are explored in the same way for each application. Table 4.3 is an example.

The use of a structure such as that provided by a decision matrix or checklist simplifies and improves the process of compiling a short-list. It ensures that all relevant factors are examined, and irrelevant factors are excluded from consideration. It also provides a means of coordinating views, if more than one person is involved in drawing up the short-list. It creates a lasting record that enables the decision to be checked. This can be particularly helpful if the selection process fails to result in an appointment, and there is cause to reconsider applicants, or if a similar post needs to be filled. Records of the reasons each application was chosen or rejected are also helpful as they provide evidence if the employer has to withstand challenges about the fairness and equity of the process.

Table 4.2 *Decision matrix for compiling a short-list*

Post:	Branch manager Criteria	E/D+W *	Mode of assessment	Assessor 1 2 3
Attainment	GCSEs (or equivalent) in English and Maths	E 2	Application	
	Evidence of post-16 training	E 4	Application	
	Management or supervision training	D	Application	
Achievement	Customer service (including dealing with complaints)	E 3	Application and interview	
	Staff supervision	D	Application and interview	
	Keeping financial and other records	E 5	Application and interview	
	Use of computer-based systems	E 4	Application and interview	
Abilities	Leadership	E 6	Application (?), selection activities and interview	
	Independent decision making	E 7	Application (?), selection activities and interview	
	Planning and organization	E 8	Application (content and presentation), selection activities and interview	
	Promotion techniques	D	Application and interview	
Aptitudes	Social skills	E 1	Selection activities and interview	
	Financial acumen	E 5	Selection activities and interview	
	Coaching	D	Interview	
	Concern for quality	E 10	Application (content and presentation), selection activities and interview	
	Assertive	D	Interview	
	Working with other people	E 6	Application (interests given) and interview	
	Concern for improvement	D	Interview	

* E = essential   W = weighting   D = desirable (importance 1–10)

Table 4.3 *Short-listing checklist*

Criteria Does the application contain evidence of:	Source of evidence	Indicators
demonstrable social skills?		
an interest in other people?		
coaching others and helping them develop their skills?		
possession of GCSEs (or equivalent) in English and Maths?		
experience of direct customer service, including dealing with complaints?		
assertiveness?		
the use of promotional techniques?		
any post-16 training?		
experience of keeping financial and other records?		
financial acumen?		
experience of using computers?		
leadership skills?		
any management or supervisory training?		
experience of supervising the work of others?		
making independent decisions?		
planning and organizational skills?		
concern for quality?		
any interest in making improvements?		

Decision matrices and checklists speed up the process of short-listing, simplify it and help to maintain consistency. They speed it by enabling the short-listers to concentrate on the absolutely essential criteria, by eliminating the need to read every application in full. Reading application forms can be boring, but the loss of concentration and the attraction of red herrings can lead to inaccuracies and inconsistent application of judgement. Therefore the use of a structure focuses short-listers on specific criteria. This will help them maintain their concentration and avoid following potentially irrelevant areas of personal interest. The concentrated search also means that the chances of distraction or missing a vital piece of information are reduced.

Which decision aid is used will depend on the culture of the employer and the way in which candidates have been asked to make their application. Different ways in which they can do this are described below. Some methods eliminate the need for devices or aids to support short-listing, as the application itself will provide a mechanism (such as Biodata). Others require more sophisticated decision aids. For example application forms and letters of application encourage the candidates to use their own words and structures when presenting their submission. Some way of analysing and comparing the varied and various styles used by each applicant is needed to organize what otherwise could be incomparable information.

FORMS OF APPLICATION

The advertisement or the additional information will tell those interested in the post how to submit their application. The most common methods are:

▌ Application form obtainable from the employer. This has set questions for required details and often space for additional information to support the application.

▌ Curriculum vitae (or CV) – traditionally, this is a brief summary of the education, qualifications and previous occupations.

▌ Letter of application – a narrative in which applicants are asked to describe in their own way (and often in their own hand) their suitability for the post.

▌ Telephone calls – some employers, and many recruitment agencies, use this as a way of conducting a preliminary screening, by asking applicants a series of questions to discern their suitability for the post.

▌ Attending an initial selection event such an open day, during which the applicant may be asked to complete some preliminary tests or do some tasks. This may also give the applicant chance to meet existing employers and ask questions.

▌ Applying online. Some employers are supplementing online application forms with online psychometric tests. The main difficulties are that the employer cannot be sure who is completing the test, and only those with access to a computer and the Internet can apply.

Some employers, especially those trying to encourage applications from underrepresented groups, provide guidance to potential applicants, advising them of the preferred form of application and indicating the desired contents. Let us examine each method in greater detail:

Application forms

The use of an application form enables the information wanted by the employer to be presented in a uniform fashion. The biographical data needed by short-listers and selectors is arranged for them in a standard way. This allows them to compare the separate applications. A form also offers some advantages for applicants. Once the skill of completing a form has been learnt, submitting another is relatively straightforward.

Torrington and Hall (1995) point out that the application initially was intended to form the basis of an individual's personnel record, rather than as an aid for selection. When forms were first introduced, most appointments were made after an interview of sorts, which relied on the fact that the interviewer was a good judge of character. Since then workers' mobility has increased, the labour market has changed from being local to national, and employment legislation has become more prescriptive. Reliance on face to face interviews as a fair means of making such contractual decisions is no longer seen as sufficient.

More systematic methods were needed to transform applicants into candidates. Consequently the application form developed from an administrative record into a means of conveying the information needed to aid decision making. The standardization of the way in which the information was presented was found more useful than idiosyncratic letters of application. It ensured that all required facts were obtained, gaps made obvious and the work of the selector simplified, as all applications had the same information in the same place. A typical application form seeks information about the following.

Personal details

- Name, address and contact details.
- Interests.
- The names of people able to supply a reference.

The questions included on the application form should be limited to the information required for the selection process. The Data Protection Act 1998 now specifies that information should be gathered and kept for specific purposes and only used for those purposes. The person providing the information should be told what use is to be made of the information and who will have access to it. Successful candidates can provide the information needed for their personnel records after they have been offered and accepted employment. There is no need to gather that data for all applicants.

However, information is needed to ensure that decisions do not lead to unjustified discrimination, and to monitor the effects of equal opportunities action, including:

- gender and ethnic origins;

- disabilities or medical conditions affecting the applicant's abilities to carry out the job, and information about any adjustments needed;

- unspent convictions (these are statutorily required for some occupations);

- the need for a work permit.

Some employers require information about marital status, age and children, though the reasons for wanting this information can be questioned.

Education and training

- Schools, colleges and universities attended with dates and qualifications attained.

- Training received.

- Details of other development activities that have led to skill or knowledge acquisition.

Employment history

- Present and past employers and their business.

- Dates of periods of employment.

- Main duties of each job.

- Salary.

- Reasons for leaving.

Additional information to support the application

This section can be the most taxing for applicants, for in effect it offers the same scope as a letter of application and asks applicants to 'write their own thing'.

Application forms are mainly used by large organizations (and often those in the public sector). The variability of CVs can cause difficulty to these employers, as they have to satisfy the inevitable bureaucracy and need for standardization that size brings. They also tend to be more concerned about demonstrating equality, the use of best practice and complying with the law. There is a cost associated with the use of forms and a delay in filling the post, and like any method, application forms have other pros and cons. Some people cannot imagine running a proper recruitment and selection process without them.

Others see them as an unnecessary encumbrance that prevents applicants from expressing themselves fully, thus showing 'what they are really like'. Some of the benefits and negative aspects are outlined below.

Drawbacks

▮ The style and format of the form can be constraining.

▮ The applicant may omit vital information if it does not fit into the standardized form.

▮ Having to fill in the application form may be off-putting to some applicants. It can take a considerable amount of time and effort to complete some of the more complex forms.

▮ The additional information section can lead to lengthy discourses that are difficult to analyse and compare. Even when applicants are advised what to say, the open nature of this section, after the tightness of the previous ones, can encourage some applicants to include everything they have ever done in an attempt to prove their suitability for the post. Alternatively applicants can be so brief that they provide no information worth speaking of.

This section works best when applicants are told what is expected of them. If they are then too verbose or wide-ranging, the short-lister is able to draw conclusions about the applicants' comprehension and communication skills. Similarly, if the conciseness is uninformative, this too tells about their abilities to convey their suitability for the post in question.

▮ Should an application form be competed in the applicant's own hand or should it be processed? Some short-listers prefer to see applicants' handwriting, confirming the impression that graphology is used more extensively than is acknowledged. There are, however, questions about legibility and space. Some people write in a small script; others' handwriting is large. How much space can be reasonably provided on a standard form?

▮ When typewriters were commonly used, it was possible to type the form and include a handwritten covering letter, thus applicants were able to supply an example of their handwriting and present a neat, legible form. However, as word processors have replaced typewriters it is becoming increasingly common to see returned application forms filled with 'please see attached sheets'. How much longer can preprinted application forms last? Some employers counter this trend by insisting 'no CVs', and the advent of online applications may further hasten the demise of applications.

▮ Short-listers expect to see a customized application for each job. They believe that if the applicants are really motivated and committed to the particular job, they will make the effort to fill in the form. However, is it realistic to expect applicants, particularly if they are in full-time employment, to spend the considerable amounts of time needed to complete an application form for every post?

▎ Application forms are part of the public relations effort of an employer. They transmit a message to the outside world about its style, and so contribute to its image. Even if that image is simple, the cost of printing and distributing the form can be considerable. There is also the cost of design and reproduction. Against this, the cost of the time saved by having standardized applications should be offset.

Benefits

▎ The application form draws the applicants' attention to information required by short-listers. One of the weaknesses of less structured methods is that applicants have to guess what is wanted (unless, of course, they have been told). A form can also discourage applicants from concealing gaps or weaknesses in their history. If for example they are requested to give dates of each attendance at college, it is more difficult for an applicant to hide a fact such as having spent a fourth year completing a three-year course.

▎ Asking applicants to present factual information in a standardized form makes it easier for short-listers to search for particular aspects, and makes it simpler to compare applicants.

▎ The information provided on the application form gives openings for interview questions. This is the occasion when gaps (such as reasons for leaving previous employers), over-egged achievements or ambitious statements can be checked. Analysing the information given on the forms requires the ability to read between the lines. As there is a tendency to take things on face value, the level of skill needed to spot what is not said is not commonly found in managers who recruit only occasionally.

▎ The application form can be used to obtain information other than that needed to support short-listing and selection. Details needed to form personnel records, monitor the effectiveness of recruitment activity and the effect of equal opportunities can be requested.

To summarize, application forms can facilitate systematic short-listing by asking applicants to structure the information they are providing about themselves, but at a cost. The use of a form can reduce the opportunities for applicants to demonstrate their individuality. On the other hand if applicants wish to demonstrate their idiosyncrasies, they will do so. Using forms is most cost-effective for employers that recruit regularly enough to justify the printing and production costs. They are also cost-efficient when the employer receives enough applications for each vacancy to require a mechanism to enable comparison between them.

Curriculum vitae

Submitting a CV is perhaps the most common way of applying for a post. They are cheap for the employer, and because they are used almost universally, their presentation is almost standardized. Templates can be found in many word processing packages, and job seekers are advised on how to lay them out in help books and during training courses. Typically a CV comprises:

I Name, address and contact details.

I Date of birth and perhaps marital status and the number and ages of children (but not other dependants!).

I Education and achievements.

I Employment history, with brief description of main areas of responsibilities and duties. (Salary and reasons for leaving are frequently omitted.)

I Professional activities such as membership of professional bodies, training and so on. (Personal interests are often excluded.)

I References may or may not be given.

The main omission from a CV is 'the additional information supplied in support of your application' section. This can be rectified if applicants send a covering letter outlining their case for being appointed to the position. However, this depends very much on the applicants. The contents and length of the CV can vary considerably. There is an accepted wisdom that a CV should be only one piece of paper, but this brevity can mean that the information actually provided is scant, and thus handicaps the short-listers.

As with the application form, there are arguments for and against using a CV as a basis for short-listing and selection:

Drawbacks

I There is no additional information.

I The mode of presentation and amount of detail will vary, making it difficult for short-listers to compare applications.

I The length of each CV submitted may vary from brief (one side of A4) to lengthy (a full narrative).

I All the information needed for short-listing may not be provided.

Benefits

▌ There is no cost to the employer.

▌ There is no delay while the application form is sent out and returned.

▌ It is possible to draw inferences about applicants' skills of communication and presentation.

▌ Generally CVs tend to be shorter than application forms, and can be easier to use for short-listing. The reduced amount of information makes it easier to isolate essential details.

For employers that recruit infrequently it is more economic to ask applicants to submit their CVs. It is possible to reduce some of the drawbacks by providing potential applicants with guidance in the advertisement, or with the additional information about the desired form of the application. This can be done tactfully, while helping applicants decide whether they match the person specification, like this:

How to apply
You are asked to outline how your attainments, experience, skills and abilities fit those required. Your CV should demonstrate your match with the profile of the ideal post-holder.

Letters of application

An advert can instruct that a letter of application should be submitted. Invited letters tend to be the opposite of CVs. While CVs draw out the factual aspects of an individual's history to demonstrate their suitability for the post, a letter tends to be a narrative 'selling' the individual's abilities and fit. Of course, a letter may include a brief resumé of qualifications and experience, but it tends to contain what the individual wants to tell the employer rather than what the employer may need to know.

It is not uncommon to see advertisements asking for interested parties to outline in writing how they meet the requirements of the job. The major disadvantage is that each letter will be different – unique to the individual. This will make straight comparison difficult. However, the letter form does allow each individual the opportunity to demonstrate his or her own approach. Some shortlisters believe that this provides invaluable insights on which to base decisions about suitability. Asking for letters does not cost the employer, and advice on form can be given as indicated above.

Alternatively, an individual may decide to approach a potential employer in writing, submitting what is known as an unsolicited application. Many job seekers are advised to do just this, as some employers find it useful (and cheaper) to use such letters rather than carry the cost of advertising vacancies. At one time it was regarded as courteous to acknowledge these letters and then keep them on file for examination when a vacancy arose, but the massive unemployment in the early 1980s meant that the number of letters outstripped the possible vacancies, and the cost of replying became excessive. Therefore the practice of using these letters as a pool of potential applicants fell into disuse. Moreover, the belief that commitment to equal opportunities required all jobs to be open to competition discredited using a file of previously received letters. There was something secret about them, possibly a 'fix'. However, changes in the labour market have led to this practice being reintroduced, as there can be a place for unsolicited letters. If they were ineffective, specialists and consultants would not advise job seekers to send them to possible employers!

The main disadvantage for the employer is that the letter contains only what job seekers want to say about themselves, not what the employer may need to know. Another disadvantage is that letters of this kind are sent when the job seekers are looking, not when the vacancy exists. The obvious advantage of these letters is that they cost the employer nothing. The cost of maintaining files and checking them does take time and resources. However, when compared to other recruitment methods, this cost is low.

The chance of the right letter arriving at the right time is pretty small, yet speculative letters have resulted in spectacularly successful appointments (and some outstanding failures!). If these letters are to be useful, the employer will need to set up a database or a filing system which is kept up to date. Recruitment agencies do this as a matter of course. These records are examined when a vacancy arises. However, it is always possible that in the interim the 'best' applicant will have been successful in the hunt for a suitable job, so will be no longer interested.

Telephone calls

Some advertisements ask interested individuals to telephone the prospective employer. This approach is used by search consultants and agencies, as well as employers. The main advantage of this method is its speed. However, it can restrict the field to those individuals able to gain access to a telephone during the normal working day. Some staff still have restrictions on leaving their place of work or making private phone calls, and of course it is possible that the place of work does not provide the degree of privacy an individual applying for another job would want. It is possible to widen the opportunity by offering the chance to call during an evening or weekend.

Regardless of when the call is made, its cost is carried by the applicant. The anonymity of the telephone can preserve confidentiality, while allowing factual information to be exchanged about both the job and the applicant. It is possible to envisage a situation when an employer does not want to give away too much information about a vacancy for competitive reasons, yet needs to attract applications. The telephone conversation thus enables the employer to find out who is calling, for example by offering to return the telephone call as a means of checking the identity and validity of the enquiry.

The telephone conversation can also be designed to act as an initial screen. If this is the case, callers should be warned that they will be asked to give information and answer questions that will be used for decision making. The employer is advised to make use of a structured approach, similar to that used in a face to face interview. Callers can then be asked for information about their qualifications and experience, and discuss some of their perceptions of the job in an organized fashion. This will enable:

▌ a comparison to be made against the requirements of the post and between applicants;

▌ the creation of a record for use in later stages of the process;

▌ the demonstration of fairness and consistency of treatment between applicants.

Likewise the employer can give out details about salary, location, purpose of the job and expectations. If a match is achieved, the enquirer can be asked to submit a written application, further information can be sent out to help the applicant, and a meeting arranged.

The advantage of this method is that it can be used to reduce the number of applications received. An enquirer can use the personal contact achieved during the conversation to obtain the information needed to decide whether to submit an application. Similarly the employer can assess on the basis of the initial questioning (and inform the enquirers) whether they fit the basic requirements. This will prevent the enquirer from spending a lot of time and energy in submitting a futile application. Short-listing is thus simplified. The applications actually submitted will be from those who have already attained a certain degree of fit.

One problem is that a manager, or someone else responsible, will have to devote some time to answering the telephone calls and carrying out the initial screening, but this should be quantified against the time spent later on processing applications that do not meet the criteria. The benefit obtained from the early personal contact between potential employee and employers should also be added into the equation.

Online applications

Asking candidates to submit their applications using an online form in principle is the same as using a paper-based form, except it has some unique advantages and drawbacks.

Benefits

■ Speed.

■ Ease of completion for applicants, particularly with disabilities.

■ Ability to manipulate the data supplied to examine applications by specific criteria separately.

■ Potential for automatic scoring.

Weaknesses

■ The selectors cannot be certain exactly who has completed the form.

■ Automatic scoring may lead to flawed decisions and be contrary to the Data Protection Act 1998. Under this act those subjected to automated decision-making techniques have the right to know the logic being used, to receive feedback or the right to appeal.

■ Only those with access to a computer and the Internet can apply.

■ There may be pressure to decide too quickly, thus excluding those who cannot submit their application immediately.

These difficulties are not insuperable, and the massive growth in the use of e-mail and the Internet suggests that asking applicants to express their interest in a job in this way will expand. The biggest advantage is the way in which online, computer-based applications open up opportunities to people whose disabilities have made traditional methods of submitting an application difficult. Once an employer has accepted that application forms can be other than paper-based, accepting voice tapes, disks, videos or Web cam becomes more possible.

SCREENING METHODS

Some means to analyse the contents of each applicant and compare their degree of fit with the role requirements and specification has to be devised, once the applications have been received. Some short-listers prefer to read all of every application, then try to decide which to reject and which to carry forward. This can be a totally unsystematic approach which does not facilitate consistent and fair judgements. The short-lister is faced with the task of processing a considerable amount of information – too much to allow simple yes, no, or not sure decisions to be made. This tends to lead the short-lister towards comparing the applicants against each other rather than the criteria. Trying to deal with the whole application at once also creates the opportunity for biases and human error to affect decisions. Personal preferences and prejudgements come into their own, and can dominate the process. If several people are involved there is a potential for unresolvable conflict. Each individual will rightly be using his or her own personal decision frame, which will be different from those of the other short-listers.

Various methods, some of which will be described below, can reduce the potential for this unhelpful conflict and lessen the negative impact of the flaws of human decision making. This is achieved by focusing short-listers' attention onto the specification and job or role requirements rather than their own internal criteria. Ideally those involved in making the decisions will be trained how to use the tools provided for them. They should also do some work aimed at helping them gain insight into their own personal preferences and how unsystematic decision making can, unwittingly perhaps, lead to unjustifiable discrimination. Some of the tools available to help short-listers structure their examination of applications and focus their decisions are given below.

Biodata

The biodata technique (or a biographical inventory) is based on a profile of the ideal role-holder. This is built from the biographic profiles of previously successful occupants. The profile thus highlights certain discernible features as an aid for the selection of future employees. The profile is developed from a database which can include personal details and typical career paths. The type of personal data may include family background (such as whether previous successful occupants were the first or youngest child), the sort of schooling received (such as type of school, subjects studied, roles played in school activities), social life and preferences (involvement in clubs or social groups, theatre-going, sporting activities and so on). It is also possible to include attitudinal issues and judgements (such as what factors candidates think influenced their personal success). Smith, Gregg and Andrews (1989) claim that biodata is one of the best predictors of job performance. However, Cook (1988) reports that applicants dislike this method more than others, but notes that it has been successful in predicting performance for sales occupations and in the insurance industry. However, the technique is used more widely in the United States than elsewhere. It is possible for applicants to fake the responses, and its fairness in equality of opportunity terms is questionable.

Several stages are used to collect the data needed to create the profile:

1. The job and the performance of previous role occupants are analysed, to identify the skills and characteristics needed for effective performance. This establishes the dimensions to be used.

2. A pool of items (examples of behaviours or background factors) relevant to these dimensions is created, and an instrument devised that enables the characteristics of the applicants to be compared with the dimensions. Multiple questions are used, with built-in checks and a scoring system.

3. The questions and scoring system are validated through testing against a sample of existing role-holders whose standard of performance is known for example, from the results of appraisal. Smith, Gregg and Andrews (1989) recommend that this sample consists of at least 300 people.

4. The findings are analysed statistically to see which combination of questions best predicts the performance of the sample of role-holders. Checks must be made to ensure that no gender or ethnic bias exists in the system, and it is consistent and reliable.

Obviously this approach is usually found in large organizations with sufficient numbers of employees in a particular role, and the resources available to fund such an approach. Moreover, repeated analysis is needed to ensure that the dimensions remain up to date. Despite Smith *et al*'s endorsement, as a short-listing device from which to predict future performance biodata contains several weaknesses:

■ It is expensive to construct and maintain valid profiles.

■ It assumes that certain factors outside the control of an individual (such as family size) have a direct effect on performance.

■ Using existing and previous employees for the sample population limits the profile and assumes future requirements will replicate those seen in the past. History does not always predict the future. If it did, very little growth, development and innovation would happen. We would simply go round in a never-ending circle of sameness.

■ Biases, albeit unconscious, can creep into the system. Some of the features identified as leading to successful performance may be culture, if not ethnically or gender-bound. For example it would be difficult for a young person to develop an interest in theatre-going if he or she grew up in rural Northumberland. Team sports have in the past been considered by some local education authorities to be unhelpful to the development of socially responsible, collaborative adults, and therefore have not been encouraged in schools. Similarly team sports can be seen in some schools as a male rather than a female pursuit.

The main value of biodata is the way it can help to sift a large number of applicants for a large number of similar vacancies. It enables factual comparisons to be made between the applications and the requirements and desired features of the successful post-holders. This acceleration and systematizing of the short-listing process allows it to be completed by comparatively junior staff. This and the predictive validity of biodata can compensate for some of the high set-up costs.

Graphology

The use of graphology, as a means of predicting success or failure in a job has been subject to some heated debate among personnel professionals and occupational psychologists. One reason for the revival of interest in this method is its widespread use in Europe. Some recruitment agencies have developed graphology services, and run workshops to explain the benefits and practicalities of the method to employers. However, very few British employers admit to using handwriting. Reviews suggest that the lack of interest is well founded, as the method has a low predictive validity. Smith, Gregg and Andrews (1989) say:

> Many systems have tried to use handwriting to predict personality. The simplest, and most scientific methods have used physical characteristics such as pressure on the page or speed of writing. The second approach focuses upon single features such as slant, regularity and connections between letters. The third, holistic approach is the method adopted by most graphologists and uses complex analyses which are based on combinations of features.

Unfortunately many of the studies of graphology have been flawed. Tests have shown that people are able to change their handwriting at will, and handwriting has been shown to have no correlation with an individual's subsequent actions. Cook (1988) notes that research has found that it 'is not a viable assessment method' as consistency between analysts is not high. He reports that 85 per cent of companies in France use this technique but only 7–8 per cent of British employers acknowledge its occasional use.

Nevertheless, it can be argued that handwriting is used extensively as a method of screening and short-listing applicants, albeit subconsciously and unsystematically. If it were not so, why do many employers expect applicants to include at least a letter supporting their application in their own hand? Some advertisements still ask for this to be done. One possible explanation is our tendency to make assumptions about people based on evidence from direct sources such as an individual's handwriting. We must remember that:

▌ Handwriting style is influenced by school teachers, who over the years have had fashions and have taught different generations of children differently. We have passed from copperplate through forward-sloping script, via italics to big semi-printed letters.

▌ We make unsubstantiated assumptions such as believing that tidy, small handwriting is produced by a neat, introverted individual and that large, scrawly script comes from an extrovert. Of course these are blatantly untrue, but they illustrate how easy it is to form truisms.

▌ Short-listers, as noted above, have their own personal preferences and prejudices which inform their decisions. If one of these concerns hand-writing and prejudices are allowed to lead to assumptions, subsequent decisions will be influenced accordingly.

One way of dealing with these biases is to be aware of them, and to use techniques that have more validity and are less open to unfettered subjectivity to aid decision making.

Tests

Testing is a well-known way of exploring applicants' knowledge and mental abilities. The use of such instruments has increased dramatically over the last 20 years. An IRS survey in 1997 reported that 75 per cent of employers used ability tests, compared with 50 per cent in 1991, and by 1999 this proportion had increased further. The use, however, was mainly in support of another technique. One reason for this growth is the comparatively high level of predictive validity. This is a measure used to assess how well one selection technique can predict subsequent performance in the job. Smith, Gregg and Andrews (1989) reported that tests can achieve a coefficient of about 0.5, while interviews range from 0.15 to just over 0.3 depending on their degree of structure. However Cook (1988) points out that 'selectors should choose their tests carefully', for the difference between individual tests can be substantial. We will look at psychometric testing in more detail in Chapter 5, but there are two major forms of ability test used for screening.

Work-related ability tests

These ask the applicant to complete some sort of task, such as typing a letter, laying bricks, giving a presentation or solving a typical problem. In some cases applicants are asked to submit examples of their work in a portfolio. It is possible to buy ability tests from commercial producers, but some employers prefer to devise their own tests to ensure that they are relevant to the actual job. In all cases, it is essential that care is taken to ensure that the tests genuinely reflect typical requirements of the role, to avoid building in opportunities for unfair discrimination. This can be seen in cases where applicants have been expected to complete questionnaires using complicated terminology and printed in small type. The actual questionnaire, rather than the questions being asked, could discriminate against those who first language is not English, those with visual impairments and those who can not read or write very well.

Appointing a new director of finance gave Bruce's Burger Bars the opportunity to develop a systematic method for screening new staff. Historically the company, like many catering businesses operating in the high-volume, low-price market, had taken people on with little checking, and relied on its ability to sack them if they did not come up to scratch within the first few weeks. But the new director of finance pointed out how costly this was, and argued that it did nothing to add to the company's reputation – either as an employer or as a place to go. A change of approach was ordered.

The personnel staff analysed a representative sample of jobs with the managers to establish a set of benchmarks for substandard and competent performance. They then designed a battery of simple tasks that realistically represented the jobs to be filled. These included a test of money handling, an exercise designed to examine manual dexterity, a verbal question and answer exercise designed to explore approaches to customers, and a test to discern levels of understanding about safe and hygienic working. The tests were then administered to existing staff, and the results compared with performance ratings and earnings. (The company gave commission payments related to the receipts taken by each front-line employee, and bonuses for kitchen staff on the basis of other measures such as wastage rates.) The tests were adapted until a high level of fit was achieved between the results and the existing measures of performance.

From then on, people interested in the vacancies were asked to submit applications as before (a letter of application giving education, previous employment, preferred hours of work and personal details). After the initial sift, potential candidates were asked to participate in the test. Applicants who 'passed' the tests were then invited for a formal interview with the manager of the appropriate outlet.

As care is needed with the design, the tests should be a fair representation of the real job, rather than a series of difficult exercises designed to 'get applicants to show what they are made of'. They should be checked to ensure that they do not contain any gender or ethnic bias and are fair to those with disabilities. Similarly, the administration of the tests needs to ensure that each applicant is treated in exactly the same way as every other applicant. These imperatives have led some employers to abandon their own tests and instead rely on commercially available ones. Those obtained from reputable suppliers have been carefully researched and checked to remove any unnecessary bias.

Commercially supplied tests can be expensive, and only test the features they have been designed to test. These may not be the ones required by the employer for the particular job in question. There can be a great temptation to look through a catalogue and chose a test because it looks good, rather than decide which behaviours and knowledge need to be explored. Fortunately most test suppliers are very cautious and helpful. They also supply instructions on how to use the tests.

Cognitive ability tests

These explore mental skills rather than physical ones, and are sometimes referred to as intelligence tests. They can test specific abilities such as numeracy, understanding or cognitive skills, or they can explore general intelligence at different levels. General tests tend to be collections of questions testing specific abilities. These tests too can be devised internally, but this is not to be recommended. Nor should they be used casually.

Numeracy, reading and aptitude tests are often used for the initial screening when a large number of staff is being recruited at any one time, for example graduates to a trainee scheme. The aptitude tests can include tests of trainability as well as preferences for particular types of work. For example, clerical aptitude tests explore speed and accuracy as well as literary and numeral abilities, and mechanical and spatial reasoning ability tests can be used to assess potential for engineering tasks.

Mental ability tests are also available to explore more advanced cognitive skills such as problem solving and reasoning abilities. The choice of the test should be driven by the needs of the job as revealed by a systematic analysis, for as before, it is important to be sure assumptions, bias and halo effect are excluded. For example, it would be wrong to believe that graduate engineers have acquired well-developed critical appraisal skills simply because they are used to carrying out experiments as part of their degree course.

Sternberg (1988) claims that there are seven different forms of intelligence:

I verbal abilities – the ability to use and understand speech;

I quantitative abilities – computation such as adding, incrementing and interacting between numbers;

I problem solving – the ability to represent problems and to identify solutions;

I learning abilities – to remember through repetition and rehearsal;

I inductive reasoning – the ability to perceive relationships between related terms and concepts;

I deductive reasons – the ability to draw conclusions from information provided about a problem;

I spatial abilities – forming and identifying visual representations.

Not all of these are considered routinely when setting down the requirements of the job.

Generally, tests are administered and interpreted by occupational psychologists or those licensed by the test suppliers as being suitably qualified and experienced. These safeguards are necessary as cognitive ability tests are powerful instruments, and in the hands of inexperienced or careless individuals they can do damage to the individuals taking the test, as well as exposing the employer to accusations of unfair treatment.

The test results are usually interpreted with the aid of data tables which compare the individual's results with those obtained by others in a similar sample population, such as entrants to the army, sixth formers, students in their second year at university, or senior executives. These tables are generally standardized and based on norms, but their validity is dependent on the size and composition of the sample used to compile them. Using a small sample or one which is biased in some way leads to inbuilt discrimination. Most test suppliers are very careful to ensure that their samples are as large and as representative as feasibly possible, and are statistically valid.

The opinion of others

Many search consultants offer to carry out initial screening as part of the commission. This will reduce the number of applicants the potential employer needs to consider. Typically, applications (on a form, or more usually a CV, or perhaps a telephone interview) will supply preliminary information from which the consultant draws up a long-list. Applicants deemed to match the requirements and specification are identified and invited to a preliminary interview. The quality of screening is totally dependent on the quality of the consultant's skills and understanding of the employer's requirements. The benefits and disadvantages of relying on a consultant's opinion were discussed in Chapter 2, and it should be recalled that a one to one interview is regarded as a poor predictor of performance in the job.

The benefits of relying on a consultant to carry out preliminary screening are:

I   The preservation of confidentiality and anonymity for both parties. Some employers do not want their search for a new appointee to be public. Some applicants do not wish to divulge their interest in another job.

I   Paying an agent to conduct the screening can save time for the employer.

I   The consultant can bring expertise. This is particularly so if the employer does not recruit new employees very often.

I   The consultant can ask questions that a potential employer cannot. Similarly applicants are likely to give information to a third (independent) party that they would not be prepared to give to a potential employer. (For example, not many applicants would admit to a prospective employer that they did not get on well with their current boss.)

The disadvantages are:

▮ Interviewing is a poor predictor of job performance.

▮ The consultant will be seen by applicants as a representative of the employer, and therefore the way in which they are treated will be taken as indicative of the organization's treatment of staff. (There are anecdotal reports of search consultants treating female applicants aggressively to see if they can take the heat.) This does not reflect well on either the consultant or the employer.

▮ The interviews, being one to one, are prone to all sorts of poor and unfair practice, with little redress available on the part of the applicant.

▮ The briefing given to the consultant needs to be thorough, and action taken to check understanding. The consultant will naturally use personal interpretations and prejudices, which may be contrary to those implicit in the employer's culture.

Competencies

The use of competencies and competences has also increased as the importance of systematic selection has become more widely accepted. The difference between the two terms has been debated hotly in some quarters, while in others they are used interchangeably. For the purposes of this book, competence is taken as a measure of the output of performance. Competency is a definition of ability or skill – what individuals put into their performance. The main use of competence and competency statements was initially in development, but now they are being applied to other areas of human resource management. Application forms and supplementary questionnaires can be designed to elicit experience, attainment, skills and knowledge against behavioural statements.

In a way the use of these statements can be seen as updating weighted application blanks. In their original form these were very similar to biodata, as they were designed to elicit information about the applicants for comparison against an idealized profile of a successful post-holder. Cook (2001) describes how a profile is created from empirical data. In the case of a department store assistant, the 'perfect' individual is between 35 and 54 years old, has had 13–16 years of formal education and over 5 years of sales experience, weighs over 11.5 stone, lives in a boarding house, and so forth. The application blank is designed to explore these and other desirable features of applicants' make-up. The criticisms of this approach are very similar to those levelled at biodata.

The modern use of competency- or competence-based applications is much more systematic, depersonalized and forward-looking. They can be used together or separately to develop a structured application form that will facilitate short-listing, as can be seen from the example in Figure 4.1.

Application for the post of Training Officer

Please complete the following questionnaire. You should give actual examples of activities that demonstrate your achievement in each of the areas. You should also indicate your level of skills, using the ratings given below, remembering you will be asked about your answers if you are called for an interview.

- poor (you have very little experience or skill in this area)
- satisfactory (you can make some significant improvements to the level of your skills or experience)
- competent (you are able to perform this area of work at a level regarded above average most of the time).

Area of work	Evidence
1. Identification of training and development need: is able to analyse complex situations and distinguish between training and other problems. Rating: ☐ poor ☐ satisfactory ☐ competent	
2. Design training and development strategies and plans: is able to organize resources for the achievement of objectives and implementation of plans and prepares contingencies. Rating: ☐ poor ☐ satisfactory ☐ competent	
3. Provides learning opportunities, resources and support: is able to implement and monitor the plans designed to achieve objectives and accommodate the needs of individual learners. Rating: ☐ poor ☐ satisfactory ☐ competent	
4. Evaluate the effectiveness of training and development: is able to review actions on the basis of information gathered from a range of sources. Rating: ☐ poor ☐ satisfactory ☐ competent	
5. Support training and development advances and practice: engages in action to ensure own professional learning and development and is prepared to innovate. Rating: ☐ poor ☐ satisfactory ☐ competent	

Figure 4.1 *Sample competence-based application form*

From the information given, the short-lister can judge which of the applicants best matches the requirements for the job. Obviously there are risks of applicants over-estimating their own abilities, but the warning in the introduction should be sufficient to safeguard against all but the most determined boast. The evidence column should provide examples of previous experience (either from work or life). For example, in response to question 4, a typical answer might be:

> I conducted an employee survey to assess the staff's views of training and development. I designed a questionnaire which covered how needs were identified, what action had been taken to satisfy the need and how the staff were able to implement the results of the training received. The answers to the questions were analysed by staff group and section. The section results were discussed with the respective managers and the overall findings of the survey reported to the Management Group.

The value of using such statements is that the questionnaire is related directly to the requirements of the role, and that the applicants are asked to use their own words and examples as evidence. At the initial screening stage, only the word of the applicant is available, but subsequent checks can be made. The applicant can be asked to provide factual evidence of achievement, which is checked via references, or other selection methods can be used to assess the applicant's level of ability. These are discussed at greater length in Chapter 5, and include, for example, criteria-based or behavioural event interviewing and work samples.

The use of competence or competency statements directly related to role requirements offers short-listers a practical way of comparing applicants in a systematic and fair fashion. The use of a matrix to record decisions can enhance the process further.

SHORT-LISTING MATRIX

The matrix allows applications to be compared against the criteria, and each applicant against the others. It also creates a record to demonstrate the grounds on which each applicant was short-listed or rejected. This latter consideration is important, for applicants have the right to ask employer's to justify their decisions – in front of an employment tribunal if the applicant believes he or she has been subjected to unlawful discrimination.

The matrix takes the job or role requirements and specification criteria as one of the dimensions and lists the applicants along the other. The use of a simple grid means that the applicants can be given a number, thus providing anonymity. This is one way of removing bias or reducing the halo or Satan effect, if for example some or all of the applicants are existing employees or known to the short-listers. The matrix also provides a mechanism for pooling the opinions of several short-listers.

Some employers hold short-listing meetings during which several short-listers exchange their opinions of each application and collectively decide on the short-list. This method is prone to all the dynamics of group working, and can result in decisions being made on criteria that are very different from those required for the successful performance of the job. Even if this type of short-listing is a part of the employer's way of work, the use of a matrix can facilitate the decision making and reduce some of the negative effects by following the steps outlined below.

1.   Each short-lister is asked to complete the matrix before the meeting.

2.   When the short-listers come together in person they are asked to compare their assessments of each application against the criteria.

3.   The applications failing to achieve the minimum or essential criteria are eliminated immediately (in a way that can be evidenced factually).

4.   The applications best fitting the criteria, as agreed by all short-listers, are carried on to the next stages of selection.

5.   The applications over which the short-listers disagree remain. The short-listers compare their views using the matrix, and articulate the reasons for them. If there is a need, further discussions about the fate of the application can take place, and informed decisions can be made.

On the evidence recorded in the sample matrix shown in Table 4.4, applicant number 4 would be short-listed and number 2 held as a reserve. Numbers 1 and 3 would be rejected. The grounds for holding number 2 as a reserve would be the lack of supervisory experience. The criteria not evidenced are gaps, not negatives. Application number 3 has similar gaps, but the poorly presented application could be taken as indicative of the standard of communication skills or a lack of concern for quality and accuracy. Applicant number 1 has not had leadership experience and the application has many other gaps.

Used in this way, the matrix can aid decision making because:

■   It makes the criteria explicit.

■   It provides a tool that simplifies the process.

■   It facilitates the pooling of several short-listers' opinions.

■   It enables comparisons to be made between short-listers and between applications and the criteria.

■   It provides a record of the decisions and the grounds on which they were made.

Table 4.4 *Sample short-listing matrix*

Criteria for Office Manager	1	2	3	4
Attainment				
Successful completion of a post-16 education course	Yes	Yes	Yes	Yes
Some job-related management training	Yes	No evidence	No evidence	Yes
Achievement				
IT office applications	No evidence	Yes	No evidence	Yes
Customer service	Yes	Yes	Yes	Yes
Staff training and supervision	Yes	No evidence	No evidence	Yes
BS 5750 (or other quality system) and record maintenance	No evidence	Yes	Yes	Yes
Abilities				
Communication skills	Untidy application	Yes	Application badly produced	Yes
Leadership skills	Trainer with no supervisory responsibilities	No evidence	No evidence	Yes
Planning and organization	Poor organization of information on the form	No evidence	Application badly produced	?
Training and instructional skills	Yes	No evidence	No evidence	Yes
Aptitudes				
Customer-focused	No evidence	Yes	No evidence	Yes
Accuracy	No evidence	?	Application badly produced	Yes
Concern for quality	Untidy application	Yes	Application badly produced	Yes
Additional factors				
Involved with people	Yes	Solitary interests	No evidence	Yes
Learning and self-development	No evidence	Yes	No evidence	Yes

■ It gives a mechanism for checking the validity of decisions. If needed, the applications can be re-examined and the decisions checked to see if other short-listers reach the same decisions on the evidence supplied.

SUMMARY

This chapter has looked at how applicants are invited to express their interest in the vacancy, and the strengths and weaknesses of various methods were discussed. Each has its own advantages and difficulties which need to be taken into account when deciding how to request applications. The different methods also have different impacts on how applications are sifted and the short-list drawn up.

Short-listing is the first point in the recruitment and selection process when judgements are made about people and their abilities. These should be made in relation to the role or job requirements, for without explicit criteria employers can easily discriminate unfairly, and potentially expose themselves to complaint and criticism. Without due care, it is possible to lose the best candidates and carry forward weaker applications.

Ironically there has been little research into how the decisions are made during short-listing, but the normal biases and errors made during selection are widely reported. We have looked at these to explore what practical actions can be taken to reduce their negative effects, and ensure that the applications carried forward to the next stages of the process are those that best fit the criteria. Not only do employers need to ensure they are considering the best applications, they also need to be fair and demonstrate the quality of their processes. Aggrieved individuals do have the right to claim discriminatory treatment, if they feel that they have been subjected to illegal discrimination. It is up to employers to maintain adequate systems and records to demonstrate that this has not happened.

Various techniques, particularly the use of checklists and matrices, have been suggested as ways of structuring decision making and recording why one application was preferred over another. These approaches have been found to be useful for both personnel staff and line managers, and as a decision aid, they can provide vehicles for combining the views of short-listers against the criteria. Regardless of the method used, it is important that all those involved know how the decision is to be made, their part in the process, and the criteria to be used. Similarly applicants need to know what is happening to their application and when they are likely to get a response.

The next chapter will consider the selection process – when the applicants become candidates and meet the employer in person. We will look further at the effects of biases and prejudgements, for person perception has a major influence on decision making and needs to be taken fully into account when choosing selection methods. The usefulness and use of the different techniques will be assessed in the context of their validity and feasibility. Techniques, however, do not make decisions; they facilitate them. It is the human beings involved who must exercise their flawed judgements, and we will keep this firmly in mind.

5

Selection methods

We have accepted that getting the right person in the right job at the right time is a vital part of any manager's job. It follows that unless the decision to appoint an individual to a job is 'good', the chances of the appointment being 'successful' are severely limited. A good selection decision can be defined as one that results in the person appointed attaining a satisfactory level of performance in an acceptable amount of time at an acceptable cost.

This chapter will be used to explore some of the methods and techniques available to support managers when making those critical decisions. We will also return and look again at some of the common pitfalls and danger points that litter the process and inhibit the use of best practice. From the outset, we should recognize that many mistakes are caused because many employers give little thought to the critical nature of the decisions. They are then surprised and disappointed when an appointment fails. Often the person appointed is blamed and labelled as a failure, rather than weaknesses in the process and poor application of methods being identified.

The previous chapter outlined some steps that could be taken to reduce the chances of some of the most common errors occurring, and so create a sound basis for selection. Nevertheless, the techniques are not 'fail safe'. Using these as a basis, we will now look further into the research that has been carried out into recruitment and selection methods, practices and procedures. This has examined the validity and impact of selection techniques, and highlights areas of concern. It also indicates where changes may be needed to affect the quality of the process and its outcome. We will also look at how the decisions can impact the well-being of all the individuals concerned. It is comparatively easy to accept that the process is stressful for candidates, but do we acknowledge the stresses of the managers involved?

The main research findings will be summarized briefly, so they can be used to draw attention to the scope for error contained in best practice and even the soundest of techniques. Some of this can be attributed to the methods themselves, but the main source is the frailty of the human decision makers. We will also look at the different selection methods most commonly used, and the pros and cons of each will be explained. The reason for this is to provide guidance and help decide which method will be best suited for a particular purpose.

When a selection method is chosen, account should be taken of:

▌ the nature of the job or role in question;

▌ the impact the method will have on the candidates;

▌ the impact the method will have on the manager and key others;

▌ the feasibility of running the method in terms of:

  – cost;

  – resources required (space, materials, equipment);

  – skills needed to design and operate the method;

  – the time required from the manager, the candidates, experts and others;

▌ the likelihood of the method achieving the desired outcome;

▌ the effect on the employer as a whole.

This chapter will conclude by offering some ideas on how to improve the final stages. As far as many employers are concerned, this is the decision to offer the job to the candidate deemed to be the best and reject the others. They may be aware that even a verbal offer is a binding contract and therefore needs to be made with care. However, it is not always remembered that in reality, this is not the final decision. The final decision is made by the candidate, to accept the offer or reject it. The candidate decides whether to close the deal.

> A *verbal offer of employment is a binding contract but the best candidate may turn it down.*

Shortages of skills and high levels of employment mean that candidates are in a stronger position when negotiating their reward packages and other terms and conditions. Even though the balance has shifted, many employers still believe they have the ultimate power, and neglect the possibility of the preferred candidate turning down the offer. The consequences of this can have a wide-spread effect including:

▌ the demoralization of those involved;

▌ blaming and fault-finding;

▌ public embarrassment;

▌ uncertainty and delay to projects and the introduction of changes;

▌ confusion for other staff.

Herriot (1989a) argued that the process should be seen more as a negotiation. If this advice is followed, much can be done to reduce the chances of the best candidate rejecting the offer. Therefore when discussing the design of selection and decision-making methods, we will take account of their impact on candidates, and how they will help us maintain our focus on the full range of possible outcomes, including the loss of the best candidate.

Filling a post is a negotiation between two parties – the potential employer and the potential employee.

WHETHER SELECTION METHODS CAN PREDICT SUCCESS IN POST

The aim of using decision-making techniques is to increase the chance of selecting the best candidate and not appointing one without the abilities and experience needed to do the job. The methods used should therefore be designed to assess capabilities, experience and competency, and to predict how well the candidates will fit into the role being filled and the organization as a whole. However, research into the various selection methods commonly used suggests the chances of predicting a perfect match between candidates and their ultimate success in post are lower than one would wish (and possibly believe to be the case).

Cook (1988) draws together the results of the most important research into the validity of selection methods. These findings indicate that the most common selection methods can be poor predictors. He suggests six criteria to aid the choice of selection method. These are cost, practicality, generality, acceptability, legality and validity. Validity is a measure of value – whether something is worth doing, whether it does what it claims to do, and whether it predicts an outcome with meaning. When assessing selection methods, several different types of validity can be used to assess their comparative worth. The most important of these is the ability of a particular method to predict performance in the post. The standard of performance can be judged using a number of different factors and techniques relevant to the post and employer, and can include supervisor appraisal, trainability, production and achievement of objectives.

The probability of the method being able to forecast the level of performance is measured by a statistic called a coefficient of predictive validity. A perfect selection method is one that predicts accurately every time it is used which candidate will be the one who will perform to the standard required. This has a coefficient of 1. A method with a coefficient of 0 may or may not predict the candidate's performance – the employer may as well appoint the first person met on the high street. Generally, a coefficient of over 0.5 is regarded as an excellent predictor, 0.4 – 0.49 as good, 0.3 – 0.39 as acceptable and less than 0.3 as poor.

The available methods have been subjected to extensive testing over the years, in organizations of all types and size, and using jobs of different kinds. The results of the research have been combined using a technique called meta-analysis. Hunter and Hunter (1984) refined the approach, which is now regarded as a way of removing sampling errors. The coefficients of predictive validity in Table 5.1, taken from Smith, Gregg and Andrews (1989) are widely quoted and generally accepted as they are based on meta-analysis:

Table 5.1 *Coefficients of predictive validity*

Assessment centres (for promotion)	0.63
Work sample tests	0.55
Ability tests	0.53
Assessment centres (performance)	0.43
Personality tests (combination)	0.41
Biodata	0.38
Structured interviews	0.31
Typical (unstructured) interviews	0.15
References	0.13
Graphology	0
Astrology	0

The methods most commonly used for short-listing and appointment – unstructured interviews, references, and judgements made about an individual from their handwriting – have the lowest predictive validity. The methods with better coefficients tend to be used less frequently, particularly in smaller organizations. The reasons often given for their lower popularity focus on the time and level of expertise needed, and hence they are regarded as expensive. Yet any selection decision represents an investment of at least several thousand pounds, and potentially many hours of unproductive work can be needed to correct a bad decision.

Some managers may be reluctant to use more reliable and rigorous methods because they believe they are good interviewers and good judges of character. Which of course they are, but . . .

ERRORS AND BIASES

We first discussed how we all form our initial impressions of other people in Chapter 3. When we meet someone for the first time, as is often the case in a job interview, we take in the evidence presented to us from the very first moment of meeting, and assess it using our own personal system of beliefs that has been constructed throughout our lifetime. These beliefs underpin the judgements we make about situations and people, and enable us to make sense of what otherwise would be a confusing, unpredictable world. They help us reduce the anxiety engendered by uncertainty, and fit what could be seen as random events into a picture that makes sense to us. This system of personal beliefs (or constructs) is used to explain the past, interpret the present and predict what is likely to happen in the future. We use our constructs to prepare for situations and rehearse the part we are to play. We also use them to prejudge the people we will meet and predict how they are likely to behave. Some of our constructs are conscious, and we are well aware that we hold them and why. Others are so deeply entrenched in our subconscious that we are not aware of them, even less why or where they came from. That is, until something happens, usually something out of the ordinary, that challenges them or that brings them into contrast with other beliefs.

We form a initial view within 30 seconds of meeting a person. Changing this view can be hard work.

When we meet someone for the first time, we use our construct system as the starting point from which to judge the other person. We use scant information as the building blocks for subsequent decisions. We also use mental shortcuts known as heuristics or rules of thumb. They are so called as we know they work because we have used them before. They are generalizations and half-truths, and save mental energy by reducing the need to gather and process data. They can be wrong and unreliable, but are rarely called into question. As more information is exchanged, it is used to confirm the initial impressions and firm up our opinions. We actively seek further information to do this, and discount anything that serves to disprove our initial assessment. In this way, we reaffirm our rules of thumb and preserve our self-image as a good judge of character. This is known as self-serving bias.

Another source of error lies in the way we tend to focus on the person who is the centre of attention and ignore other factors that might have influenced their previous behaviour. We tend to assume that individuals are responsible for what has happened around them. This can happen, for example, when applicants are asked to describe a successful project they have worked on. It is easy to believe that the applicant contributed to the success and so is a competent worker. It could be that the reason for the success lies in the actions of others, and the applicant was a passenger. We attribute failure in the same way. If a person is unable to answer a question during an interview, it can be taken as a general reflection of his or her ability and knowledge. In fact, the person's failure to answer may have been caused by a confusing question.

We see people in isolation – giving a soliloquy centre stage – rather than being part of the play that takes place in a greater scheme of things. If a person has been assessed as being successful in one area of work, it is taken that he or she will be as good in all other aspects of the job. This is called the 'halo effect'. A similar effect can be formed by associating an individual with the success and achievement of other people or organizations with whom he or she has had contact. If you hold a poor opinion of the organization that employs one of the individual's referees, you are likely to transfer that opinion onto the individual, without necessarily being aware that this mental process is happening.

We base our first impressions on what is witnessed. Judgements are based on what we see and hear the other person say. We can also use our senses of smell and touch. Using all of these inputs, we make assessments about personality traits. Conclusions are drawn, and then used to predict how the person is likely to behave in other, non-related situations with different people. Our conclusions tend to be gross generalizations and over-simplifications. Nevertheless, unless something makes us challenge our view, the information so gathered is regarded as reliable.

We use stereotypes as another way of saving mental energy and providing shortcuts to decision making. A stereotype is a set of broad truisms used to describe all members of a group, who are assumed to share similar character- istics. Individuals are classified, and it is then assumed that the common, general characteristics are found in all individuals classed as members of that group. The use of these generalities denies uniqueness and the potential of individuals, and can be grossly misleading, leading to false conclusions. For example, it is well known that Irish people often have red hair and names beginning with O. They are also likely to get things wrong, but have good luck. People with red hair are known to be quick-tempered. When a young women called O'Donnell with fiery red hair walks into the interview, it is easy to leap to the conclusion that she is Irish and that the interview will have some lively exchanges.

Even when we are aware of these dangers, we are susceptible to some of the other traps and errors. For unless we try and deliberately use other evidence, our impressions, opinions and conclusions are naturally formed from:

▌ **Appearance** – hair, facial appearance, dress, demeanour, use of cosmetics. For example hunched shoulders can be taken as indicating timidity. (It could be the individual is simply cold.) The use of perfume (or aftershave) can be seen as an indicator of extroversion. A quiet voice demonstrates a lack of confidence.

▌ **Behaviour** – conformity to social mores, conventions, patterns, body posture and language. Everyone knows to wait before being asked to sit down at the start of an interview. Someone taking a seat before being asked is lacking in courtesy and is presumptuous. Leaning against doorframes indicates sloppiness, which implies careless work. A hand tremor is a sign of nerves rather than another indicator of coldness. Someone who cannot handle an interview will not do very well with a complaining customer. A regional accent is still regarded as a sign of poor educational achievement.

∎ **Role** – roles occupied or assumed to be occupied are used to predict behaviour and state of mind. A teenager in jeans and a studded leather jacket is likely to be disobedient and disruptive. A senior manager will not move easily into a lower-paid position even though the application says otherwise. Someone with experience of the private sector will not understand the publicly funded services, and vice versa. People aged over 50 do not like change and cannot learn. If they do, it takes them longer than younger people.

Research also shows that, in addition to the above errors and biases, our memories of other people are prone to distortion. We tend to remember the first and last people we meet better than those who were encountered in the middle of a sequence of interviews. We also recollect a person who had an outstanding feature – like a big nose or a facial mark – or someone who did something out of the ordinary (such as suffered a coughing fit) better than those who were 'normal'. The outstanding feature may not have any relevance to the situation, but it still fixes the person in our memory. These effects are known as:

∎ primacy;

∎ recency;

∎ saliency.

These effects can influence decisions simply because the decision makers are able to remember those individuals better. This does not necessarily mean that the decision is likely to favour the individual best remembered. To the contrary, the 'best candidate' may be rejected because the selectors were unduly and negatively influenced by the after-effects of a common cold.

We prefer to be surrounded by people who share the same values as ourselves. At our first meeting the exchange of information aims to seek common ground. If our initial impressions are favourable, we tend to ignore differences later revealed and assume agreement. We seek harmony and consensus, and avoid conflict and disagreement. We like to be with people we like and who like us. If the early indicators are favourable, we tend to play down or ignore potential areas of difference. This can be based on the slimmest of evidence, but early signs of the potential for disagreement and later conflict are given considerable weight. Being risk averse, we are likely to prefer a candidate that does not appear to present this threat.

No technique can totally eliminate these errors, biases and distortions.

The reasons these subconscious processes exist is to safeguard us by protecting our physical and mental health. They can play a useful role in ensuring coopera- tion and effective working, by helping us to find like-minded people who share our values. They help us avoid unnecessary stress caused by internal conflict within the work team. They save time and mental energy that could be expended when making decisions about other people. These errors and biases should therefore be seen for what they are – part of the normal human perception and decision-making processes. But as they contain prejudice and unfounded assumptions, they should not be allowed to govern modern recruitment and selection practices.

It would be misleading to suggest, however, that decisions taken by one person about another could ever be totally objective. We all use our personal construct system to inform our judgements. Therefore selection methods should take account of the existence of these processes, and provide ways of gathering information to enable decisions to be made on objective and relevant evidence. No selection method can (or should) take over from human judgement, but it can help to structure the process. Using explicit criteria, developed from the analysis of requirements and organizational need, rather than the selector's personal preferences, prejudices and assumptions will also enable subjectivity to be contained. Linking evidence gathered systematically with explicit criteria will help decisions to be made within a robust framework that can be applied consistently to all candidates, and can be explained. This approach will reduce the risk inherent in predicting the behaviour of another person.

SELECTION METHODS

Selection methods do not make a subjective process objective. They do not remove bias, nor do they prevent errors. The use of a method does not make the decision, or remove the responsibility for that decision and its consequences from the individual manager. Selection methods provide a systematic means by which information can be gathered about candidates and help predict their performance in that particular job. A method will only explore the aspects of human skills and abilities that it has been designed to explore. Some are more valid than others, but a good method badly applied will not do its job effectively.

The starting point of the selection process is the creation of the job descrip- tion or role outline, and the specification of the competencies and attributes required for effective performance. Having these written in clear terms and based on a thorough analysis makes choosing the selection methods straight- forward, and means that decisions can be made against predetermined and explicit criteria. If the description is too general and unfocused and the specifi- cation written in unspecific terms, no matter how sophisticated the selection method, the information gathered will reflect the vagueness of the initial thinking. If you don't know what you are looking for, how will you know when you find it?

Validity

The choice of selection method should reflect the level, context and content of the post in question, and have some demonstrable reason for being used. We have already discussed the importance of predictive validity, and touched on other ways of assessing the value of different types of selection method. These included cost, practicality, generality, acceptability, legality and validity.

The cost of a method and its practicality sit close to each other. Some methods may seen costly in terms of design and application, but their effectiveness in the longer term may prove worthwhile. Therefore while these factors are important, they should be assessed using a cost–benefit analysis rather than just expenditure and how difficult they are to arrange. Generality relates to how widely a method can be used. One of the main advantages of interviewing is that it can be used for all posts. However, the needs of a particular post should determine which method is the most appropriate. There should be no debate about the need to use a legally acceptable method, but the legality of the use of a method is a different matter, and in particular, equal opportunities legislation is a major consideration. We will return to this question again. Meanwhile, the following aspects outline how the worth of a method can be assessed:

▌ **Face validity.** Candidates should believe that they are being asked to carry out an activity that is relevant to the post for which they are being assessed. They should feel that it has some meaning. They should not be made to think that they are being asked to jump through hoops for the amusement of the selectors, nor should they see the selection activities as games. The method should be acceptable to them.

▌ **Content validity.** 'Experts' should agree that the contents of the selection method are relevant to the post in question, and that they reflect accurately the type of work normally or likely to be encountered by post-holders. This is achieved by using real-life aspects of the work and situations encountered during the design or choice of the method. The 'experts' can include existing post-holders or the manager.

▌ **Construct validity.** The selection method, activities and instruments should test aspects of behaviour that are meaningful in the context of the job. These should be those aspects identified as being essential for effective performance in the specification, and become the criteria used as the basis for decision making.

▌ **Criterion validity.** The selection method should explore what it sets out to explore. If a selection instrument purports to measure a candidate's skills in social situations, the instrument should do so on each occasion it is used. The results of the one activity should not be assumed to demonstrate the candidate's ability in other areas.

▮ **Reliable validity.** The selection method should be consistent. It explores and predicts performance against the criteria it is designed to examine, because it has done so in the past and can be relied upon to do so again in the future. The result should be the same regardless of who uses it (providing they have all been trained in a similar way).

▮ **Impact validity.** The impact or effect the selection method is likely to have on candidates should be considered. This is different from face validity. Even if the candidates regard the method as valid, the impact of the method can still be adverse. Ideally those applying the method should have experienced similar sorts of activity under similar conditions. We will return to impact again, for it can influence the subsequent decisions of candidates and have a lasting effect on candidates.

When deciding on the choice of method and designing the process, consideration needs to be given to the likely effect resulting from the following:

▮ **The behaviour and role of the assessors.** Will they interact with candidates, and in what capacity? Will they be intimidating? Are they at an appropriate level in the organization to give the 'right' messages about the level of the job?

▮ **The number of assessors.** Will the number of internal people involved overwhelm the process? Will there be sufficient involved to give a balanced, all-round perspective of the candidates?

▮ **Obtrusiveness.** The assessor's behaviour needs to be suitable so that it does not intrude and disturb the candidates' performance.

▮ **Degree of involvement.** Only have assessors when they are needed. For example, there is usually no need to invigilate. It is not likely that candidates will 'cheat'. It should be clear when they are carrying out formal assessment as part of the process and when they are acting informally. For example, the part being played by the assessors during the lunch break should be unambiguous.

Strengths and weaknesses

Each method has its own particular strengths and weaknesses. Even those shown to have a low predictive validity have a legitimate role to play in the selection process, if they are chosen for the right reasons and their weaknesses are acknowledged. In the following section, the comparative strengths and weakness of the methods most often used will be discussed. In doing so we will make some assumptions about the ways in they will be applied. It is not possible to describe all the possible variations, as some are prone to the idiosyncrasies of the selector(s), and it must be stressed that any method is only as good as the way in which it is applied.

Interviews

One to one interviews

This is perhaps the most widely used method of selection interviewing. Typically each candidate is questioned by the interviewer about his or her background and experience. The application form, if used, or CV forms the basis of the discussion, which can flow freely in the direction the parties wish to go. It enables topics and issues to be explored at some length and in depth, and allows the interviewer to probe any particular areas of interest or concern. However, despite this benefit, as an approach it contains many potential pitfalls for the interviewer:

■ It is not easy for a sole interviewer to ensure consistency of treatment between the candidates.

■ It can be difficult for an interviewer to probe in depth and remember fully what was said. Note-taking, observing and questioning simultaneously is not easy.

■ The process is open to all the biases and error of perception described above. The sole interviewer does not have the benefit of a co-interviewer who can add a different view and enable perceptions to be checked.

The 'safety' of the process has also to be considered. The interviewer is very open to accusations of malpractice. It is not unknown for disappointed candidates to level accusations of unfair treatment and discrimination. Without the evidence from another party, it can be difficult to present a defence. The one to one interview also exposes the candidate to unfair treatment and bad practice. Therefore, any complaint is one party's word against the other.

One way of avoiding these pitfalls is to ensure that the questions are preset and each candidate is treated in the same way. The questions should be asked in a similar fashion, and detailed contemporary records should be maintained. Another way is to have the company of another interviewer.

Panel interviews

Panel interviews tend to be used by larger and/or publicly funded employers. They are used widely, and tended to be a trusted method of selecting candidates.

Nevertheless, research suggests that this method is not very good at predicting which candidate is likely to be the most successful in the job. The reasons for this are mainly found in the errors outlined above, if the interview process is unstructured.

Panel interviews have additional problems that may contaminate the selection decision:

▌ Without proper planning and preparation, the interviewers are liable to use their own criteria and apply different standards with different weightings. Even when explicit criteria have been developed, consistency can be difficult to achieve.

▌ Every interviewer wants the chance to ask her or his own questions. The need to allow each interviewer a fair amount of time with the candidate can inhibit the opportunity for one interviewer to probe the candidate in depth in a particular area, for example if a potential weakness is suspected.

▌ Candidates can easily be confused by the rapid changes in the direction of the questions. This may be seen as a reflection of their abilities rather than a flaw of the process.

▌ The dynamics of the interviewing panel may take over. Interviewers can try to score points off each other at the candidates' expense, or strive to influence the decision by tripping up less favoured candidates.

Even though they are extremely problematic, panel interviews do have a valid contribution to make in the selection process, for as research carried out by Herriot (1989a) suggests, the interview is a social event. It is the main formal occasion when employers and candidates meet face to face. It is also the occasion when the negotiations regarding the nature of the role and the employment contract begin. As such, it has a useful purpose. Therefore, rather than the abolishing the panel interview, ways of improving its contribution and separating it from the other parts of the selection process should be introduced. Some ways of doing this follow.

Structured interviews

Rather than follow the candidate's application or the interviewers' preferences, the interview's underlying format is planned in advance. The various stages of the interview are identified, and each question is designed as part of the whole, to flow from the previous into the next. The mnemonic WASP is used as a guide:

Welcome (and introductions).
Acquire (information from the candidate).

Supply (information to the candidate and answer any questions).
Part (by describing what will happen next and thanking the candidate).

The structured approach means that each question has a purpose, and is designed to elicit information required to aid the selection decision. The questions should aim to explore the requirements contained in the specification, explore issues raised in the individual's application, and amplify any points that remain unclear. It is also the opportunity for the candidates to ask questions. The type of questions asked by each candidate also provides information that contributes to the picture assessors are building of the individual.

Members of the interview panel should do some preparatory work, preferably together. They need to be clear who is going to do what, when, and ask which question. Thought also needs to be given to the ways in which each candidate may be probed and challenged in ways that are appropriate to the situation, if any one of the interviewers detects any area in need of further exploration. Having a chair of the panel is useful here, for an interviewer can indicate to that person his or her wish to carry out further questioning. The chair is then able to manage the interview with an eye to the flow and the importance of keeping to time.

It is important that each candidate is asked questions about the same areas in the exactly the same way. This ensures that required information is obtained and candidates are treated consistently and fairly. However there should be some flexibility, for excessive rigidity can waste the opportunity for social interaction. Face to face interviews provide the chance to explore particular issues in depth with individual candidates. Therefore, even though the same structure should be followed for each candidate, there should be scope to allow some deviation.

Some employers have found the use of detailed questionnaires useful to supplement the information given on the initial application form. Others ask candidates to submit essays, papers and other forms of ancillary data to complement and inform the interview. There are also additional ways of probing in depth without distorting the structure – providing the interview is planned, and the panel members understand what is happening and what they are expected to do in the process.

Needless to say, notes and a record of the interview should be maintained. These are required as aides memoire for use when making the final decision, to reduce the distortions of saliency, primacy and recency, and to demonstrate that the correct procedures, designed to ensure that each candidate was treated fairly, have been followed.

Competency-based interviews

Structured interviews are based on preplanned standard questions, which range over all aspects of the post. Competency-based interviews focus directly on the elements of the specification – the abilities and behaviours required for effective performance of the role. The interviewers, the structure of the interview and the questions are selected to explore these elements in some depth. Thus the range of questions is deliberately more limited than those posed in the structured interview. The aim of this type of interview is to probe. Their use has increased as the weaknesses of the traditional interview format have become recognized more widely. They are comparatively easy to set up, providing the initial analysis of the post requirements has been carried out thoroughly.

Focused interviews

Focused interviews are similar. The difference lies in the emphasis of the questions. They are designed to cover the tasks to be completed. While a competency-based interview might explore decision-making skills, the focused interview would ask how the candidate would approach and complete a specific task, for example implementing a major change initiative or managing the breakdown of the working relationships between two members of staff.

If the job or role has several distinct elements, it is possible to hold several focused interviews, each designed to explore a particular area. This is known as serial or sequential interviewing.

Behavioural event interviews

Behavioural event interviewing was initiated in the United States, where it was developed to identify the differences between average and superior performers to specify significant competencies. The purpose of this type of interviewing is to explore at some length and in some detail the skills used by a candidate during a particular event or set of circumstances. Typically questioning would follow this sequence:

■ Tell me about a successful project you have worked on.

■ What part did you play in its success? (This is probed in detail as many candidates find it difficult to articulate their own part, as opposed to that played by the others in the team.)

■ What was your most useful contribution?

■ What leads you to that conclusion?

■ How did your contribution help the project's success?

■ What makes you think that?

■ Could you have taken other actions that might have meant the project was even more successful?

■ Did you do anything that might have hampered the work of the others in the team?

And so on. The aim is to help the interviewers assess what candidates have done and are able to do, as opposed to what they say they can do. The probing can help candidates to identify skills they may not know they possess. The questions can be based on aspects of the post that are critical for success, and enable each candidate to choose suitable tasks from their own experience. Alternatively, projects cited by the candidates on their application forms can be used.

Situational interviews

Situational interviews (or scenarios) are used to project the candidates into the future by asking 'What if' questions. The questions can be chosen to reflect aspects of the job that are known to present difficulties, or those which will be critical for future successful performance. These should stem from the analysis used to draw up the role outline, description of duties and specification.

Ideally the scenarios should be challenging, but realistic. There can be a temptation with this sort of interviewing to play games with candidates by asking them impossible questions. Asking questions candidates cannot answer does not provide the information needed to predict their future performance. It may test their abilities to respond to direct pressure and challenge, but, unless this is a real feature of the work, such 'game play' should be avoided. Instead, the questions should be designed to enable the candidates to think themselves into the situation, and explore with the interviewers how they would deploy their skills and experience.

Informal interviews

We considered informal meetings when discussing how to facilitate the provision of information about the job and employer to prospective candidates. Informal interviews held as part of the selection process are different and have another purpose. The interviewers are expected to feed their assessments to the members of the final interview panel or appointment board to help with the final decision. Mostly unstructured, this form of interview allows candidates to be questioned on a broad range of topics, superficially or to some depth. As the interaction between the candidates and interviewers is on an informal footing, the flow of the conversation can be less in the form of a question and answer session and more of a discussion, an exchange of views on a topic. But care is needed in its management, for if the interview is too relaxed and informal, it can confuse the candidate as to its real purpose. This confusion can be caused by the following:

▌ If the discussion focuses on one aspect of the job, this can be given undue importance and be taken out of proportion.

▌ The name 'informal interview' can also be a misnomer, with its exact contribution to the final decision being unclear to the candidate.

▌ Informal interviewers are not always certain of their role in the final decision, and may present themselves as having more influence than is really the case.

▌ The process, being a social interchange, is prone to all the errors and biases of perception described above.

▌ The effects of group dynamics and internal politics within the organization can take over the process. If this happens, the assessment of candidates can be subordinated to other (unrelated) considerations.

However, this social interaction is important. It helps candidates decide whether they are likely to fit the organization and its existing staff, just as much as it allows the interviewers to assess their potential colleagues.

Final interviews

It is possible to combine the above forms of interview. In this case, care is needed to ensure consistency and maintain a clear separation between different modes of interviewing. Candidates should know what is expected from them at each stage, and the interviewers should be clear about their role.

When other selection techniques have been used, the final interview's role is to ensure that all required information has been obtained from the candidates and that the candidates have the information they require. Some employers use the preliminary selection methods to enable some of the short-listed candidates to be eliminated (either by their own choice or by their demonstrable inability to meet the requirements). The final interview is the 'last' chance for selectors and candidates to talk to each other before the decision to offer, accept or reject the post is made.

The decision can be made in one of several ways. (Guidance is given below on techniques to help this.) Whichever method is used, candidates need to be assessed systematically against the job's requirements and specification. It is also the time when the candidates are compared against each other to assess who is likely to be the best in post. While this is happening, candidates, too, will be making their decisions about whether they will accept the job if it is offered. All too often selectors forget that, in reality, the candidate makes the final decision.

Structured activities

The reason for using structured activities as part of a selection process is to explore areas of knowledge and skills in ways not possible in interviews. Various techniques, all of which are known to be valid and reliable predictors of performance, are described below. However, it should always be remembered that they can only achieve their potential if they are designed and administered properly. They should conform to the criteria listed above, and be designed to elicit evidence that enables the candidates' ability to satisfy the requirements of the role and the specification to be assessed. They should also be fair and uniquely unfamiliar to all candidates. This means:

■ They should not require candidates to possess information not generally available.

■ No candidate should need knowledge about the internal workings of the organization.

■ The activities should not have been seen previously by candidates. (It has been found that prior knowledge can actually disadvantage some as well as advantage candidates.)

Work samples

Herriot (1989a) argues that work samples are the most accurate predictor of performance, as the candidates are assessed directly on the way they complete activities relevant to the job or role in question. However, research shows that when the output of the work sample is rated rather than measured, the potential for unfair bias remains. In the context of most administrative, managerial and professional work, assessment would need to be on a rating scale. Measurement of output is only possible in jobs where a quantity is produced, for example in secretarial work where speed, accuracy and volume can be measured, in technical work where similar measures can be used to quantify the standard of work, or in customer handling roles where the number of calls made and results achieved can be set. In some occupations it is possible to construct benchmarks or have norms of standard achievement levels. There are questions concerning the quality of the work done, but provided these can be assessed in other ways, asking candidates to carry out a relevant task or part of the job and measuring the results of their efforts can be a valid, reliable and appropriate means of assessing abilities.

The choice of task or aspect of the job needs careful consideration:

■ It should be closely and clearly related to the main purpose of the job or role.

■ It should be discrete (that is, stand on its own and not be dependent on the input of others or ancillary information for its completion).

■ It should be possible for the candidates to complete it in a reasonable time.

■ It should be meaningful, so candidates can see the relevancy of what they are being asked to do.

■ Candidates should not need inside information or specialist knowledge.

■ The means of assessing the results of the activity should ensure consistency between candidates.

■ Each candidate should be asked to perform the work sample under the same conditions as the others.

When the sample is chosen and it is decided how to assess the result, it should be remembered that the candidates are not being asked to perform the task under normal conditions. If it is desirable for the task to be performed under similar conditions to those normally encountered as part of the job, it may be necessary to make special arrangements to stimulate these, for example by providing equipment (such as computer facilities) and ensuring that the candidates are free from undue distraction. However, the circumstances under which the activity is being carried out inevitably mean that the candidates will be under abnormal stress, and account should be taken of its effects. For example, it would not be reasonable to compare a candidate's work carried out in a simulated situation under stressful conditions to that of an experienced employee who was working under everyday pressure. Therefore the sample should be chosen to reflect the content, level and context of the job in question but it should not represent the hardest part.

Tests

The most commonly used test of knowledge is the achievement of an academic qualification or level of qualification. For example, a degree is taken to represent a certain level of cognitive ability. Some employers therefore recruit graduates regardless of subject area, believing they will obtain the desired standard of intellectual ability. However, changes to the levels of qualifications and the introduction of different types of qualification have meant that comparing them can be difficult and confusing.

Some employers use their own tests to explore a particular skill or area of knowledge, rather than the candidates' ability to carry out an aspect of the job. For example, a typing test would contain a variety of measures chosen to examine the typist's capabilities across a range of activities. A work sample would consist of a number of typing tasks normally encountered routinely in the job. The latter would not necessarily explore all the skills a competent typist could normally be expected to possess.

When using a test, it is important that the following conditions are satisfied:

▌ The tests should be piloted to ensure they actually test the knowledge and skills they purport to examine.

▌ They should produce the same results each time they are used and be reliable.

▌ Mechanisms are needed to ensure that marking is fair and consistent.

▌ Marking or assessment should be carried out by someone who is not involved in the final decision.

▌ The administration of the test should be consistent.

▌ Care is needed to ensure that nothing happens to distract the candidate unduly.

Presentations

Presentations should be intended to explore candidates' abilities to expand their ideas and arguments in a public forum. They provide candidates with the opportunity to demonstrate their abilities in three ways:

▌ making presentations – testing communications skills, such as clarity and comprehensibility of speech, use of the language, style of delivery, use of aids and use of time;

▌ convincing the audience of their case and arguments – exploring the structure of content, logic of arguments, credibility with audience, engaging with the audience, building rapport, use of influencing skills and so on;

▌ demonstrating the level of knowledge – soundness of arguments, use of evidence, correctness of facts, choosing the right level for the right audience and so on.

When using this method, consideration needs to be given to the choice of presentation topic and the wording of the brief given to candidates, and to when to brief the candidates. If told in advance they will want to know the size of the audience and its composition, the aids to be made available, and how long their presentation should last.

Some employers simply tell the candidates they will be required to make a presentation, then give them the topic on arrival, with a limited time to prepare. This ensures that the work is exclusively that of the candidates, but it means that they are not able to consider or reflect on the content of their presentation. It also restricts their use of aids. Candidates should also be clear about the expected way of taking and responding to questions from the audience.

The size of audience and the roles its members are to play in assessing the presentation also need to be decided. The assessors will need to be briefed, and their role in the assessment of the candidates explained. Some mechanism and structure will be needed to collect feedback and ensure that the assessment is consistent. Some employers find the use of pro formas ensures that assessment is made against the criteria contained in the specification. They also help in collating the assessments of individual assessors and creating records, and facilitate feedback. If only a few members of the audience are to carry out the assessment, the remainder need to have this explained so they are clear about their role and contribution to the process.

In-tray exercises

In-tray activities could be called work samples, but a well-designed in-tray exercise is more than a collection of typical communications encountered routinely in the job. Yes, they are a collection of letters, memos, reports, messages, e-mails, fliers and so on that the post-holder could expect to receive during the course of a normal working day.

A well-constructed in-tray contains items that have links with each other. This explores the candidates' abilities to make connections, discern issues, make inferences and give appropriate responses. Normally a time limit is imposed to introduce an element of pressure. Additional items (for example an urgent e-mail) can also be fed in while the candidates are working through the in-tray, to create an added source of realism – interruptions are a fact of life for most people at work.

A range of skills may be explored by this method, including decision making, planning and organizing, problem identification and solution, communication skills and delegation. The in-tray can be rated on the written replies and notes. Alternatively or additionally, a follow-up interview can be held. The latter provides for the assessment of additional aspects of performance such as assertiveness, interpersonal and influencing skills. It also allows the assessor to explore the reasoning behind the candidates' decisions.

The in-tray should be designed to reflect the content, context and level of the post, but it should not require specialist or internal knowledge. The size of the in-tray should also reflect reality. It would be unfair to give candidates vast quantities of items to deal with, if in fact the job-holder will receive very little when in post. Similarly, it would be misleading to give only a few items if the job-holder is likely to be inundated with such matters.

Case studies

Case studies are designed in similar ways to in-trays. It is possible to ask candidates to prepare to work through the case study before participating in a selection event. Alternatively, they can be presented with it on arrival. If candidates are asked to prepare in advance, it must be accepted that candidates will devote different amounts of time and energy to the study, and may draw on others for help.

A case study normally presents the candidates with a scenario that contains a problem. The task is to analyse the problem, and distinguish between symptoms and real issues. Depending on the level of the post, the case study can be straightforward, with all the necessary information contained in it – a bit like an Agatha Christie novel. Everything that is needed is given, just concealed. For more responsible roles the case study can contain gaps, misleading or contradictory information, so candidates have to deduce and use their intuition to get to the 'right' answer. In the latter case, the case study is used to explore candidates' abilities in decision-making processes: that is, their abilities to investigate and resolve problems. In the former case, it is used to explore their use and analysis of information. The case study should not assume that the candidates have any inside knowledge about the employer or its business. Any necessary facts should be contained in the case study, or be provided as an additional resource. Whether the candidates make use of such resources can be another measure used to assess their abilities.

One of the outcomes of the task could be a written report. If this is required, the candidates should be given some indication of the expected format, as style and presentation can be a product of organizational style rather than skills. For example, some employers expect reports to be a narrative arguing the case, with a brief executive summary. Others expect a punchy analysis with short recommendations. How the report is to be produced will also require some thought. Some candidates will be very competent in using a word processor, so will be able to write and finish their own document. Others will be used to preparing a draft and asking someone else to produce the finished product. The report can be the only means by which the candidates' work is assessed.

Another outcome, used instead of or as well as a report, can be a presentation to an 'audience', for example playing the role of an internal committee. The audience will include the assessor, but the other members will need to be clear about the role they are being asked to play. The candidates should be told what to expect and who will be in the audience. They should also be given appropriate materials and access to aids. The use of PowerPoint and OHPs is now widespread, but the points made about expectations and abilities to produce the finished product apply here as well. The assessment of the content and analytical processes should not be subordinated to the abilities to use the media – until these matter.

The candidates' findings can be reported verbally to an assessor acting in the role of the manager. This enables an in-depth discussion to be held to explore the way the candidates approached the task and their thought processes. The discussion provides the opportunity to assess additional skills, such as communication, interpersonal skills and influencing abilities.

Problems

A problem differs from a case study mainly in the way in which the situation is outlined. In a problem, the situation to be resolved is not 'hidden' in a scenario. It is presented directly as the question 'How would you deal with this problem?' Problems tend to be shorter than case studies and more specific. Possibly they are more suitable for middle- to junior-level posts, as they are best used to explore skills such as problem identification, decision making and contingency planning. Case studies, being capable of being more complex, enable 'senior' skills (such as strategic analysis and complex problem diagnosis) to be explored.

Group discussions

Asking candidates to discuss a topic or problem as a group is a common selection activity. It can provide a valuable means of observing the ways in which candidates behave in a peer group and during a 'meeting'. Most other selection activities focus on candidates in isolation, or during interactions with assessors and existing employees. A group discussion can enable selectors to witness candidates interacting with each other as equals.

The candidates need to be briefed adequately about the task, and the assessors should be clear about the criteria to be assessed. However, unless the situation is carefully designed and set up, conditions can be created which enable candidates to play games with each other, and demonstrate their skills of taking over meetings. That is fine if these are the skills being sought. If not, the following steps need to be taken:

■ The skills to be explored should be clearly defined and written as specific behavioural criteria.

■ The assessors should be well prepared, trained to observe and understand the criteria.

■ The discussion should be organized so that each of the candidates has an equally fair chance to display his or her own abilities without detracting from those of the others.

■ The assessors should be provided with appropriate paperwork to enable them to record and report their observations.

■ Some means of collating the observations and assessing each candidate's performance should be planned and prepared for in advance.

There will always be the chance of the candidates 'playing the game' and being nice to each other. This can lead to the task being approached superficially, or the candidates might collude (sometimes unconsciously) to avoid disharmony, competition or stress. If these dynamics occur, it is possible that the intended skills will not be exhibited. The design of the task should take account of this, and if necessary other ways of assessing those criteria be found.

Another way of dealing with the possibility of unhelpful dynamics is to provide the candidates with a detailed briefing. The task can also be written in a way that gives the candidates indications regarding the direction they should be following, without giving them a route map. They can then compete, collaborate or challenge each other, or accept each other and what is given. They can complete the task as it seems, or probe and explore the boundaries.

Interactions

As Herriot (1989a) points out, the social fit between candidates and future colleagues (as well as the boss) is an important aspect of the selection process. If this is properly recognized and formalized, some of the traditional inbuilt unfairness of the interview process can be reduced. It provides a valid reason for building in less formal activities and interactions into the selection process. However, it must be clear to all involved exactly what part each activity plays in the formal assessment, and those involved should understand the contribution they are to make to the final decision. It is not unknown for internal power games; point scoring and feuds to be conducted around selection activities, for the less formal activities create opportunities for these internal dynamics to be acted out. As they contribute nothing to the process and tend to be apparent to candidates, they should be avoided at all costs. Nevertheless, social events have an important part to play provided their purpose is clear, they are well planned, and the roles of the various participants are understood by all involved.

Informal visits

Pre-selection visits were described above, as they provide the opportunity for candidates to see the place where the post is to be based, and give them the chance to meet future colleagues in their own setting. As well as seeing the physical conditions, candidates are able to pick up a 'feel' of the organization's and work group's culture. This advance information means candidates are better able to decide whether they are likely to fit. It will help new appointees settle in more quickly, as the visit during the selection process will help individuals to prepare and think themselves into their new job. These impressions will also help to build the picture of what it will be like to do the job.

Sometimes there is a temptation to hide what may seem to be unattractive features, but it is a mistake to pretend that the working environment is different from what it is really like. The successful candidate will soon find out the reality. In any case, what seems unattractive to insiders may not appear so to others. Some employers are worried about exposing people to certain existing employees, and try to control who is met. But dissidents and atmospheres can be detected, and 'difficult' employees will be met at some point. Being clear and open about the purpose of the visit helps candidates to identify the role of existing members of staff, and giving everyone in the work group a proper and active role to play can be a better way of dealing with the situation.

However the reason for the visit should be clear, for in certain situations it adds nothing. For example, a trip round an ordinary office will do little more than show the candidates the location of their future workspace and let them say hello to their potential colleagues. Conversations about 'What is it like to work here?' are likely to be superficial. A way of making a visit more meaningful would be to ask candidates to perform a work sample task in the office, and involve existing staff in it. This would provide real interaction, and allow existing employees to contribute to the assessment on more than a social level. Visits to laboratories, workshops and other specialist sites could involve demonstrations, detailed explanations of machinery, equipment processes and so on. This would engage existing staff in a more purposeful dialogue, which could allow them to assess, for example, interest, understanding and technical knowledge. Staff involved in assessment should be prepared, and understand both the criteria and the contribution their views will make to the final decision.

Group discussions

Rather than simply bringing candidates and existing staff together in a social interaction, focused discussions can be organized. As these are more purposeful, they allow a more systematic assessment to take place. The topics chosen for discussion can include burning topical issues (such as the evergreen how to improve internal communications), contentious areas (such as whether to charge employees for car parking spaces), aspects of importance (such as how to improve quality), or other matters provided they affect everybody and do not require internal knowledge. Topics to avoid are those that would stimulate fierce debate between the individual members of staff, rather than discussion between them and the candidates.

Each candidate should be met separately and a discussion leader, preferably someone from outside the work group, should be appointed. This role is necessary to ensure that each candidate is treated consistently and that the discussion, which will inevitably vary each time, contains enough common features to ensure that treatment and assessment are fair. The discussion leader will also be responsible for collating the views of the group members against the criteria, and combining them to create a feedback report on each candidate for the selectors.

Social events

The Civil Service Selection Board was famed for its assessment of dinner table behaviour. While for some jobs these social skills may be important, they are not required in most. Nevertheless, some employers believe that assessment by fork and wineglass is a legitimate way to predict future behaviour in the post. However, considering the increased awareness of allergies, and the increase in alternative views about diet, this sort of social event can cause candidates more stress than the rest of the selection process. Formal dinners also restrict interaction, as it is only really possible to talk to one's immediate neighbours. The other guests can only be watched from a distance. As other people (for example chefs and waiters) are involved in the process, the success of the event can be dependent on their skills and organizational abilities. If there is a wish to expose candidates to key individuals in a social setting and give them the opportunity to interact, some less formal type of activity, such as a reception or buffet, may be preferable. This type of event allows for more interaction, less can go wrong, and stress levels for everyone are lower.

Regardless of the nature of the event, those charged with the task of making an assessment need to be clear what role they, and the event, are to play in the final decision. The criteria should be determined and the event carefully planned in advance. The assessors should be briefed so they are aware of the pitfalls that can easily befall candidates during such activities, and prepared to use the criteria systematically.

Psychometric tests

The use of psychometric tests has increased rapidly in recent years, and this trend looks likely to continue. One reason for this is that they are relatively simple to administer. A number of tests, which perhaps only take one hour to run, are available commercially and can be generally applied. Careful marketing and development have increased the awareness of their existence, and the outcomes appear easy to use. Many produce graphs and numbers as well as a written narrative that describes the individual. Many are now available for use on computers or online; this gives an added impression of scientific measurement and apparent accuracy.

It is tempting to believe, that because psychometric tests measure the psychology of an individual, they will tell the whole truth about that person, forever. The tests, which come in several forms, are in reality assessments and indicators of individuals' psychological make-up and personality. These can alter over time; they can also be influenced by the circumstances in which the individual is placed. Fierce debate has raged in the professional press in recent years about the appropriateness and validity of the use of such instruments. An interesting exchange on the topic took place in *People Management* (10 December 1998, p 29), in which Robert Sternberg argued for ability testing (or successful intelligence) to replace accepted and traditional definitions and measurements of IQ. Recent developments have led to an increasing focus on the assessment of ability, as the limitations of psychometric tests have become accepted. The current view appears to be that using such tests is a legitimate activity provided the tests are used in combination with other activities, and are administered and interpreted by appropriately qualified and competent practitioners.

The tests can be extremely powerful instruments, and if not used carefully they can be intrusive. Therefore they should be only administered with the candidates' permission. However, this is not easily withheld during selection events. Guarantees regarding the use of the information generated and its confidentiality should be given. Candidates should be offered feedback and be assured about the competence of the administrator. The Data Protection Action 1998 gives the subject of tests the right to know the logic behind the test, and the right to appeal or get feedback on the results. This right applies to both manual and computer-based tests.

Will candidates have the right to refuse to take part in psychometric testing?

There are other ethical issues surrounding the use of the instruments. The ones that have caused most concern relate to gender or cultural bias, and whether the test itself is a unjust barrier to those with disabilities. Most reputable suppliers claim that their tests have been designed to be free of bias. The leading producers have issued guidance on how the test can be used fairly by candidates with disabilities, and the Employers Forum on Disability has issued some useful advice. Despite the reassurance, there continues to be some concern about inbuilt bias and potential unfairness, because of the predominance of the white male, able-bodied view of the world of work and its grounding in the values of the dominant culture.

A simplistic approach often taken by the untrained is to regard the norm tables supplied with the tests as descriptors of the ideal profile against which candidates should be compared. This reduces what should be a sophisticated process involving the individual's reaction to the results to a level which merely catalogues individuals into types. The reputable publishers advise that the norm tables provided alongside the tests should be used as indicators of the results found in a particular population at a particular point in time. They also warn that tests are not a perfect predictor of performance in the post.

Concern about the use of psychometric tests led the Chartered Institute of Personnel and Development to issue a Code of Practice. The British Psychological Society has also been instrumental in setting standards and levels of competency. The main suppliers require evidence of competence before supplying their materials. However, publishers and professional bodies can only advise; they cannot control how employers administer and interpret the results.

Tests should be administered only by fully trained and competent professionals.

Despite the efforts of the professional bodies and suppliers, it is possible for untrained or non-registered individuals to obtain such tests. The Internet has made it even easier to obtain psychometric tests. Some of the Web-based tests purport to be based on highly reputable products (and some claim validity by association). It is not unknown for employers to make use of tests they have managed to obtain in this fashion, and to be less than scrupulous in their administration. However, if they do use tests obtained from dubious sources and base their decisions on what could be unreliable instruments, they should not be surprised if performance in the post is not as anticipated.

While the predictive validity of psychometric instruments is higher than many of the commonly used selection techniques, as with any method, this validity can only be obtained when the technique is administered in the way intended. There are many ways in which the tests can be abused. The different types of psychometric test in common usage can be separated into two categories, discussed below.

Cognitive ability tests

These were discussed in Chapter 4. In some ways they are similar to the intelligence tests that were used to assess and categorize children, and that are critiqued by Sternberg above. Typically these tests explore mental abilities ranging from numerical, spatial and mechanical skills through to critical reasoning. The test chosen should reflect the needs of the job or role. There is little point in checking candidates' numeracy and mechanical aptitudes if the job in question is entirely clerical in content. Similarly, testing individuals for their creative thinking skills would be irrelevant if the job demands strict adherence to instructions.

These tests can be bought singly, to explore one or several related dimensions, or in a battery. This approach enables several tests to be combined to measure a range of dimensions. Typically the use of a battery of tests is regarded as preferable, as a more rounded picture of a candidate's abilities is obtained. The results can be used as individual indicators, or can be compared to normative tables. If the latter is used, care must be taken to ensure that like is being compared to like, and the results are used as indicative, as we discussed above.

Administration is straightforward provided that the instructions are followed and the chances of contaminating the scoring are reduced. There are no judgements about an individual's personality, so the influence of subjective interpretation by the assessor is limited. The output tends to be in a straightforward form that makes the scoring system and results accessible and understandable for users and candidates. The provision of feedback tends to be a discussion of facts, as there are right and wrong answers, and if necessary candidates can question the reasoning behind the answers. If the results are compared to norms, with caution, they can provide useful insights into individuals' cognitive abilities.

Personality questionnaires

The use of personality questionnaires in selection has been the subject of more heated debate than cognitive ability tests. Their use has also increased rapidly in recent years. One of the drivers has been the desire to predict how people will behave in different settings. Personality questionnaires, or inventories, can be administered in paper or computer form; the latter makes it easier for non-specialists to administer and score them. Some providers will carry out the scoring and provide an analysis of the results, sometimes online. Thus it is possible to carry out a measurement of personality and assess the fit of an individual's personality to the job and employer, in a short space of time.

A test will only measure what it is designed to test.

However, the main source of the debate about the use of personality tests arises at the very start of the recruitment process. 'We know what sort of person we want' is a common opener when starting to compile the specification. The first difficulty is met when we try to define precisely what this person is like. What do we mean when we say we can identify a good leader? How do we know such people when we meet them? The definition of personality traits varies between the schools of thought used to underpin the different instruments. We find it difficult to agree on the basic terminology that we use to describe units of personality. Are we measuring traits or aptitudes, characteristics or dimensions?

Additionally, the methods used to measure personality can differ. Cook (2001) identifies seven different ways of assessment:

▌ observation;

▌ situational or behavioural tests;

▌ questionnaires or inventories;

▌ ratings and references;

▌ projective tests;

▌ biodata or weighted application blanks (described above);

▌ laboratory or physiological tests.

Some of the above are not appropriate for use in employment, as they were developed for use in clinical or therapeutic settings. The type of test most often found in recruitment and selection is the self-completion questionnaire or inventory. These usually comprise a series of questions with either/or or don't know-type responses. Candidates are asked to indicate the option that best fits their preferences. The scoring mechanisms usually contain safeguards to check the candidates' consistency of response and to indicate whether the candidate has tried to guess the 'right' answer. The test can be administered in paper form, or the candidate asked to complete the questionnaire using a computer. Computer use can be either on a free-standing PC or one connected through the Internet. This provides for online analysis. In either case, computer scoring is very fast. Even so, it does not remove the need for the specialist skills and training that are required to interpret the scoring.

Typically the answers to the questions are scored, by either the computer program or the practitioner using the laid-down format, and the results are interpreted using norm tables for guidance. The computer-driven analysis produces a profile based on the norm tables and the philosophy on which the test is based. The human analyst therefore needs to understand this philosophy and the way scores are compared against the norm tables. The norm tables are usually based on a number of statistical methods that also require the analysts to be trained and competent in their use. A report is produced for the selectors, usually comprising a profile, possibly in graphic or pictorial format, and a narrative. This report should be augmented to show how the dimensions of the test relate to the specification and the requirements of the job.

Good practice indicates that the results should be fed back to candidates and discussed before the selectors are informed. This enables candidates to respond and give any information they feel is necessary to explain the results. This process needs to be handled skilfully, carefully and sensitively. Real psychological damage has been caused by the bad provision of feedback to unsuccessful candidates.

Factors that merit consideration when using personality questionnaires include how the results are to be interpreted and whether feedback will be given to candidates. As the results tend to be in the form of tables, numbers, graphs and other seemingly scientific outputs, they have a semblance of undeniable and scientific accuracy that it may be difficult to question or disprove. Also, the results have a high face validity. This means that subjects tend to be very ready to accept the results and believe them to be a good description of their personality. The technique leads selectors to the creation of a preferred and idealistic profile, possibly using some of the norm tables. The high face validity can result in a candidate whose profile does not fit the desired one believing that his or her personality has failed; that as a person he or she is not good enough. In reality, there is no right or wrong personality. We are all uniquely different. However, the use of profiles and norms can mislead us into believing that there is an 'ideal' model that will match the job requirements perfectly.

In spite of this some questionnaires have been widely used, piloted and validated over a number of years, and are generally regarded as being sound, comparatively free from bias and reliable. Research indicates that they have good predictive validity if used correctly. For example, 16PF and OPQ are well known, and being founded on a reputable theory of personality, are generally regarded as being valid – provided they are used with care and ethics. Similarly, the Myers-Briggs Type Inventory has been subjected to thorough scrutiny.

However, others have been developed with less rigour, and their theoretical basis is possibly less sound.

There are a number of issues surrounding the use of personality inventories. The reputable suppliers have made great efforts to ensure that their products are free of gender and ethnic bias, but some practitioners remain concerned because of the deep and inherent nature of bias. There is also concern about the way the use of such instruments may disadvantage candidates with disabilities. The Disability Discrimination Act (1996) requires employers to make reasonable adjustments to make sure that any test is fair. This requirement demands that the employer considers both the content and the way in which the test is administered.

The increased use of these instruments means that some candidates will be asked to complete the same inventory several times. Even though the better tests have inbuilt checks of internal consistency and safeguards against faking, it is possible for a thoughtful candidate to remember the results and learn how the questions fit together. Some employers provide written feedback for the candidates to take home. This can help the candidates remember the test, which may enable them to recognize connections between the questions, the measures used to underpin the inventory, and the requirements of the role, when asked to complete the test in future. This could allow candidates to fit and shade their responses, without faking or providing incorrect answers.

When choosing a test, we need to remember that:

▌ It should be equally unfamiliar to all candidates.

▌ The test should assess the requirements of the job.

▌ A test can only measure what it has been designed to measure.

▌ The test should be used by trained and competent practitioners.

▌ The results should be seen in light of the selection criteria and used to supplement information obtained from other sources.

Assessment centres

Assessment centres were originally developed during the Second World War to distinguish between candidates for promotion from the ranks to officer positions. The strength of the technique lies in its ability to predict performance where there is no track record of achievement to use as a basis for forecasting future behaviour. They were further developed mainly in the United States, to help appoint managers from supervisory staff. They were subjected to intense scrutiny by the exacting US equal opportunity legislation. As a result, a Task Force on Assessment Center Standards set out detailed criteria for the design, implementation and training of assessors. It is claimed that a properly designed and run assessment centre has one of the best predictive validities of all the selection methods.

It can be argued that one reason for this superior predictive validity comes from the fact that it is a combination of assessment methods. Sadly, the quality and reputation of the technique has been compromised by practitioners who believe that is all it is. There are examples of selection activities that have included a personality inventory, cognitive ability test and a presentation, all slung together and called an assessment centre.

In reality an assessment centre is more sophisticated than this. To obtain the predictive validity claimed by the research, the centre needs to be built on well-defined principles. The first stage is the development of behavioural criteria against which candidates are assessed. A number of different activities are designed to reflect the content, context and level of the job in question. These can include an in-tray, a work sample (which may be a presentation), a case study and a group exercise. The candidates are asked to work through the activities, during which they are assessed by one of several assessors. The candidates may be asked to rate their own performance either during or after the event. The assessments are then pooled after all the activities have been completed, and a conclusion is reached.

The use of assessment centres has extended from their original purpose into career and management development, and the output used to form personal development plans. They have high face validity, and research has shown that candidates feel that the variety of exercises gives them a fair chance to show their strengths and recover from any weaknesses displayed. Because the development of an assessment centre is rooted in specification of role requirements for the behavioural criteria, and the use of typical tasks for the activities, they have been found to be less prone to bias.

The assessors are trained to use the technique. They need to learn:

I What the behavioural criteria mean in practice.

I How to observe and assess behaviour.

I What needs to be done to complete the activities. Normally the training involves the assessors themselves doing the tasks.

I How to carry out the assessments. This enables consideration to be given to the impact of gender, ethnic or other bias.

The assessors are also trained how to pool their observations and assessments.

The main problem with assessment centres is the cost incurred in their development. Their development also requires the involvement of skilled professionals who have a good understanding of the job and organization. Their operation is also time-consuming, and therefore costly. Ideally managers should be closely involved in the design of the centre and its operation. Typically a centre-based assessment lasts at least one day. Some assessment centres used for graduate recruitment can extend over two days. The assessment (or wash-up, as the pooling of observations can be called) can last another two or three days, depending on the number of participants.

Rating and competency frameworks

Interest in competency frameworks has grown out of the use of assessment centres. Their main use is for development purposes, and sometimes team building. However, some employers have found that they can be useful in selection, particularly when all the candidates are existing employees. They have been used to help reassign employees to new roles, for example following a restructuring exercise or a period of major change when roles have been redesigned.

Individuals can be asked to assess their own performance against a set of predetermined statements of behaviour. These can be in the form of a set of linked and incremental statements for each main competency, called behavioural anchored rating scales. Individuals identify which statement best describes their current level of performance. They can also be asked to state the comparative importance of each competency to overall effective performance of the role.

This assessment can be extended by asking others to assess the performance of the individual. This is known as 360-degree assessment, which can involve the individual's manager, colleagues and appropriate others. Whether it is an appropriate method for use in selection decisions is debatable, particularly if individuals are in competition with other candidates.

If the method is used, great care is needed to ensure than any relationship difficulties between the individual being assessed and those carrying out the assessment are not allowed to affect the decision. It should also be remembered that under the terms of the data protection legislation, individuals have rights regarding information maintained about them by their employer (and others). The information gathered should only be used for the purpose it was gathered, unless the individual gives permission for other uses.

References

While the use of references alone has low predictive validity (less than 0.15), they do have a value. However, their use depends on the willingness of previous employers to provide comments about the individual. Some are reluctant to do so; references take time to write, and some employers fear the consequences. As a result many references tend to describe the individual's performance in terms of excellence, regardless of how well they have done the job. Some unscrupulous employers have been known to give glowing reports to incompetent performers in the hope of 'off-loading' them onto another employer. However, since the case of Spring v Guardian Assurance in 1994, the High Court judgement placed a duty of care on past employers to provide the potential employer of an individual with an accurate, evidenced reference.

If that reference contains factually incorrect information or unsubstantiated statements that might harm an individual's reputation (and prevent him or her from being offered a post) that individual may have a claim for damages. Similarly if an employer makes an appointment based on a reference that contains information that is not correct, the employer might be able to take legal action because of the deceit. No wonder employers are cautious about providing references! Nevertheless their use is very common, and many employers rely on them when making their decisions.

One reason their predictive validity is so low is that they tend to be unstructured, unfocused, and ask the provider sometimes inappropriate questions that are difficult to answer. It is normal practice for contact to be made with a candidate's current employer, and comments sought on the individual's suitability for the post for which he or she has applied. This requires the current employer to speculate about the post and make assumptions about the context and the organization's expectations. Even when the job description and specification are supplied, the current employer has many gaps to fill. It is little wonder that many references are full of generalizations and bland statements.

References can be improved if account is taken of their weaknesses. In addition to the above, these include:

▮ the referee's ability to write references;

▮ the referee's ability to assess candidates against the job requirements;

▮ the referee's relationship with the candidate;

▮ what is not said;

▮ the selector's ability to read between the lines and avoid the temptation of guessing what lies behind the words used in the reference.

One strength of using references is the opportunity to check the accuracy of some of the statements made by the applicant. Research by the Chartered Institute of Personnel and Development has found that one in eight candidates falsifies or exaggerates his or her qualifications. The reference also provides a double-check on the assessors' reading of the individual candidate.

If a candidate does not cite his or her current employer as a referee, this should sound a warning bell. The reasons for the omission should be explored during the face to face interview. No offer of employment (and it should be remembered that even a verbal offer is a legally binding contract) should be made before references have been taken up, at the very least, to confirm some of the candidate's claims.

Checks for honesty and substance abuse

High-profile incidents, particularly relating to child abuse, have focused attention on the importance of exploring candidates' suitability for the area of work. Other occupations also require prescribed checks to be carried out. An employer also needs to be sure that a candidate has a legal right to employment in the United Kingdom. There are limits to the amount of checking a potential employer can carry out. The Human Rights Act gives for the right to privacy, and under the terms of the rehabilitation of offenders legislation, once a conviction has been spent it is expunged.

An employer may need to make other checks before offering employment to a candidate. The use of these tests reflects the areas of work, and they are usually used in occupations that contain a higher than average element of risk, such as train driving. These tests can only be applied with the agreement of the candidates, but how much choice they have can be limited to the way in which they are asked to take the test. The final decision might rest on their compliance, as much as on the outcome of the test.

FACTORS INFLUENCING THE CHOICE OF SELECTION METHOD

The purpose of any selection method is to provide enough and adequate information to support decision making to ensure that the right candidate is appointed. Therefore, the method must make a positive contribution to the utility of the recruitment and selection process. To do this the method should:

▮ increase the predictive validity of the whole process;

▮ be cost-effective;

▮ be practical;

▮ make sense to the selectors and candidates;

▮ be acceptable to the selectors, the manager and candidates;

▮ be acceptable and transparent to existing staff and key others;

▮ enable good quality feedback to be given to candidates;

▮ begin the induction process;

▮ inform the creation of development plan;

▮ contribute to the organization's image as a reputable employer;

▮ contribute to the development of the managers and others involved.

There is a very great danger of deciding to use a selection method because it is fashionable and thought to be the thing to do. However, a bad choice or application of a selection method can do untold damage. Not only can it increase the risk of appointing the wrong candidate, it can also reduce the chance of the right candidate applying for the right job in the future. An employer's reputation as a good employer is fragile. In a fluctuating job market, damaging it by treating candidates poorly even once can cause lasting harm.

With careful planning and considered choice and professional operation, the use of a systematic means of assessing candidates against the requirements of the job can do a great deal of good. It will improve the chance of a successful appointment, make the candidates feel as though they have been given full and equitable chance to demonstrate their abilities, reduce the risk of an accusation of unfair treatment, and contribute to the image of the employer, internally and externally.

DECISION MAKING

Once the assessment has been carried out, those responsible for making the appointment are faced with the task of making the decision – which candidate is the best for the job. This final decision, as with any decision, can only be made by the humans involved. The various selection methods may inform decision making but they cannot apply judgement – this is the domain of humans and the responsibility of managers.

The selection process is made up of a number of phases, each one producing information about the candidates. In the final stage, this information needs to be brought together in some way. Usually this is done in the minds of the selectors. Some of it will be conscious (and the more conscientious selectors keep notes). Other pieces of information will be stored in the subconscious as impressions. This information will have been based on:

■ the factual information provided by the candidates, both in their application and by their behaviour during the various meetings with the selectors;

■ the evidence experienced by the selectors – what they have seen, heard or felt about the candidates;

■ the information given to them by others, such as other assessors, referees and the other people involved in different ways.

Cumulating the different pieces of information can be formalized to ensure that the information used to make the decision is explicit instead of being based on impressions and memories. The rigour this introduces focuses selectors' attention on the criteria and away from personal preferences and biases.

A matrix is a simple way of combining the information gathered from the different phases of the selection process. It comprises two axes, one for the criteria from the specification and the other for the separate activities used in the selection process. Cells can be marked to show that a particular selection activity is intended to explore a particular skill. A simple matrix is shown in Table 5.2.

Table 5.2 *Assessment matrix*

Criterion	Application form	Focused discussion	References	Case study	Final interview
Attainment					
Degree	x				x
Achievement					
Supervisory	x		x		x
Research	x	x	x		x
Abilities					
Communication	x	x		x	x
Decision making		x		x	x
Aptitudes					
Team working		x		x	x
Resourceful		x	x	x	x

A scoring system can be devised to allow the candidates' degree of fit against the criteria in each activity to be assessed. A weighting can be given to the criteria to differentiate between them. Totalling the scores and combining them with the weights produces a total score for each candidate. This will reveal, apparently, which candidate is the 'best'.

However, this quasi-scientific approach has some dangers. There is a risk of the numbers taking over from the judgement. Take the case where, for example, Candidate A obtains a score of 28 and Candidate C 32, Candidate B achieves only 15 and Candidate D 40. While Candidate D obtained the highest score, this might conceal the fact that only 2 marks were given for team working, the most important of the criteria. The use of a weighting can help to reduce the chance of this happening, but even so it is still possible for a candidate to obtain high marks in the other criteria and few in the ones deemed to be more important.

Decision trees can help to steer a course through a complex, lengthy process, and separate aspects of performance that are more important than others. The tree also provides a way of sifting the candidates. Figure 5.1 gives an example.

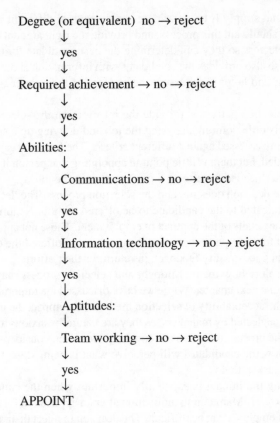

Degree (or equivalent) no → reject
↓
yes
↓
Required achievement → no → reject
↓
yes
↓
Abilities:
↓
Communications → no → reject
↓
yes
↓
Information technology → no → reject
↓
yes
↓
Aptitudes:
↓
Team working → no → reject
↓
yes
↓
APPOINT

Figure 5.1 *A sample decision tree*

SUMMARY

The choice of a selection method should be driven by its underlying purpose: to contribute positively to the entire recruitment and selection process. It should aim to:

▌ get the right person into the right job;

  – as quickly as possible;

  – in a cost-effective and efficacious manner;

▌ add value and contribute to the quality of the process.

In summary, it should be fit for and do its job.

The selection method should not be over-fancy, nor should it dominate what is really happening. The real business of the selection phase is to gather information from, and supply it to, candidates using several different media. Any method used should aid this process, and provide the right amount of information to the selectors so they can determine the best candidate for the job. The selection phase also provides the candidates with information about the job and the employer, and helps them assess the chances of their expectations being met.

Quality selection activities provide the information the selectors need to know. There is little point in analysing the job and drawing up a specification if candidates are assessed against different criteria. The favoured candidate may be highly skilled, but there is little point in appointing that person if those skills are not the ones needed for effective performance in the job.

Making the decision does not end the selection process. The decision needs to be communicated to the candidate to be offered the job. Negotiations then begin about the details of the contract of employment. Those not appointed need to be thanked for their participation in the process and offered the opportunity of being given good-quality feedback in return for their efforts.

We will explore how the recruitment and selection process may affect the candidates in the next chapter. While we have discussed the importance of face validity and the acceptability of selection methods, the impact the process may have is often neglected by managers, as they are naturally anxious to make sure their part of the process is carried out correctly. However, consideration should be given to how the candidates will perceive what is being done to them and what they are asked to do.

Considering the impact is especially important when the candidates are existing employees. Maintaining motivation after an application for another job with a current employer can be difficult. The decision to reject their applications can also have a wider impact on other employees. The consequences therefore should be considered. We will look at ways of managing the process in a positive way to ensure that everyone involved comes out with some benefit; so it is turned into a win/win experience.

6

Impact on the candidates

We have already considered the two-way nature of the recruitment and selection process, and the importance of satisfying both parties' expectations and needs.

The employer has a job to be done and a role to be filled, and is prepared to offer the best person rewards and benefits in return for that person's contribution. The employee has experience, skills and potential to offer in return for the agreed salary, other rewards and a future. This concept is well accepted, and the importance of the psychological contract widely recognized.

However, in practice many of the systems and procedures are designed to reduce the load on managers and to ensure compliance with legal requirements. Managers are trained, prepared and briefed, and paperwork designed to make the process simple. But, what about the applicant? Changing job is known to be one of the top 20 most stressful life events, yet we find that the impact the chosen methods may have on applicants does not receive as much attention as the other aspects of the process. Some employers deliberately load on the stress to see if candidates can jump through the hoops. Clearly the needs of the employer must be given high priority. The most important of these is ensuring that the offer of employment is made to an individual able to perform the job and fill the role to the standard required. The processes used to find and employ that person need to be effective, efficient and suitably economic of time and money.

As far as the applicants are concerned, what amounts to success will be determined by a range of possible outcomes, some of which will be unique to each individual. Perhaps the most important, and probably common to all, is their self-efficacy. This embraces the sense of self-worth, self-esteem and the amount of control individuals can exercise over what is happening to them. The successful candidate usually comes out of the process having achieved the desired outcome with high levels of self-esteem and confidence. His or her sense of self-efficacy will been strong, and he or she will be looking forward to the future. Success in the process will have provided some external benchmarks that confirm and strengthen the individual's assessment of his or her abilities, and often that person is given positive feedback by the selectors.

But what of the unsuccessful candidates? How often do we, as selectors, think about the consequences of our actions on the people who are not successful? The number of candidates who are not appointed – in other words rejected – is greater than the number appointed. They deserve consideration; they will have put some time and effort in making their application, and possibly invested their hopes and aspirations in it as well. Sometimes there are particular circumstances when the rejected should be given special consideration. These include when applicants are already employed by the organization, and may feel that by not being successful, they have blighted their chosen career path and future with their employer. The sense of rejection could have a long-term impact on their effectiveness in their current post and their ongoing commitment to their employer.

This chapter looks at recruitment and selection from the applicants' points of view, and explores what an employer can reasonably do to reduce any negative consequences. By careful forethought, even rejection can give the candidates not appointed something positive to take away from the process. It is also possible to build in some simple steps to maximize the chances of the appointment being of long-term benefit:

- **For the successful candidates:** after the offer of employment is made, negotiations begin about details of the terms and conditions of contract. These discussions usually concern the explicit terms, but they can be broadened to include the implicit terms and development needs. Induction and inclusion can be integrated.

- **For the unsuccessful candidates:** instead of just a 'thank you but no thank you' letter or telephone call, feedback can be offered. This conversation can change a cold rejection into an event that includes some positive comments and practical guidance.

- **For the manager:** the selection process enables investment decisions to be made systematically following structured assessments of the candidates' ability, suitability for employment and the potential for development in the context of the job and employer. The process creates the opportunity for the formation of development plans based on a rigorous assessment. The skills learnt to carry out this assessment can be transferred to other human resource management functions such as appraisal, performance management and reward allocation.

- **For other managers:** they will have the chance to gain an increased understanding of how different sections work, and make a different contribution to the organization. They will be able work with other managers on a shared task, and will acquire additional skills that will aid their overall development.

▌ **For existing employees:** they will able to interact with potential colleagues in a meaningful way and contribute to decision making. As the person to be appointed will have been met before the start date, his or her assimilation into the work group should be facilitated.

We should also consider some of the less pleasant features of the recruitment and selection process, if we are to learn what should be avoided and what needs to be improved. All too often, when discussing what to do attention is given to best practice, as defined by the employer – the party with the power. Sadly there are occasions, even when the employer believes that best practice has been used, when candidates emerge from the process as losers. The winners move on and let the occasion slip into the memory of another everyday event at work. In the worst cases, the pain caused by being a loser can form scars that remain and influence career decisions for a long time. No one deliberately sets out to create a process that does damage, but the whole nature of the process of assessment and scrutiny can make the participants vulnerable.

CANDIDATES' PERSONAL CONSIDERATIONS

When a candidate decides to submit an application for a job, the individual has made the first of a series of judgements. Assuming that person is already in employment, the decision to apply for a new job, according to research carried out by the Audit Commission to investigate why public sector employers change jobs (2002), is driven by one of several factors:

▌ the sense of being overwhelmed;

▌ insufficient resources;

▌ lack of autonomy;

▌ feeling undervalued;

▌ pay is felt not to be fair;

▌ the need to change is imposed and irrelevant.

In other words, they want to leave more than they want the new job.

The research also showed that, when considering whether to apply for a particular job, people assess how well it will match what they want from their working lives, how well rewarded it is, and its image and status. These are weighed up as a package against other options open to them. The biggest attraction for the public sector employees was the opportunity to make a positive difference to the lives of services users and communities.

There is no reason to suppose that some of these factors are very different for people working in the private sector. The desire to do a good job and succeed is very similar to the wish to make a difference. And other research, by the Institute for Public Policy Research (2000), confirmed the importance of the quality of work factors. Thus the decision to submit an application requires individuals to weigh:

I   Their future career and prospects with their current employer. This means thinking through where their current job is likely to take them and what chance there will be of obtaining their desired outcomes.

I   The prospects and opportunities in the new job. However, the amount of information on which to make the assessment is limited, and that available is often presented in glowing terms. Therefore, the judgements have to be made on a very partial and biased picture.

I   The likely impact on life outside work. Changing employers may have a knock-on effect on the individual's domestic and social life. Moving employers may involve moving house, thus partners and other members of the family may be affected. Dual career partnerships are known to suffer strain as one member's career goes in one direction and the other's in another. Social life is also often built around our work. After all, we spend a considerable amount of time there, and the chances of meeting and making friends outside can be limited.

I   When to tell colleagues, the boss, family and friends about the application. Once other people have been told, they will probably ask questions later on about its progress. While these are no doubt posed out of genuine interest, they can add to the stress of waiting to hear about success or failure. If the latter is the outcome, there is the chance of losing face and being embarrassed.

I   Family members may be unsettled and made anxious about the impact on their lives. Alternatively, they could be excited about the prospect of change. In this case, the application's failure is a let down for them as well.

I   Friends may start making plans that do not include the individual; after all, he or she will not be there, or may not have the time or interest because he or she will be too busy in a new job. Some employers regard applying for other jobs as being tantamount to treason. (In fact, some require those moving on not to work in similar areas.) Thus the individual telling the boss he or she applying for other jobs risks blighting his or her future career prospects.

I   But then if no one knows, where does help with the application and critical feedback on its contents and presentation come from? Where does the support and encouragement come from during the days of doubt and uncertainty? And how can the individual prepare for the interview if he or she has no one to talk to?

Most people do not think about the chance of failing when they submit an application for a new job. Yet if they are making the application because their present position is unsatisfactory, it may be wise to develop contingency plans just in case leaving is not an option. Pedler and Boydell (1985) give some helpful advice on how to make the most of the current job.

For those out of paid employment, the rejection letters can make it seem as though the person is being rejected, not just his or her application for the particular job. The determination needed to continue with the submission of applications is not easy to maintain. This is where assistance and guidance can be invaluable. Some recruitment consultancies offer this moral support alongside practical assistance to job seekers. The government's New Deal programme and support from Job Centre advisers are also intended to provide the same service.

Personal disclosure

When individuals decide to apply for a job, they submit themselves to a process of examination and assessment. They are expected to be totally honest and open with an employer who may or may not consider their application. They will be expected to disclose their:

▌ **Employment history.** Some employers require a checkable work history. Even if this is not specified, the applicant is expected to give details of every job ever held. Even though there have been periods of high levels of unemployment, a period spent out of work is taken as a negative indicator by many employers. Salary details and reasons for leaving previous jobs are also expected.

▌ **Educational successes and failures.** On a CV or application form, the applicant has no chance to explain, for example, why a year at college had to be repeated or A levels were not taken at the age of 18 at school. Judgements tend to be based on today's practices rather those current at the time. There have been significant changes in the structure of examinations in the last 20 years, and it can be quite difficult to keep up to date. However, this is important if an employer faced with GCEs and NVQS is to weigh their comparative value.

▌ **Personal details.** These may not be relevant to the job yet the applicant may be asked to give information, for example about interests and reasons for leaving previous employers, with no guarantee of confidentiality. The Data Protection Act has gone some way to providing protection, and requires that information is only gathered if needed and used for that purpose alone. It also gives individuals the right to check the correctness of the information held about them. Some employers request information about ethnicity, gender, age, martial status and the numbers and ages of children. It is also common to ask for details of disability, medical history, and recent criminal convictions. These may be needed to help monitor the effectiveness of equal opportunities policies, and applicants may be told that the information they supply will be separated from the main body of their application. Even so, and despite the legislation, it is still possible for others to gain access to these details without the applicant's knowledge and permission.

Lack of confidentiality

Despite the legislation, applicant confidentiality is not always respected. It is almost as if the individual, by applying, has given permission for this information to be shared. Of course it is proper for application forms or CVs to be circulated to all those with a 'legitimate' interest in the process. However, some employers copy applications to short-listers, but exercise no control over who else is able to see them.

From the applicants' point of view, this lack of respect does not consider the individual's future relationships in the organization, and takes no account of who might know whom. There are no promises made to the applicants about the retention of the material and method of destruction. The application form's initial purpose was to create a personnel record, but the forms also now act as a record of the recruitment and selection process, as well as conveying the information needed for decision making. Some employers keep application forms on file for a time so they can refer back to them if a vacancy for a similar post arises later. Not all employers destroy their old records with care; some dump waste paper rather than shred confidential documents.

We have already discussed the disproportionate distribution of power in the traditional recruitment and selection practices found in the United Kingdom. European practices, as reported by Iles and Robertson (1989), seem to have more concern for the vulnerability of the individual. This includes the rights of applicants and the use made of the information they supply.

Unequal amounts of information

Employers, particularly if competing in a tight labour market, try to sell themselves and paint a very positive picture of their current situation and future. Implicit, if not direct, suggestions are made to applicants about career prospects and opportunities for growth, tempting applicants with promises of multiple rewards and benefits. Job seekers are advised to carry out research into potential employers, but the amount of information available tends to be limited. The information they are able to obtain tends to concern the employer's business and its performance. Information about the individuals the applicant will be working with and for will be difficult to obtain.

On the other hand, applicants are expected to give considerable quantities of personal information, and the employer will check their details, reputation and track record with previous employers and others with relevant knowledge of the individuals.

The employer very carefully considers what information is sent to applicants. Anything that may prove 'sensitive' or could give 'competitive advantage' to others tends not to be readily available. Even though this may be the very information applicants need to help them decide whether they wish to apply and prepare their submission, the competitive consideration tends to take precedence. Opportunities to test out the truth of the information provided by the employer without affecting the applicant's chance of success are limited. Making contact with existing employees, unless they are known personally to the applicant, is not the 'done thing'.

It is interesting that the standard texts of recruitment practice make little reference to shifting the balance of power more towards the candidate. Chambers (2001), writing for US recruiters, states, 'today, candidates interview and evaluate organizations and managers just as much as they are being evaluated . . . Highly creative and productive people no longer accept the new job offer; they evaluate the best job offer . . . They ask, "Is this a manager I want to work for? Will this job enhance my career? Is this an organization that I want to be part of?" Many candidates shop for managers just as much as they shop for new jobs.'

Domestic considerations

If the individual is applying for a job in another part of the country, decisions about lifestyle, domestic arrangements and social relationships need also to be considered. Of course, personal decisions of this nature are outside the control of an employer and may seem to be none of the employer's business. Yet they do have an effect. It is not uncommon for a successful applicant to turn down a job because his or her partner does not wish to move or cannot find work. Perhaps a worse scenario occurs when the appointee and family move home, only to find they cannot settle in the new area. Problems of commuting, the difficulties of selling the previous home, negative equity and the problems of relocating can hinder the new employee's first critical months.

Some employers provide help with house moving. This ranges from the repayment of costs to the provision of temporary accommodation and increasingly extensive aid packages. Even though these tend to be confined to executive, senior or other key posts it is worth paying attention to the difficulties facing staff at other levels. Some employers based in areas with high housing and travel costs, particularly those in public sector, have to find ways of dealing with this problem. Some pay additional allowances, others provide accommodation, some pay travel home costs, and others struggle to recruit staff.

For those employers in areas not facing such acute problems, an easy way of helping (and attracting) applicants is to provide information about the locality, housing, its amenities and details of other employment opportunities. This comparatively low-cost service can assist newly appointed employees to settle in more quickly by alleviating some of the other sources of stress inherent in job change, and make them feel welcomed.

Uncertainty

Once an application has been submitted, the applicant enters a period of uncertainty and unsettledness. As we discussed above, research suggests that most applicants currently in work look for another job because they are dissatisfied in some way with their existing position, rather than because they want the advertised job or to work for the particular employer. Simply submitting an application can add to the individual's sense of disenchantment, as the opportunity of leaving comes closer and the person mentally prepares to move on. This could lead individuals to say or do things they would otherwise not do.

Herbert Hunt was dissatisfied with the working relationship with his boss. The boss tolerated the other employees sitting with their feet up, chatting all day, while the work got further and further behind. This was allowed to go on until the customers started to complain. Then everyone was reprimanded and expected to work overtime. This happened so often that Herbert could not wait to get out. He had been watching the situations vacant columns for months. Eventually a job was advertised that perfectly matched his experience and skills. The application form was sent off, and Herbert was convinced that he would be offered the job.

As the backlog mounted again, Herbert's anticipation of getting out increased. When the boss announced that overtime would be required again, knowing that he was soon to leave, Herbert could not resist the impulse of telling his boss what to do with the overtime. The next day the letter of rejection arrived . . .

Recruitment consultants, in seeking candidates to fit a profile, are able to approach individuals who are not job hunting and are not necessarily discontented with their current positions. The interest of the consultant and invitation to apply for another post can be flattering, and will inevitably contain prospects of enhancement and improvement. There will be hints of the grass being greener, and it is not easy to resist such an invitation. If the individual agrees to consider the job, there is a chance that he or she will examine his or her current situation with greater scrutiny than before. This examination may reveal features of the job that are satisfying, and tempt the individual to stay. However it may also reveal features that, once exposed, become the source of dissatisfaction. If the individual had never been approached these issues might not have ever mattered, but once raised they can become a lasting irritant.

Lasting effects

The recruitment and selection process can have a long lasting affect on applicants, especially those who are not successful. Some of the selection methods described in Chapter 5 can be invasive. An individual's personal life, aspirations and aspects of his or her personality can be explored in ways that exceed those needed to assess an individual's abilities to perform the job. Some interviewers take pleasure in asking probing questions, and requiring candidates to give explanations for decisions made years before.

Robyn had applied for a supervisor's job at the local factory. She had worked steadily on the shop floor since leaving school, and had recently completed the relevant NVQ course successfully. She felt ready and qualified to take charge of a section of her own.

The job she applied for was with a large multinational organization. Her previous employers had been small companies. Even so, she was confident that her experience equipped her to work effectively and gain the respect she would need as the supervisor of a multi-trade work group. She was pleased when she was called for an interview, expecting to meet perhaps one or two managers and someone from personnel. She was not prepared for what was to come. First she was asked to complete a test to see if she was a suitable sort of person to be a supervisor. Then she was asked to take part in a group task with other candidates. The task was a sort of game to see who could 'earn the most money'. This was not a pleasant experience. One of the other candidates was extremely aggressive and nasty to the others. The people from the company just sat and watched as this person was rude to everyone. When the candidates had a coffee break in private afterwards, they all agreed that it should have been stopped.

Each candidate was then interviewed by one of the managers. Robyn came out feeling as though she had been grilled. She had been asked all sorts of questions about her personal life – what she read, how she spent her spare time, what aspirations she had for the rest of her life. She was challenged and made to doubt her choices. She had been asked to prove that she was up to the job in a way that made her doubt her existing levels of competence and wonder if it was worth all the bother.

When she left the factory, she questioned why she had exposed herself to such an experience and decided that she didn't want to be a supervisor after all. The company wrote offering feedback, but she burnt the letter, not wanting to make herself vulnerable again.

The boxed example illustrates how selection activities can put candidates 'through the hoop', regardless of whether hoop-jumping is a requirement of the job. It is not uncommon for selection events to be loaded with stress to see if the candidates are 'up to it', but the appropriateness of taking this approach can be questioned. The whole recruitment and selection process is stressful enough, without adding in additional stress – unless of course the job really does require high levels of resilience. However, given the health and safety issues in jobs with high stress levels, if this is the case perhaps the job should be redesigned to eliminate such extraordinary demands.

Sense of rejection

Herriot (1989a) says that 'all too often rejection results in a loss of self esteem. Whilst one or two rejections can be attributed to the stupidity or poor selection procedures of organizations, more result in self-attribution for failure: I must be useless if everyone thinks so.' The applicant may not just feel rejected as an employee; he or she could feel rejected as a person. If the application contained dreams and aspirations, the sense of rejection could result in damage, and make the individual reluctant to go through the same degree of hurt again.

Post-hoc rationalization is another way in which rejection can be handled. Individuals seek reasons beyond themselves to explain why they have not been successful. This search may lead them to conclude that they have been treated unfairly or less equally than other applicants. Sometimes these feelings are based on truth, and under these circumstances, when an individual believes he or she has suffered illegal discrimination, he or she is rightly able to seek redress by appealing to an employment tribunal. However sometimes distinguishing between genuine grievance and disappointment can be difficult, particularly if the individual has submitted several applications to the same employer.

UNFAIR DISCRIMINATION

There is ample evidence to suggest that women and those from minority groups continue to be treated unfairly and disadvantaged in the recruitment and selection process. It is over 30 years since the first Sex and Race Discrimination Acts were passed, but there is still evidence of illegal practice against members of these groups, despite widespread reporting. On the plus side, some employers have led the way in demonstrating good practice and the benefits accrued from recruiting a diverse workforce. Increasingly the adverse treatment of those younger or older than the majority, and those whose sexual orientation is different, is being recognized as well, and it is likely that legislation to address age discrimination will come into force.

Much research into the discriminatory processes has been conducted in the United States, partly because of their more searching equal opportunities legislation and partly because of the litigious nature of US society. During the 1970s and 1980s steps were taken to redress previous imbalances and to ensure that members of minority groups were treated more fairly. Some of these were intended to make sure that selection techniques related to job relevant criteria. In the United Kingdom, despite similar legislation, examples of indirect (and some times direct) discrimination can be found. For example, advertisements for 'an office supervisor with man management experience' can still be found in newspapers.

The new concept of institutional racism was introduced following the inquiry into the murder of Stephen Lawrence. This term was used to illustrate how deeply ingrained unfair and unjustified discrimination is in organizational systems and procedures. The Race Relations Amendment Act was passed to oblige public sector employers to do more to promote racial equality. They are required to audit their systems, redress any weaknesses and build a workforce more representative of modern day society. The rights of those with disabilities are being extended following the Disability Discrimination Act of 1996, and age discrimination will be outlawed in the foreseeable future. It is likely that in future similar action will be required to tackle other forms of discrimination against minority groups.

The reality and depth of discrimination experienced by members of minority and disadvantaged groups means that sadly, even employers actively pursuing diversity policies find it difficult to convince them of the genuineness of their intent and their real wish to receive their applications for employment.

Previous unfair discrimination can make it difficult for an employer to enact its genuine commitment to recruit members of under-represented groups.

Another sad fact is that despite the legislation and examples of best practice from leading employers, some deny the issue and others find it difficult to understand how their systems and practices serve to exclude members of minority groups; they cannot see the problems. Statements such as, 'We do not discriminate, it is just that they never apply' are commonly used to justify why their workforce is dominated by members of just one group of people. Undeniable evidence, such as statistics, is one way of convincing those who have difficulty in understanding the nature and effect of unfair discrimination.

Statistical evidence

Statistics proving the extent of imbalance and unequal treatment are published frequently by various agencies and researchers, including the government. These will be referenced to illustrate how members of certain groups are disproportionately found in organizations.

Investigations into the reasons for this have found ample evidence of perceptual barriers in addition to unjust discrimination. The 'glass ceiling' is perhaps the best-known and most widely reported barrier. Evidence that demonstrates the level to which people from black or other ethnic minorities, those with disabilities and other disadvantaged groups are unfairly excluded and denied equality of opportunity is becoming increasingly available.

Equal opportunities policies

Policies and practices have been introduced by employers to help them ensure that breaches of the law are avoided and to promote fair treatment. Many of these policies relate to recruitment and selection, with the intent of giving equal access to employment opportunities to people from both genders and all sections of the community. These policies tend to include statements on recruitment practice, particularly advertising, and the use of systematic selection methods based on the assessment of abilities against predetermined criteria. Other policy statements relate to access to training and development, the fair distribution of rewards, and ensuring that other management or personnel practices do not treat members of any group more or less favourably than others. The effect of these policies can be seen in the statistics that demonstrate that despite the legislation and efforts of some leading employers, members of under-represented groups are still under-represented in many high-status occupations, and paid at lower levels than members of the majority group.

There has been some confusion between equality (ensuring everyone had fair access to opportunities, facilities and rewards) and equity (treating everyone the same). The UK legislative base is about equality of opportunity. Employers are allowed to take positive action to enable members of under-represented groups to reach the same starting position as the advantaged group, but then decisions must be based on merit and fit against criteria. This approach is different from positive discrimination, which can be found in practices such as quotas and giving members of certain groups preferential treatment.

Managing diversity

Managing diversity encompasses all that is best about equality of opportunity, and goes to a deeper level. This draws attention to the ways in which organizations can benefit by having a mixed and diverse workforce, made up of people with different backgrounds, attitudes, abilities and assumptions. The variety reflects the make-up of modern society and enables organizations, particularly those providing services to the public, to understand their customers' needs and adapt their operations to meet them. It also means that the contribution of the different individuals is valued for what it is worth to the organization, not suppressed or ignored.

Recruiting a diverse workforce requires an employer to make determined efforts to attract applicants from different backgrounds.

Managing diversity successfully involves more than making sure recruitment and selection practices are designed to ensure that applicants are not unfairly treated or disadvantaged during the process. It requires that positive steps be taken to attract applications from people from 'non-traditional' backgrounds: that is, people with the required competencies but different cultural upbringings, different religions, different attitudes from those previously employed. Employers who have tried in the past to recruit staff from diverse backgrounds have learnt that one component of success is looking at their organization from the perspective of the potential applicants to identify what may discourage them from applying. The following section looks at some of the factors that are known to be important to applicants.

Domestic responsibilities

There is significant evidence that those responsible for the care of others, particularly women, face considerable difficulties. In addition to the work responsibilities shared with their male counterparts, they have substantially heavier domestic responsibilities. As long ago as 1988, Nicholson and West said, 'what every working woman needs is a wife', and gave information about the different sorts of home life enjoyed by female and male managers. Even though the figures in Table 6.1 are over 10 years old, the number of women in positions of power has not altered significantly enough to suggest that these figures no longer reflect the current situation.

Table 6.1 *Domestic responsibilities of managers, 1988*

Married managers with:	*Females %*	*Males %*
No children	48	11
One or more children	52	89

Moreover, the number of men whose partners were at home or in part-time paid employment was considerably greater than the number of women in similar posts. Marshall (1994) reported that she found, as part of her investigations in to why women leave senior posts, that 'a linked theme was tiredness and wanting a rest'.

Women's participation

The following information has been obtained from the government's *Labour Force Survey* for Spring 2002, and shows how these commitments limit women's choices and their participation in the workforce. At this time, around 12 per cent of all women of working age were economically inactive because they were looking after family or their home. In 1992 this figure stood at 17 per cent. About 2 per cent of men were looking after others; this number had doubled in the previous 10 years. More than half of them were caring for an adult, but it would seem that care of the elderly, as well as childcare, is the responsibility mostly of women. Moreover women not only have care responsibilities for their immediate family, they find themselves with commitments to their extended family (their own parents and those of their partner). They also face limitations imposed by their partner's career and job prospects. On these grounds alone it is not surprising that fewer women than men submit applications, particularly for senior posts.

The age of the youngest dependent child (if any) has an effect on the number of hours worked by women, and those with children are more likely to work part-time than those without. 10 per cent of women in work occupy management and senior positions compared with 18 per cent of all men. For those women with children this was 9 per cent compared to 11 per cent for those without. Female employment is concentrated in service industries. 13 per cent of women at work are employed in administrative and secretarial positions compared with 5 per cent of men. Even though equal pay legislation has been in force for over 30 years, women still earn considerably less than men.

Childcare

Action is been taken to improve childcare facilities to encourage more women back to work, but cost, location and quality are all concerns that need to be dealt with to the satisfaction of the woman concerned. The child tax credit has been introduced to help meet the costs incurred by parents going to work.

The question of work–life balance is also gaining greater attention, as the hours worked in general in the British economy continue to increase. There is an expectation that employees, particularly those in senior positions, will dedicate themselves wholeheartedly and whole-time to their work. Reports of working 60 and 70 hours per week are not unknown. Some employers have recognized that time for recreation is needed if their employees are to remain fresh and productive. They are taking action aimed at restoring the balance between home life and work, but the majority continue to expect their staff to work when necessary. Is it surprising therefore that many women are not prepared to sacrifice the quality of their own lives and that of their family by applying for such jobs?

The glass ceiling

Even if they do submit an application for a responsible position, the figures quoted above suggest that women still find there is a glass ceiling preventing them from achieving senior positions. In 1994 Alimo-Metcalfe stated, 'Large British organizations now realize how much they need to attract and retain women, but I fear that without a serious and critical examination of their selection and assessment procedures little will change with respect to women's representation in either non-traditional female occupations or senior management positions.' She suggested that the criteria, the techniques and instruments, and the assessors used in the process all contain inbuilt bias that favour the status quo and dominance of men. Drawing from research evidence such as that conducted by Schien and Mueller (1990), Broverman (1975) and others, coupled with empirical data, Metcalfe demonstrated that the underpinning assumptions about male and female behaviours are translated into the construction of selection activities, rating scales and profiles of effective behaviours.

The figures given above describing women's participation suggest that little has actually changed despite these writings and initiatives such as Opportunity 2000 (now Opportunity Now). Women know that when they apply for a new job they are likely to be placed in a situation where they will have to prove themselves. They may find themselves disadvantaged from the outset, made to feel uncomfortable, and have their failings and weakness paraded in front of them. The chances of obtaining a successful outcome from an application are known to be slim.

If the application is for an internal promotion, women candidates know they face greater chances of failing than their male counterparts because the odds are stacked against them. Even if they are successful, the battle is not yet won. Women managers continue to face difficulties because of their gender, not their ability. Other women who may be considering applying for similar posts see what happens. Is there any wonder they decide not to put themselves into the position where they may be the recipients of such treatment?

Racial and cultural assumptions

Black people and those from other minority ethnic groups also face a host of problems in employment. Government statistics reveal that in 2001–2, 58 per cent of the working age population of ethnic minority groups was in employment compared with 76 per cent of white people. Those classified as being of mixed ethnic origin had an employment level of 61 per cent, Asian or Asian Britons 57 per cent, black or black British 61 per cent, and Chinese 60 per cent. This disguises the low levels of employment among some groups. Bangladeshi people have an employment level of only 35 per cent. Men had a higher level of employment than women.

There is no doubt that members of these groups face considerable problems. However, employers who have tried to increase the numbers employed have experienced difficulty in increasing the number of applications received from members of minority groups. Why is this so? There are several levels on which this question can be answered. The main response concerns the way in which people from under-represented groups are treated once employed. Like women in management positions, the reports of poor and discriminatory treatment are shared with other members of the group. Whether they are true or not, the employer's reputation is spread, and as we discussed earlier, this is a more important form of publicity than a simple vacancy advertisement. An employer known to allow discriminatory practice is hardly likely to attract many applications from disadvantaged groups, no matter how large the words 'We are committed to equal opportunities' appear in the advert.

Ability not disability

People with disabilities also face difficulties arising from employers not fully understanding what is required to enable them to contribute their talents at work. The Disability Discrimination Act requires employers (currently with more than 15 employees) to make reasonable adjustments and provide aids to ensure that people with disabilities do not face unjustifiable discrimination, and have equal access to employment to their able-bodied counterparts. Many employers believe this means providing wheelchair access and making considerable changes to toilet facilities. Yes, these are important features of the workplace, but many people with disabilities need other types of assistance. One of the main forms of help is the chance to demonstrate their capabilities.

Government statistics show that in Spring 2002 there were 7 million people in the United Kingdom of working age with a long-term disability. Of these only 47.6 per cent were in employment, compared with 80.7 per cent of those without a disability. People with disabilities are more likely to work part-time or be unemployed. However the economically inactive with disabilities are more likely to want a job than the able-bodied economically inactive (nearly 16 per cent compared with 4 per cent).

Action is being taken to encourage more people with disabilities to return to employment, through various government initiatives and the disabled persons' tax credit. However, as the above statistic demonstrates, the block does not necessarily lie with the people. If they want to work, and employers are required to treat applications from people with disabilities fairly, what keeps the levels of employment so low? There can only be one answer.

To some people with disabilities, there is little point in applying for work with some employers. It is evident that even though they are able to do the work, they could not hold the job because of:

▌ the attitudes of co-workers and managers;

▌ the way the work is organized;

▌ the type of equipment used;

▌ the layout of and access to the building.

Finally they do not believe that their application will be treated seriously.

Success or failure

Another reason people from disadvantaged groups do not put themselves forward for jobs is the fear of success. This taps a lack of faith in one's own skills and abilities. Research has indicated that generally men apply for a new job believing they will be fully competent from day one. Women, on the other hand, generally believe that unless they are confident that they will be able to do every aspect of the new job effectively, they should not apply. They do not allow for development and time to grow into the new job, and they do not want to put themselves willingly into situations where they believe the chance of failure greatly outweighs the chance of success. Men recognize that they will need to learn, and so apply knowing that there will be gaps between their current level of performance and that desired.

Deaux (1976) found other differences in the ways men and women assess their own abilities. She found that men tend to credit their own abilities for successes and blame external factors for their failures. Women tend to do the reverse. This suggests that men will find fault in the process whereas women find fault with themselves. If this is so, the failure to be appointed or even short-listed can have a greater negative impact on women than men.

Deaux (1976) also found that women are disinclined to 'sell' themselves. They credit past successes to the efforts of other people, and engage in other self-deprecating activities. She also identified that women will avoid the chance of success just as much as failure if they believe the outcome is likely to have a negative effect on them. Dale (1992) conducted a small study into the ways in which men and women view advertisements and apply for jobs, which suggested that for women, success was not necessarily a positive experience. The female participants in the study expressed greater concern than comparable men about the undesirable outcomes success could have on the rest of their lives.

Fear of leaving one's peer group

When an application for a new job is successful, the individual leaves behind his or her old role – and colleagues. In the case of an internal promotion, the team mate becomes the boss. The changed role demands changes to working relationships. Research, particularly that carried out by Hertzberg and co-workers

(1959) demonstrated the importance of relationships with co-workers, and found that often relationships formed at work spill over into social contexts, even involving other members of the family. It can be of no surprise that sometimes people are reluctant to alter the foundations of such friendships.

I am not welcome here

Applying for another job can represent greater levels of change. Groups at work develop their own cultures in the same way as organizations. They have symbols and routines that set them apart from all other groups in the organizations. Some of these can be quite distinctive, and membership requires members to conform to certain patterns of behaviour. Examples can include:

▌ the consortium of systems analysts that has a weekly flutter on the lottery;

▌ the managers who go to the pub every Friday evening;

▌ the sales representatives who all share a passion to drive fast cars and go to motocross every month.

What does someone wanting to apply for a vacancy in one of the above groups do if he or she does not want to gamble, drink or go to car races? Compromise his or her preferences and comply with the group's mores, chance being rejected by the rest of the groups' members, or not apply?

This sense of not fitting into the social group becomes worse when the potential applicants see themselves as being significantly different from the majority of people in the group they aspire to join. Imagine what it must be like for the first woman director, the first black accountant or the first person with disabilities employed in the organization. Will that person be able to retain his or her individuality and difference, or will the pressure to conform oblige:

▌ the woman to mimic male characteristics and become what was pejoratively called a Queen Bee?

▌ the black person to adopt white assumptions?

▌ the person with disabilities to see himself or herself as imperfect?

An individual does not need to be employed to have the right of complaint to an employment tribunal about unfair treatment. The cost of defending a case and the associated damage to reputation can have serious effects on an employer. Even employers with well-developed equal opportunity policies are not free from risk, and there are examples of cases taken against such organizations because their managers have failed to follow procedures.

The way members of minority groups are treated can range from direct to institutional discrimination.

Direct discrimination

Naseem was as well qualified and had more experience than Peter but Peter was offered the job. Peter had been to the same school as the managing director and was a member of the same gym. These factors influenced his appointment.

Indirect discrimination

Smith and Partners found that asking existing workers to tell their friends and family about vacancies saved money on advertising and attracted enough applications to fill all the posts. They also found that the workforce was mainly white even though the town in which the company was based had a large Afro-Caribbean community.

Institutional discrimination

Freezer Foods opened a factory on the new industrial estate on the edge of town. The chief executive and chairman were proud of the premises, which had won an architectural award. Fifty new operatives were required but the HR director thought there would be no problem recruiting. The industrial estate was located close to a part of the town where unemployment was higher than elsewhere in the town. Advertisements were placed in the local newspaper and the Job Centre, and an open day organized. Fifteen applications were received, none of which came from local people.

The HR director was confounded, so asked an existing employee who lived nearby what was the cause of the low response. Zak laughed and told the HR director that the lack of washing and prayer facilities had prevented members of the community from applying. Many were devout and regular worshippers, and it was known that the building lacked the sort of facilities required if they were to spend all day at work.

THE CONSEQUENCES OF NOT CONSIDERING THE CANDIDATES

Management gurus, such as Charles Handy (1994), predicted that in the future organizations would rely on the expertise of 'knowledge workers' rather than the brawn of manual workers. The realization of this prediction can be seen in the emergence of new roles, such as call centre and IT operators. The expertise needed by employers does not rely on technical knowledge acquired during initial education and training. Employers are now dependent upon their staff's abilities to learn and find new solutions to new problems. Employees need to be adaptable and capable of responding to rapid change, and flexible so they can respond appropriately to customers' differing needs.

Smart organizations have begun to recognize that different groups in society are also consumers, and the value of their pound is the same as that of the majority group. Seven million people with disabilities of working age spend money just as much as the able-bodied. Women make up more than half the population, and many make the major household expenditure decisions. Blacks and people from other ethnic groups represent a substantial proportion of the population, especially in large cities and north of England towns. They use services, buy goods and want to trade with organizations with staff who understand their needs.

Smart organizations also accept that they need to invest in their employees' ongoing development. The Investors in People initiative encourages employers to invest in training and development, not for any altruistic reasons but because it makes bottom-line sense.

New approaches to other human resource management practices can be seen in organizations adapting to meet the changed circumstances found in the 21st century. Some however hang on to traditional methods and fail to recognize the value of having a diverse workforce. Poor recruitment and selection practices can have other negative consequences on the organization. These are discussed below.

Loss of talent

The dangers of recruiting employees in the image of previously successful post occupants have been reported many times, initially by Belbin (1981). Organizations can be very effective in maintaining the status quo. Systems and procedures grounded in past values and practice conspired to ensure that conservative dynamism functions effectively. This means that it is assumed what worked well will work again in the future. Thus, competencies and patterns of behaviour deemed to lead to success will be sought again. Clones of previous postholders are sought using old criteria to select and deselect applicants.

Using old criteria may result in the employment of a person who seems initially to be a 'good fit'. However, if the purpose of the post is to develop new approaches and move the organization into different ways of working, employing a person with a background and profile that conforms to the status quo can lead eventually to decay, as the organization fails to adapt. The person may bring about some changes, but the chances are that these will be more of the same. Inevitably we are all limited by our experience and learning. If an employer needs radical changes, it needs to consider seriously bringing in people whose experiences and views are different. This may be uncomfortable, but both change and decay bring their own sort of pain.

There is a chance that the old criteria will relate more to the degree of 'fit' with existing groups and cultural norms than to defining the skills, knowledge and expertise currently required. We have already discussed the importance of diversity to organizations. The same applies to teams. A team whose members have exactly the same profile, same experiences and views is limited. Its horizons are constrained and its abilities to respond rapidly to changing conditions are restricted. On the other hand, a team made up of individuals with different, complementary skills and experiences is able to view problems and new situations from a number of different perspectives. It is better able to synthesize new approaches by drawing on its own resources.

Appointing the wrong person

Another risk of using old criteria and practices is the appointment of the wrong person. To base current decisions on what worked in the past may appear to be a safe option, but the person appointed may be under-qualified or over-qualified for the current needs of the job. Making the wrong appointment can be damaging for both the individual and the employer, and result in a number of difficult situations. These can range from the predictable failure of the person appointed to perform to the standards required to more subtle problems, such as the difficulties caused by a bored employee too well qualified for the post held, or the damage done to an effective team by the appointment of someone who proves to be too different and challenging of the existing values.

The town's largest employer, a mail order company, decided to relocate its head office. This change took some time to make an impact on the workforce. Most of the jobs to be lost were clerical, part-time and low paid. The professional and specialist computer staff were to move with the company.

Traditionally, the mail order company had recruited school leavers and returnees, trained them and then lost the more able to the other employers who were thus able to recruit competent administrative staff. Around the same time as the company's relocation, the schools and colleges began to advise students to stay in education rather than seek employment. Consequently, it was two years before the company's relocation made an impact on the town. Other employers began to find that their traditional source of office staff had dried up. Instead, to their initial delight, they found a pool of applicants who were more mature, better educated and capable of thinking for themselves. Two or three years later, this delight had changed to despair.

The recruits had found that their chances of career progression were limited; there was nowhere for them to go, yet they wanted to pursue their careers. To them, their jobs were routine and unchallenging. They began to question existing working practices, and disputes between them and long-standing employees increased. Their abilities to question and think for themselves had turned from being an attraction to being a damned nuisance.

The town's doctors, solicitors, architects, estate agents, dentists and insurance brokers wondered in the pubs and clubs what had happened to their office staff. They all found that they had a generation of rebellious, unsettled and dissatisfied administrators whom they did not understand and did not know how to help.

Being rejected

If the person offered the post decides to turn it down, a very different set of problems is created. Initially it is embarrassing, but then a solution needs to be found:

Consider the second runner

This response is rarely satisfactory, for there will have been good reasons this person was not offered the post in the first place. These may not seem as important when revisited under different circumstances. However, the areas of mismatch between the individual and the criteria will not go away. Moreover, the person will know that he or she was the second choice. This is bound to have some impact on the way in which he or she sees the job and organization, and his or her own abilities in relation to both.

Re-examine the applications from people not short-listed

The same reservations apply about this option. If the applicants had been short-listed on the basis of their match to the specification, these individuals would have been identified previously. Additionally, the passage of time will have suggested to them that they had not been successful in their application. They will have moved on, mentally and possibly physically. They may be flattered to be called in for the 'second round', but they may feel insulted.

Readvertise the post

This option has some merit, but it tells the rest of the world that the first recruitment and selection process was not successful. It will also take time. The delay may save salary costs, but the work will not be done.

Ask other staff to cover

Some employers manage this situation by asking other staff to cover for the unfilled post. Acting-up arrangements, temporary appointments, and sharing the work between other staff are all common examples of cover arrangements. In the short term this may seem a good solution, but as time passes problems can occur. Existing employees may want to develop new approaches and try out ideas but feel constrained, waiting for the new person to come. (They are bound to have their own ways.) They can feel slighted and passed over if they have not been considered for the post, and other staff can find it difficult to settle down, especially if the post vacant is the boss. The atmosphere of uncertainty will be pervasive.

If the chosen candidate turns down the job a sense of rejection can affect everyone, not just those directly involved in the selection process. Filling a post usually generates interest from other staff, and the prospect of a new team member can create some excitement. A buzz of expectancy surrounds the announcement of who has been offered the job. To hear that the person has turned it down can be a big let-down, and can make people wonder what is wrong with their employer.

The initial reaction is to focus immediately on what the organization has done to the individual to 'turn him (or her) off'. Did he or she not like what he or she saw or heard? Was the money not enough? (This is often believed to be the reason.) Was the job not what he or she had been expecting? The rewards and challenges might be too much or not enough for the individual to justify the upheaval of moving jobs. But the real reasons for the loss of the applicant's initial interest in the job could lie elsewhere.

Some individuals apply for other jobs as a means of testing their current situation, or as a lever in negotiations with their current employer, for example when discussing pay or bonus levels. The process of testing can turn what appears to be an unsatisfactory job into one that is not as bad as it seemed. Sometimes the current employer is prepared to offer what the individual is seeking to retain a valued individual. Other times the employer can say, 'Go if you really want', but the employee recognizes the job has other benefits when compared with what is available elsewhere.

Finding out why someone turns down a job offer can be difficult, yet this information can be valuable and indicate weaknesses in the selection process. We will return to the value of feedback from candidates later.

Failing to appoint

Failing to appoint can be equally as difficult to manage as the situation described above. After a lengthy and rigorous process, not being able to find a candidate of the calibre required can be seen as embarrassing. It can lead to questions about how the recruitment process was carried out and the criteria used. Critics have been heard to say, 'They can't find what they want because they don't know what they want.' If the steps suggested throughout this book are followed, such an accusation cannot be levied.

However sometimes, no matter how well the recruitment and selection processes have been carried out, the candidates do not match the specification. This should not be seen as a failure. Appointing the wrong candidate almost always leads to far worse problems than considering the following:

▌ What are the gaps between the profile of the ideal candidate and those who applied? (The answers should be expressed in terms of attainment, experiences, abilities and aptitudes.)

▌ Could the gaps be filled by any of the candidates in other ways? (Could any one of them develop the missing criteria through training or a programme of development?)

▌ Could other people fill the gaps? (If so, is it possible to separate out parts to be filled by other people?)

▌ Do all of the criteria really matter? (Was the job definition for a supra-human? Could any of the criteria be done without?)

Another reason for not being able to appoint is that an assessment of the candidates' belief systems suggests they are quite different from the employer's. This dilemma can arise in multinational organizations employing staff in one country to work in a different one, where cultural assumptions are very different. Similarly, such difficulties can occur when the employer has a clear and individual definition of certain essential skills such as leadership. One employer can define this as the application of a set of skills that result in staff being empowered to take responsibility for their own work, act on their own initiative and be able to function effectively without close supervision. Another can define an effective leader as someone who leads from the front and gives staff precise instructions, close follow-up, frequent monitoring of performance and detailed feedback on where they need to improve. Both definitions are equally valid, but it is unlikely that candidates able to operate according to the first would be acceptable to the second type of employer.

Rather than try to make do or hope the candidate will change, the best solution would be to repeat the recruitment and selection process. Even though time will be lost and more money spent, it would be better to start again than risk making a poor appointment.

IMPROVING THE TREATMENT OF CANDIDATES

The chances of the selection process having a negative impact can be reduced if the procedures outlined throughout this book are followed. If only it were so easy! Recruitment and selection is a complex process, made up of several stages that are put into operation by different people. These people need to work together, but they may have their own interpretations of how procedures should be implemented. They may interpret rules and systems differently, and most importantly, form opinions about the candidates during the separate stages that could influence final decisions. Consequently, actions additional to setting down the procedure are needed. These include the following:

Allocating responsibility

Who will be responsible for managing the whole of the recruitment and selection process? This seems to be a simple question, but particularly in larger organizations, actual responsibility may be shared between several key players.

The personnel or human resources department

The professionals will be responsible for setting down the procedure and the rules, and they will endeavour to establish good practice. In some organizations they will carry out various tasks on behalf of the manager whose subordinate post is being filled. However unless it is clear who is doing what and responsible for making which decisions, there will be scope for mistakes, duplication of effort or actions not being taken.

There are examples of organizations where the professionals make selection decisions on behalf on managers. For example, with graduate trainee schemes or where large numbers of staff in the same occupations are employed, a specific person may be responsible for appointing and placing staff within the organization. However if this approach is used, care is needed to make sure that appointment decisions are made with some input from the managers who will be ultimately responsible for the staff employed.

The manager

In most organizations now the manager to whom a post-holder reports is responsible for the appointment. The personnel or human resources department provides managers with professional advice and support, but the success or failure of the managers depends on the performance of the staff who report directly to them. Therefore they should have overall responsibility for making sure that staff with the competencies needed to achieve the standards and output required are recruited and appointed.

If staff are appointed centrally and then allocated to managers who are not involved in their selection, the managers can easily avoid responsibility for any subsequent performance problems. If there are other compelling reasons for the recruitment and selection process to be controlled by others, it is advisable to find appropriate ways of involving managers.

The selection process

The way in which candidates experience the selection events will have a major impact on how they perceive the employer and the way in which they are treated. We have discussed how this could affect:

▌ the way they view themselves;

▌ how they assess their abilities in comparison with the criteria;

▌ how they frame their aspirations;

▌ their memories of the employer.

The latter point is as important to the employer as it is to the candidates, for they are likely to tell other people about their experiences after the event. If they report that they have been well treated, and feel they were given a fair chance to demonstrate their abilities, the reputation of the employer will be enhanced. Alternatively if they have grounds for telling colleagues and peers how badly they were treated; the employer's reputation will suffer. Candidates' memories and perceptions are influenced by factors other than the contents of the process. The operation of the process as outlined below will have an impact.

Choice of method

The choice of selection method should be driven by the criteria outlined in Chapter 5. Reference was also made to the different forms of validity a selection activity should possess. These factors are intended to demonstrate the quality of each method from the employer's perspective. These will be important to the candidates as well, for they will want to be assured that the particular methods they are being exposed to relate to the job in question. Candidates will also be interested in the effect the selection process will have on them. Acceptability and face validity are also measures that may be more important to candidates than the employer and its managers.

Face validity

This is a measure to demonstrate how candidates view the particular method, and whether it is plausible. It assesses whether they see it as being appropriate to the job or role for which they are applying and whether it contains activities that are relevant to the work they will be asked to do.

Acceptability

Acceptability is a separate measure that assesses whether candidates see the method as valid; whether they are prepared to put themselves forward to go through the exercise or activity. For example, a test, work sample and a series of case studies may both have high levels of face validity and acceptability, but a formal dinner may satisfy neither criteria. Candidates want to know that the methods being used to assess their fit for the role are realistic, relevant and appropriate for the post in question.

Impact validity

This measure is defined by Robertson and Smith (1988) as 'the extent to which a measuring instrument has an effect on a subject's psychological characteristics'. When choosing a particular method, we should consider the following pointers.

The relevancy of the method to the job in question

The method should reflect the employer's context, and its core values should be incorporated into any activity. More importantly, the content of the method or activity should have some reasonably obvious link with the vacancy. Sometimes this can be difficult to demonstrate when 'off the shelf' activities are being used. However, this link should influence the selection of any test or other selection device. The level and degree of difficulty should also be similar to those the candidates will encounter if appointed.

One of the exercises that candidates for the post of branch manager with a leading high street bank were asked to complete concerned trading in shares, bonds and equities. One of the successful candidates knew from the feedback received after she was appointed that she had not done very well in this exercise, but the high standard she had achieved in the other modes of assessment had carried her through. She therefore spent her first three years waiting, with some dread, for a customer to appear with a portfolio of shares.

> Eventually she plucked up courage to ask her regional manager why she had
> not been asked to sell or buy. The reply, 'We don't trade in shares at branch
> level' both surprised and angered her.

The candidates should not feel as though their privacy has been invaded

Candidates have been asked inappropriate questions or asked to reveal information about their personal lives that has nothing to do with their ability to do the
job. The classic examples of such questions relate to domestic arrangements,
such as 'Does your husband mind you being away from home a lot?' to a
candidate for a role that involves a lot of travel, 'How will you manage school
holidays?' or 'What did your father do?'

Requiring candidates to participate in activities such as those that involve the
examination of personality traits or motivational factors, without giving them
the power to refuse, can also be invasive. Some activities may take candidates
into areas they would prefer not to go. For example, the use of biodata may
return an individual to an unhappy childhood.

The method chosen should make use of technology that is understandable and challengeable

Data protection legislation gives candidates the right to know how computer-
based assessments make decisions that affect them personally. Some people find
the idea of being 'black-boxed' highly intimidating and are concerned about the
results. Therefore a person of reasonable intelligence and the experience
required for the particular post should be able to understand the underpinning
rationale and operation of any method that relies on any form of technology.

The candidates should feel treated fairly and with equity

Candidates should not feel as though they have been the subject of games
played at their expense. Some employers enjoy using methods to find out just
what candidates will or will not do and say. They use pressure interviews,
during which candidates are grilled and subjected to hostile questioning, just to
see if they are up to it, rather than because this type of experience is part of the
job. Other inappropriate activities include using an interview as a fishing
expedition: for example during an organizational restructuring, when candidates
are asked to pass opinions on the competency of colleagues. Some employers
believe that it is best practice to use extensive selection activities regardless of
the level of post. Even candidates for comparatively junior jobs are expected to
spend a whole day going through tests with no regard to the amount of time they
are obliged to take away from their current job. The use of activities that expect

a level of knowledge that can only be gained from direct experience in the particular organization would appear to favour internal and disadvantage external candidates.

Operation of selection events

Conduct of staff

Usually the people involved in running a selection event are from the personnel department or the support staff of the manager responsible for the appointment. Regardless, they should know what they are doing and appear competent and confident to the candidates. The way in which the candidates are treated by these staff can have a major impact on their perception of the employer, and can form a lasting impression. Examples of poor behaviour include staff who:

■ appear disorganized and surly;

■ seem uninterested;

■ stand in corners, chatting and giggling while candidates struggle to concentrate;

■ are unable to supply information or answer even the simplest of questions;

■ gossip about candidates' performance.

The validity of the activity can be brought into question, and the professionalism of the employer be placed under scrutiny. If on the other hand the staff are well prepared and conduct themselves in a friendly, open and helpful manner, candidates will feel as though they have been treated well by people they would like to work with in future. This gives added credibility to the process, and helps to ensure that the candidates go away feeling as though they have had a fair chance to display their abilities and their suitability for the post.

Paperwork and accommodation

Likewise, the paperwork and organization of the whole event will reflect the standard of preparation and standard of administration. Candidates are not likely to have faith in the process if:

■ the paperwork is inaccurate, poorly presented and out of date;

■ rooms are not ready, unclean and inadequately heated, lit or equipped;

■ receptionists do not know the event is happening or where it is to be held;

▌ selectors do not have the right forms, do not know which candidate they are to assess or what activity takes place where and when.

And if the coffee fails to appear, the candidates will wonder if they were expected at all.

Timetables

One of the worst failures often encountered is the inability to stick to the published timetable. Frequently candidates are kept waiting as the time of their appointment or interview is allowed to slip. Obviously rigid compliance with the clock is not always possible or desirable. However it is possible to prepare a timetable that takes account of predictable slippage, builds in time for contingencies, and allows for some small over-runs. Candidates should always be kept informed what is going on. Keeping them waiting and in the dark shows a lack of respect as well as a lack of organization, planning and courtesy.

Power to refuse

Candidates should *feel* as though they have some control over the process and are able to refuse to participate in a selection activity if they think it is not appropriate. Usually candidates are highly compliant; if they refuse to carry out a task or an activity they believe it will reflect badly on them, and be taken to mean that they are not serious candidates or are not prepared to carry out reasonable requests. If candidates are told what they are being asked to do and why the activity is relevant, the chances of them refusing to carry out an activity will be reduced significantly.

If a candidate does have reservations about an activity and is able to articulate his or her reasons, serious consideration should be given to excusing that person from that particular activity. Even though this will remove a mode of assessment, his or her views should be respected.

Candidates should be warned in the invitation to attend the event that they will be asked to carry out certain activities. How much prior information should be given is debatable. Herriot (1989a) argues that selection should be seen as a process consisting of a series of ongoing steps. The commitment of candidates to move through each should be obtained at each stage. The reason for this is to create a positive working relationship in which both parties trust the other. The mutual exchange of information was described in Chapter 3.

If the candidates have been given advance notice of the activities, there is the chance for them to discuss their personal concerns privately beforehand. If they continue to decline to participate, their position will be fully understood and need not be seen as an unwillingness to accommodate the employer's procedures. However, if they are presented with the activities when they arrive on the day, they will be in a weak position, have little information on which to base their response, and little choice in the matter.

The assessors

Even though all the general guidance recommends that those involved in the assessment of candidates should be carefully chosen, trained and competent, in reality the choice of who is to be involved is often governed by other factors. Constraints, norms and priorities, not to mention the politics of the situation, often determine who is to participate. The manager to whom the post-holder is to report should be responsible for the appointment and the decisions surrounding the selection procedure, including who should participate and what their roles in the process should be.

There are times when other people from within and from outside the organization can make valid contributions. They are able to examine the candidates against the predetermined criteria but from different perspectives. They can act as expert assessors, a contribution which can be invaluable when appointing to the only specialist role in the organization. Some employers make use of independent assessors to assist and demonstrate impartiality and fairness. Usually these people are knowledgeable about the employer's operation and values.

The choice of selectors should also be made against explicit criteria, such as:

▍ Who needs to be involved (for example existing employees with whom the post-holder will need to work closely).

▍ Who ought to be involved (for example those upon whom the success of the appointment is dependent, or whose status demands their involvement).

▍ Who has to be involved (for example those who need to give permission or authority for the appointment).

▍ Who can make a valuable contribution (for example those able to offer specialist input, such as representatives of professional bodies or particular expertise).

Even if the participation of an individual is required rather than wanted, the reasons for his or her involvement should be made explicit. If this reason is one of expediency, it is important that all those involved understand their role, the criteria, and are prepared to work within the agreed processes. There is little room for virtuosity and improvisation in recruitment and selection. Variation and deviation, once the process has started, can lead to unfair treatment of candidates and decisions being made on questionable grounds.

The assessors once chosen should be trained to use the criteria and follow the processes set out, in accordance with the employer's own ways and peculiarities. Some managers may be resistant to such training, believing themselves to be good judges of character. Often they fail to appreciate why they should be systematically trained, especially if they have with previous experience of recruiting and selecting staff.

Sara had been selecting staff for her employers since she didn't know when. She took pride in that fact that she had developed her questioning technique, and the vast majority of the staff she had appointed had proved to be good choices. Less experienced managers frequently asked for her guidance and help, and she was the personnel department's first choice as an assessor when special appointments were being made. Sadly, a reorganization in the company's site forced Sara to choose between relocation or redundancy. Due to family commitments, she regretfully chose the latter. With great relief she quickly found another comparable job with a major employer in a neighbouring town.

Sara had been in post six months before she needed to appoint a new team member. She was shocked when she was told that she could not do so until she had been through the new employer's recruitment and selection skills workshop. She was understandably irritated, but decided that it was too soon into her employment to rock the boat. She arrived at the workshop prepared to have her time wasted, but she was surprised at the professionalism and the quality of the trainer, so sat back comfortably to have her views and current practices confirmed. The first session contained some less pleasant surprises. The trainer outlined the results of research and findings of some employment tribunals. It was with some horror that Sara discovered that the previous company's practices, such as one to one interviews, obtaining character references via the telephone, and not making or keeping notes, would have made her personally culpable if an applicant had felt aggrieved enough to lodge a complaint with an tribunal. She had never heard of a specification, and after some explanation and practice found their use obvious. After the two days, Sara left a changed and sobered person. She readily admitted that she had learnt a lot and saw the value of her new organization's different approaches.

This need for training can pose an employer wishing to use best practices some difficulties. How does one tell senior managers that they lack basic observational and interviewing skills? Apart from grasping the nettle and telling them, or finding ways to exclude them, other ways to manage the incompetent but important person's involvement need to be found. It should be always remembered that the impact poor selection practices can have on candidates, their subsequent performance if appointed, and the reputation of the employer, can do far more damage than denting a senior manager's ego.

Making sure that even the competent managers behave themselves during selection events can also be taxing. Some cannot resist the opportunity of showing off or trying to exercise their power to the other staff involved in the process. It is not unknown for managers to giggle and gossip in the corner while candidates are completing difficult pen and paper exercises. Discussions about the candidates within their earshot have also been observed. Candidates can sense what is happening around them, and the way in which they are treated can have a direct impact on their performance during the event. Such bad behaviour needs to be tackled.

Iles and Robertson (1989) have showed that if the candidates like the people acting as selectors, the process is more likely to be regarded by both parties to be successful. Consequently, selectors need to behave in a professional but sympathetic manner towards the candidates. Some managers find their role in the process stressful, or believe they should be remote. There is no real reason for not being friendly and helpful. It is also important that existing employees involved in the informal interactions and activities are honest and open about the organization. There can be nothing worse for candidates than feeling that their performance is being judged by people who are hiding critical facts from them. Similarly, candidates are unlikely to want to work for an organization whose employees display hostility towards newcomers. They are more likely to choose to work for one where their future colleagues are welcoming and helpful.

Decision making

The candidates should be told how the decisions are to be made. There are different schools of thought about whether the candidates should know what criteria are being used for selection. Some employers publish the specification and say how each component will be assessed. They also indicate what evidence is being sought. Others are less inclined to be so open, as they believe that providing too much detail will encourage complaints.

Alternatively employers may believe that candidates will fabricate evidence and play to the criteria if they have been given advance information. This need not be the case, and provided the agreed criteria are explicit and used consistently throughout the process and the methods used for assessment are valid, the employer should have nothing to fear. Even if it is decided that the criteria should remain confidential, there is no reason candidates should not be told the steps to be used and timescale involved in making the decision.

Records

Adequate records should always be maintained. Readable, accurate notes should be kept, and the reasons for the judgements recorded and related to evidence. This does not demand a forest of administrative paperwork. A simple decision matrix such as that described earlier will suffice.

Operational practice

If the practice and operation of the selection method has been professional, overt and related to the needs of the job, candidates will be left with the impression of a good employer. It is even possible that they will have 'enjoyed' the process. The stress levels inherent in selection for all concerned can be made manageable, and a climate can be created that makes candidates feel they are able to do their best. If this is achieved, they will feel they have been assessed fairly in a way that is positive, helpful and informed. To achieve these ends:

▍ the selection method needs to be administered by staff who are competent;

▍ a process should be organized professionally;

▍ the timetable should be followed;

▍ candidates should be informed of what is happening, when, why and with whom;

▍ candidates should be given some control and feel that they are able to say no;

▍ the stress of the situation needs to be realistic, and irrelevant sources of pressure eliminated.

SUMMARY

This chapter has considered how recruitment and selection can affect the well-being and self-esteem of the candidates. For those of us who are involved regularly with recruitment and selection, it is easy to forget how traumatic it can be for those who are not so familiar with the processes. Involvement in selection events can be just as stressful for managers as for candidates.

This involvement can have lasting and negative consequences on candidates, and damage their self-confidence and willingness to put themselves forward again. It is worth remembering that they are applying for a job, not asking to be psychoanalysed. Employers may have the right to gather relevant information about candidates, but they do not have the right to invade their private lives or intrude into their personal background when it is not relevant to their work.

Selection methods should be chosen to explore the required skills, abilities and aptitudes; their use can also add to the employer's image and reputation as a good employer. The methods should reflect the content and context of the job in question, and should be planned and executed professionally. Even the best methods can easily be rendered invalid by sloppy administration. The operation should also be designed to ensure that adequate records are maintained. These are essential. If anyone feels aggrieved enough to lodge a complaint, contemporary records will reveal what happened and how the decisions were made.

Those acting as assessors and any other staff involved should be included because their contribution to the process is necessary; they should be trained and briefed about the sort of conduct the candidates deserve to expect. Candidates do not like being played with; they like to know what is happening and why.

Iles and Robertson (1989), talking about internal applicants for promotion, said:

> Individuals who feel unfairly assessed, by invalid techniques, presented in ways which fail to include their active consent, participation or involvement may feel alienated from the organization, uncommitted to it, think of leaving it and actively seek another job. Their work performance may also suffer if they feel insensitively treated and their future options closed off. On the other hand, if they are accurately and sensitively assessed and given constructive feedback, individuals may feel a rise in self-esteem, enhanced self-efficacy, a greater sense of personal agency, greater commitment to their organization and greater motivation to undertake further training and work experience.

Similar feelings are experienced by external candidates. A basic rule to govern the running of selection events is to treat candidates as you would want to be treated.

7

After the offer

Once the excitement of the selection event has come to its end, it is easy to think that the vacancy has been filled and the recruitment and selection process is finished. This is not the case; there remains a lot to do, and deciding which candidate is the 'best' and should be offered the post is a distinct phase in the process. Like all the other steps, it should be conducted in a planned, systematic and rational fashion and records kept. When the decision has been made, the person to be offered the job needs to be told. Many managers do not realize that a verbal offer constitutes a legally binding contract, so care and attention needs to be given to its form and content.

The other candidates also need to be informed of the outcome, and the way in which the decision is communicated to them merits consideration. Without due care and attention, damage can be caused and grounds given for complaints. These candidates, having vested energy and emotion into their application, will naturally be disappointed in its lack of success. Even though some may experience a sense of relief if the job was not what they were seeking, most will feel some sense of failure.

This chapter will explore how making and announcing the decision can provide some benefit to all concerned. We will discuss how the process of making decisions can be designed in ways that produce information for subsequent use. This includes the provision of information that will help in the negotiations with the successful candidate regarding the terms and conditions of the contract of employment. It also includes information that can be offered to the unappointed candidates as feedback. Giving feedback is not easy, particularly when sensitivities are involved. Therefore, some guidance on how to be constructive in this specific situation will be offered. Feedback can help to reduce the disappointment, as it gives something back to these people in return for their effort. It can contain practical information about how approaches can be adapted, and how to enhance their skills and experience. For the appointed candidate, the feedback is the beginning of his or her development in a new role.

MAKING WIN/WIN DECISIONS

A win/win decision is one from which both parties feel that they have gained an outcome that has some value to them. This may not be everything they sought at the outset. It may not even be an outcome they thought of at the beginning of the process as something they did not want. Nevertheless, when they look back at the decision they are able to say that it had some benefit for them. Considering that most of the candidates who put themselves forward for assessment will not be offered the job, making the decision to reject them may seem a negative. However, we need to remember that when they look back, they will consider the whole process. As we have already discussed, this can be made a positive experience for them in many ways. If they can be sure that the final decision was made in a robust manner that is open to scrutiny, at the very least, they will be reassured that their applications were considered fairly and thoroughly.

The decision to appoint or reject candidates is usually made after a final interview. Even though interviews are known to be poor predictors of performance, the leading researchers, particularly Herriot (1989a), have concluded that there is a legitimate place for them. He suggests that, at the later stages of selection, the social interaction between the candidates and the decision makers is important to the subsequent success of the appointment. This is the stage when details are verified, the final check between the individual and the specification is made, the degree of fit is established and negotiations regarding the contract are started.

The interview should be used in conjunction with other selection methods and structured in appropriate ways to ensure that all necessary aspects are covered. Chapter 6 suggests ways to enhance the validity of the interview. This includes the recommendation that more than one person is involved. Three is the ideal number. This number of interviewers allows for a balance of views and allows the candidates to be assessed from different perspectives. If only two people are involved in the final interview, it is possible that the divergence of opinion will be too great to produce a clear decision. More than three can create a panel that is intimidating to the candidates, and can mean that decision making is made complex by the dynamics of the group. However some employers, for other reasons, make use of interview panels with several members. It is not uncommon to have as many as six interviewers, and some organizations have been known to hold interviews for key or senior posts in front of committees of over 20! (The prospect of appearing in front of such a gathering may conjure up images of Romans, gladiators, and thumb signs in the minds of candidates.)

It should be clear who is responsible for making the final decision. Normally this will be the person responsible for the appointment and to whom the post-holder will report. However, whether this will be an independent decision or made consensually with the other panel members will depend very much on the style of the organization. There is no point in involving others as interviewers if their advice is not taken. They should be clear from the outset how much scope they have to influence or be party to the appointment decision.

The matrix suggested earlier (see page 192) can be used to create a device that enables the information gathered during the previous stages of the selection process and the various activities to be integrated into a report on each candidate. This report should contain an assessment of each candidate against the predetermined criteria, and indicate to the final interviewers which aspects need further exploration. A sample form is given in Figure 7.1.

This matrix should not dictate the format of the final interview. The job requirements in the wider organizational context should set the agenda within which each candidate is assessed against the criteria. The interview should also be structured to provide a consistency of treatment between the candidates, and allow for their differences to be explored in full. This requires preparation and some discipline. Managers can find it very tempting to compare candidates with each other. This should be avoided for, even at this last stage, they should be assessed against the criteria required for adequate performance of the job. This stricture can help an employer withstand claims of unfair treatment, as well as create the explicit framework for decision making.

The matrix also provides the basis for the necessary records. It is absolutely essential that the notes made during the final interview be kept in a form that is intelligible and can be checked by others after the event. The formal records required include:

I   The criteria derived, the outline of role requirements and the specification of competencies required. This should be clearly expressed in ways that are understandable to candidates and others who have a legitimate interest in the process.

I   A separate record for each candidate which is authenticated by the person responsible for the appointment.

I   Any other notes kept by members of the interview panel which should be collated to comprise a complete record.

I   The reasons outlining why applications have been rejected, based on evidence gathered about each of the criteria.

I   Information to be fed back to the unappointed candidates, should they accept its provision.

I   Reasons for offering the appointment to the selected candidate, based on evidence gathered against the criteria.

I   Information for use in the individual's initial training and development.

Another matrix, such as the one in Figure 7.2, can be used both to record the interview and as an aid to decision making.

CANDIDATE ASSESSMENT REPORT

Candidate ....

Criteria	Rating	Evidence
Understanding of organization and its environment Recognizes the impact opportunities and action have on other parts of the organization, especially with regard to resource utilization and cost		
Strategic approach Able to see ahead, determine priorities, devise plans and organize resources for his or her achievement		
Communication Able to express ideas and convey information clearly and concisely using appropriate media, and checks to make sure the messages have been understood		
Budget management Understands the concepts relating to the application of funds and cash flow, can recognize how actions affect costs, and acts to use resources economically, efficiently and effectively		
Involvement Can recognize when to involve others in a task, give them clear, precise instructions, set realistic deadlines, and provide the assistance needed to complete the task in ways that contribute to the development of others		
Team working Able to work within a group without dominating others and can influence its processes and group members in a positive way		
Resourceful Able to find other ways of doing things and to act on own initiative		
Role appreciation Able to balance several differing roles, assess the limits of authority each imposes and values the contributions made by others in different roles		
Social skills Able to develop and maintain constructive relationships with one or more people, demonstrating sensitivity to their moods and needs		
ASSESSORS		

Figure 7.1 *Sample candidate assessment report*

INTERVIEW RECORD		
Post title	Interviewers	
Candidate		
Criteria	**Weighting**	**Evidence**
Attainment		
Achievement		
Abilities		
Aptitudes		
Interests		
Circumstances		
Other factors		
Decision and reasons		
Feedback		

Figure 7.2 *Sample interview record*

The decision to offer a job to one individual is one made by human beings, and is prone to all the flaws of human decision making. It can be argued that the idea any selection can be made objectively is a myth. Any judgement made by one person about another is inevitably made on subjective grounds; we cannot remove personal perceptions and bias from the mental processes used to form these judgements. However, we can reduce errors and the undue influence of our preferences by using aids. These include mechanisms that:

▌ gather information systematically from a number of sources (such as the application form or CV, selection tests and references);

▌ assess performance throughout all stages and all activities against predetermined criteria and on the evidence gathered;

▌ weight the criteria (if appropriate) to focus on their comparative importance.

Using approaches to structure decision making will help those making the decision identify which candidate will be best able to meet the requirements of the job.

MAKING AN OFFER OF EMPLOYMENT

The final stage of the selection process is normally an interview. The candidates who have been short-listed and have successfully completed all those assessment activities are seen in turn by a panel of interviewers. The interviewers explore their applications, consider the information and evidence of competency gathered previously, then make an assessment. After seeing all the candidates the interviewers make a decision. This decision can be made immediately after the interview or in the days following. Some employers draw their conclusions, then seek confirmatory evidence and carry out other checks before deciding finally whether to make an offer of appointment. These can include:

▌ medical examinations and health checks;

▌ references from previous employers and others given by the candidates;

▌ security clearance;

▌ evidence of the achievements cited during the interview;

▌ evidence of qualifications and registrations.

Some candidates are asked to wait until the interviews have been concluded and the decision is announced to them all at once. Other employers prefer to inform the chosen candidate and then wait for the offer to be accepted before informing the others that their applications have not been successful. Sometimes the offer is made by telephone or personally, or it can be made in writing. This is a slower way, but in some respects safer, as a verbal offer of employment constitutes a legally binding contract. The contents of the offer are less prone to misinterpretation if it is made in a form that is more enduring than the spoken word. The person making the offer should be sure he or she has the proper authorization and is clear about what he or she can and cannot offer or negotiate.

Contract of employment

The contract does not have to be written, for in reality it is the formal agreement, the foundation of the bond of trust that must be developed between the employee and their employer. It contains legal rights and obligations and also has implicit terms, sometimes described as the psychological contract. The contract is two-way and can be broken by either party. That the contract is not written and that the employee does not have a legal right to a written contract may be surprising to some managers. However, all employees now have the right, under the Trade Union Reform and Employment Rights Act 1993, to receive a written statement of terms and conditions within two months of commencing their employment. The written statement must be accepted in writing.

The written terms and conditions are taken to represent the bulk explicit contract (that is, the terms formally agreed and recorded). However, some of the documents given to employees describing the job and organization may be taken to outline further explicit terms, as they will inform the parties' expectations of each other. Under the terms of the Act, employees are entitled to receive the following information within the two-month period:

■ The names of the employer and the employee.

■ The date when the employment began.

■ The date when the employee's period of continuous employment began.

■ The rate of pay, and any pay scale or method used to calculate pay, including that used to calculate commission or bonus payments if these are contractual entitlements.

■ The intervals at which the payments are paid.

■ Any terms and conditions relating to:

  – hours of work including compulsory overtime;

  – holiday entitlement including paid and public holidays, with enough information to enable the employee to calculate 'precisely' the accrued entitlement if he or she were to leave the employment;

  – any terms and conditions relating to sickness or injury, including sick pay, which may include requirements regarding notification, certificates and submission to medical examination;

  – pensions and pensions schemes.

■ The length of notice each party is required to give the other.

■ The title of the job or a brief description of the work for which the employee is employed.

■ If the job is not permanent, the expected duration of the employment, and the date of termination of a fixed-term contract.

■ The place of work or, if the employee is to work at various locations, a statement to this effect and the employers' address.

■ Any collective agreements that directly affect the terms and conditions of the employment, including, where the employee is not a party to those agreements, the persons by whom they were made.

■ If the employee is required to work outside the UK for more than one month, certain particulars regarding the arrangements for working abroad (such as the duration, currency in which the salary will be paid, additional remuneration or benefits, and any conditions relating to the return to the UK).

■ Any reference to other documents, such as those specifying disciplinary rules or references, should indicate how those documents can be obtained. The written statement should contain the name of the person to whom appeal can be made against any disciplinary decision, or with whom a grievance may be raised. The method of application and subsequent procedures should also be described.

Most of the above will give only brief details. However, collective agreements can be quite lengthy. The agreements could include the rights and responsibilities of employees relating to, for example, training and development allowances, flexible working arrangements, special leave and, of increasing importance, safe working practices. Regulations concerning professional conduct or confidentiality, and restrictions on practice after employment and exclusivity, may also be included or referenced.

These latter clauses have become more common as the ability to retain skilled staff in specialist areas has become more difficult, and competing employers are prepared to tempt staff with skills in short supply away from their current employer. However, clauses forbidding an employee to work for a competitor after the termination of the contract are not easy to enforce. Taylor (2002) discusses how theses restrictive covenants, and other means used to restrict employees' actions outside and after employment, are used to protect the employer's interests. However, courts often have found in favour of the employee unless the clauses are specific, related to the work of the employee, and have a clear timescale.

Short-term contracts

During the 1980s and 1990s there was a growth in the use of short-term contracts and part-time working. These gave flexibility to employers at times of rapid change and uncertainty. However, the way they were being used raised questions about many of these practices. New legislation introduced to harmonize UK practice with that of other members of European Community has given part-time workers the same rights as full-time employees, and has clarified the difference between contracts *for* service and contracts *of* service. The former are used when the individual carries out specific actions for the employer but does not have an exclusive or ongoing relationship. The latter are used for those who have a wider relationship with the employer, and carry out actions in response to the direction of the employer concerning standards, timescales and place where the work is to be done. These actions need to be integral to the employer's business.

Staff handbooks

Some employers provide staff handbooks to ensure that both existing and new employees have adequate information about the general conditions of employment, and the practices and rules used by their employer. There are a number of advantages of doing so. A handbook can provide:

▌ an authoritative and single source of formal information;

▌ for consistent interpretation between managers in different parts of the organization;

▌ a single place for staff to look;

▌ only one document to keep up to date (trying to make sure that every member of staff has an up to date personal copy can be both unrealistic and costly);

▌ details ancillary to the contract, but important parts relating to employment can be communicated officially and shared with all staff equally.

Guidance on both the format and content of staff handbooks can be found in Salthouse (1995).

Implicit terms of the contract

The implicit terms and conditions of employment do not appear in writing in the statement issued to new appointees. These terms are those aspects of the relationship that are understood between an employee and his or her employer. The common law aspects are fundamental parts of this understanding. For example, it is taken that employee will carry out any reasonable request, but the employer will not ask the employee to do anything that could be regarded as unreasonable or illegal. In addition, the employer will:

▌ pay wages;

▌ treat employees courteously;

▌ provide support to help the individuals carry out their work;

▌ reimburse expenses incurred in relation to the performance of the job;

■ provide a safe working place.

The employees are expected, in return to:

■ be willing to work;

■ be honest;

■ be loyal;

■ take care when carrying out their duties.

The relationship between the employer and employee is rooted in mutual trust. The meaning of this concept has been tested in court, where it was established that if an employer is able to demonstrate that the bond of trust has been eroded beyond repair, it is reasonable for the employer to conclude that the contract of employment has been broken. The dismissal of the employee would therefore be fair. As the implicit terms are so important, it follows that it should not be assumed that each and every employee understands what they are and what they mean in practice. Consequently, the more important aspects should be discussed and agreed during the final stages of the appointment process. After all, they will embody some of the expectations discussed earlier.

NEGOTIATIONS AFTER THE OFFER

Making an offer of employment to the selected candidate is not the end of the process. The use of individually negotiated contracts has increased, particularly for senior appointments or those with skills in high demand. This approach allows an employer to offer inducements to encourage the preferred candidate to accept the offer of employment rather than consider other offers or inducements. It is essential that any employer choosing to use such an approach can relate these inducements to factors pertinent to the situation and the job. These should be material (that is, they should be tangible and their need capable of being evidenced). Great care should be taken to ensure that the inducements are not related to the gender of the individual.

The effect of using individually negotiated contracts is that the terms and conditions of employment will vary between employees. Sometimes, this type of contract has been used to negotiate in changes to terms and conditions of employment, for example during a reorganization. However, any future changes will need to be renegotiated with each employee, individually rather than as a group, thus introducing a greater management load. Moreover, as employees learn of skills shortages and the scarcity of relevant experience changes the power base, they will become more confident about making demands and be able to negotiate contracts that are in their favour.

Rewards and benefits

Usually, the terms and conditions open to negotiation are those relating to pay and other pay-related benefits, such as bonus and performance payments. However, the introduction of an increased range of pay- and non-pay related benefits has made the development of reward strategies more sophisticated. Some of these benefits are well used and accepted, but some are novel and their use depends on their availability and how much value they would have to the employees. Even in the public sector, where pay, terms and conditions were traditionally subject to national negotiations between trade unions and representatives of the employers, there has been a growing use of locally agreed packages of benefits.

The benefits can include:

▮ holiday allowances;

▮ sickness benefits;

▮ pensions;

▮ private insurance;

▮ health schemes;

▮ professional subscriptions and related fees;

▮ cars;

▮ relocation and housing costs;

▮ loans;

▮ school fees and childcare;

▮ shopping and preferential purchasing benefits;

▮ service-related rewards;

▮ performance-related payments including bonus pay, commission, achievement of target payments, and share ownership schemes;

▮ gifts and rewards for achievement, including prizes for performance points, which can range from pens, food and drinks to holidays and cars;

▮ subsidized catering, parties and so on;

▮ employee assistance (eg counselling services);

▮ training and continuous development;

▮ sabbaticals and career breaks;

▮ home or flexible working arrangements;

■ policies designed to ensure that the treatment of employees is of a high standard (eg dignity at work, equality of opportunity, work–life balance and the quality of the working environment).

Changes to the income tax regime have made some of these, for example cars and parties, less attractive.

The psychological contract

Just after the offer of employment is the time to clarify the implicit terms and conditions and other less tangible aspects of the contract. The psychological contract is the term now used to describe the factors that define the nature of the relationship between employee and employer. These are driven by expectations and aspirations, and each party's ability and willingness to satisfy the needs of the other. As these are often the source of misunderstanding it is vitally important that these and other assumptions are checked and clarified early after the offer of employment has been made.

The negotiations can clarify, for example, access and resources for training and development, standards of work practice, and should certainly include key objectives and priorities to be achieved. They can include other areas that could easily be misunderstood and could lead to conflict. These tend to concern the underpinning values of the organization – those unique features of the employer's culture that everyone in the organization takes for granted, but that may not be obvious to those coming in from outside.

Fred's previous employer allowed staff to borrow equipment, such as laptop computers, as working at home was accepted practice. When the machine was at home, there was no problem with the children using it to help with their homework and for the occasional game. Files left on the machine by his family were sometimes the highlight of Fred's Monday mornings.

When Fred moved jobs, he had no reason to doubt that his new employer would have the same approach. He was somewhat embarrassed to find himself summoned to the boss to explain why that he taken his laptop from the office. Even though the employer knew staff took work home, borrowing machinery and equipment was regarded as misuse of property.

Other aspects of the psychological contract define how staff treat each other and what are regarded as acceptable standards of behaviour. An employer has a vicarious responsibility for ensuring that staff, particularly those in management positions, do not adopt any pattern of behaviour that is best described as inappropriate. This includes bullying and harassment, particularly if the bad behaviour is related to the other person's gender, sexuality, ethnicity or any disability.

Arthur had just the sort of industrial and academic background the research institute needed. He was a red-hot find and the director could not wait for him to start; he was looking forward to the many new contracts Arthur was sure to win. Arthur's credibility with his colleagues was very high and he had brilliant ideas for future developments.

Everything seemed to promise a bright future for the institute and Arthur. Then he hit his first obstacle. It was only a minor difficulty really, but his temper flared. He shouted at the secretaries, told the technician he was incompetent and threatened to sack a research assistant. The director was shocked. He had never seen a member of staff behave so outrageously. When he challenged Arthur, the latter was genuinely puzzled. 'Why?' he said. 'That was nothing out of the ordinary. You should have see Bill, a colleague in my last institute. When he got mad, things really flew.'

The director struggled to explain that a less emotional expression of frustration was the norm in the institute and began to wonder if the appointment was 'red hot' in the way he had originally thought. Would Arthur be able to make the changes to his behaviour that would be demanded if he wanted to stay at the institute?

The time spent during the negotiation stage can prevent later misunderstanding, and lay the ground for the induction phase that starts when the new employee begins work. Induction and initial training and development are discussed more extensively in Chapter 8. It is enough to say here that research indicates that if employees are given good quality information early in their employment, there is a greater chance of it being successful.

TREATING UNSUCCESSFUL CANDIDATES WELL

It may be hard to believe that unsuccessful candidates can obtain any benefit when they fail to be appointed to a job they really wanted. Submitting an application requires the commitment of time, at the very least. Most applicants invest some emotion as well. If the applicant is short-listed this emotional investment is increased, as the individual psyches him- or herself up for the selection events and final interview. Consequently, failing at the last hurdle is disappointing. Even if an unsuccessful candidate had decided that he or she would not accept the job if it was offered, there can still be a slight sense of rejection and let-down.

Individuals can be vulnerable after an application has not been successful, and they deserve sensitive treatment. If the process is designed as an opportunity for learning and development from the outset, and candidates are told that this is the case, the chances of all the candidates obtaining a positive outcome can be increased. Experience of running assessment centres and other selection events has shown that if candidates are treated with respect and consideration through-out, even when they do not progress to the final stages, they generally say that they feel that they have had a fair chance and have gained some additional insight and learning.

However, this approach is not commonly found. It requires skill and con-sideration from those involved, and needs to start at the very beginning of the process. If applicants are given information describing what the employer will ask them to do as part of the selection processes, in addition to details of the job for which they are applying, they are able to prepare themselves for what is to come. This means that they are also prepared for the offer of feedback. Research carried out by Mabey and Iles (1991) found that candidates tend to prefer procedures that are forward-looking rather than those that concern only the past. Some of the other considerations candidates deserve are reported in Dale and Iles (1992).

A considerate approach is especially important when internal candidates are involved. Mishandling of internal candidates can have long-term consequences on their morale and that of others. There is little point in letting them (and helping them) lose their commitment to their current employer by lowering the levels of their motivation by mistreating them when they are putting themselves forward for positions with greater responsibility. It is likely that these people are well regarded by peers, so how they are treated will be witnessed by their colleagues and friends. If they believe the applicants have not been treated well, they will see this as a manifestation of the employer's attitude to its staff in general, and this can feed other sources of discontent. Some simple steps can be taken that both enrich the recruitment and selection process and help the candidates not appointed retain their self-esteem and dignity. These steps will also demonstrate to the rest of the workforce that the employer is capable of acting on any commitments to good employment policies and practices. This is achieved by making sure that:

▌ the methods and criteria to be used are explicit and open;

▌ the candidates are treated with consideration and respect throughout;

▌ the candidates are kept fully informed at every stage;

▌ the reasons for taking particular approaches are explained;

▌ the assessment is seen as a diagnostic, not a pejorative, process;

■ decision making is used to inform action planning to help longer-term learning and subsequent growth;

■ feedback is given constructively and confidentially;

■ action results and follow-up happens.

A number of career grade system analysts had been recruited during a period of expansion. They were very much of an age and possessed similar qualifications. However their interests were very different, as were their career aspirations. After a period of low turnover, one of the three section heads left. It was decided to advertise the post internally because of the specialist nature of the department. Only two members of staff applied.

This was obviously a difficult situation to handle. Only one could be promoted, and that person would supervise the other. The whole selection process was carefully planned to be both thorough and sensitive. The debriefing and feedback sessions were seen as being critical to the successful implementation of the appointment decision. Not only did the employer have to select the best candidate, that decision would have to made in a way that was open, with an outcome that had to be acceptable to all the staff in the section. The process had to be fair, and seen as fair by all.

When the deadline for applications had passed and it was clear there were no other candidates, the department manager met with the two people who had applied. The process to be used to make the appointment was outlined to both. This included an explanation of the criteria and the way in which their applications would be assessed. They were told that the person not appointed would be expected to meet a careers counsellor after the event, and support would be given if that individual wished to consider his or her future in the organization.

Nicola was promoted, Dennis not. Naturally he was very disappointed and felt extremely devalued. He didn't really want to see the careers counsellor, but the meeting had been scheduled for 10 days after the final interview. As the meeting approached, Dennis wished he could forget the whole business. Nicola was being very careful and his other colleagues were keeping well away. They seemed afraid of hurting him.

When he met the counsellor, he was pleasantly surprised. The meeting was not the warm and fuzzy non-event he was expecting. The counsellor took a very practical and focused approach. There was no beating about the bush. He was asked about his feelings and encouraged to express his anger and disappointment. Then the counsellor asked him to examine the criteria, consider the feedback and explain why he thought his application had not been successful. He was not asked to compare himself with Nicola in any way. (This was something he had been dreading, as they had previously been very good friends.) The counsellor encouraged Dennis to stand back and focus on the areas of mismatch between the criteria and his skills. Once that had been done, they moved on to what Dennis wanted from a job.

Several meetings were held between the two of them. Gradually Dennis came to realize that he did not really want to be a manager. His skills were professional, rather than those required for management, and his weaknesses lay in the very areas needed for effective management. He was good at breaking down systems, relating to service users and finding innovative ways of meeting their needs. His job satisfaction came from pleasing people. He did not enjoy dealing with conflict, planning workloads, or dealing with the bureaucracy needed for the smooth running of the section.

Dennis finally decided that his future lay in computing rather than management, so he applied to take a further course of study that would lead to a postgraduate qualification. He also turned his attention to producing articles for professional journals. Over the next few years his reputation grew, and increasingly he was invited to present his work to his colleagues at conferences.

Meanwhile Nicola became more and more removed from her professional role. Even though she was enjoying her job, she was being drawn into business and workload planning, and was working longer and longer hours to keep on top.

Who was the most successful applicant in this example?

GIVING FEEDBACK

Selection methods have become more sophisticated and probing, and candidates want to know the 'results' of tests and findings of the assessors. More employers are prepared to provide information about the outcomes, but some are still nervous about doing so, believing that unhappy candidates will use any information they can get hold of to inform a complaint. This defensive view does not respect the effort made by candidates in applying, and how much information they have revealed about themselves in the process.

Moreover, the term 'giving feedback' puts the emphasis on the wrong side; candidates should be *offered* feedback only *if they so wish*. Forcing feedback on to unwilling listeners is likely to do more harm than good. Reference has been made above to the vulnerability of candidates after selection, and the imbalance of power between the potential employer and candidates. Often candidates feel obliged to take up the offer of feedback; a failure to do so will be seen as another negative. This fear is more real when the appointment has been entirely an internal process and everyone else is receiving feedback.

Feedback should not be forced on to the unwilling.

During the process applicants will have raised their hopes and aspirations, and these will grow as they progress on to the later stages. They will have thought about the impact success will have on their personal lives, and may have discussed the implications with family and friends. Very few people, when psyching themselves up for a new job, prepare for failure. They are busy 'going for it', preparing themselves for the interview, considering the possible questions, the sort of events they will be asked to go through, and thinking themselves into the new job. It is not that normal for candidates to think about how they will react and what they will do if they do not get the job. Even if asked, they will probably only say 'carry on as before'. They do not prepare themselves for disappointment and the sense of failure.

For some people, not getting the job will come as a shock. Likely responses will include denial, rationalization and blaming the process:

I   The tasks were unrepresentative.

I   The activities were too hard/easy.

I   The process was not valid.

I   The assessors were unfair and behaved badly.

I   The whole process was a game to justify appointing the favourite.

While some of these responses may be justified and there are occasions when candidates do have grounds for complaint, most often they are examples of post-hoc rationalization. Imposing feedback on to people in this psychological state can add to any damage already sustained to their self-esteem. Feedback may well contain information about their performance and skill levels that individuals are unable to deny. Forcing this on to them could erode the candidates' psychological defences at a time when it may be important for them to protect themselves and rationalize any sense of disappointment and failure. Consequently it may be better to let candidates know they may have feedback, but only if they want it.

If the appointment has been an entirely internal affair, it is possible that receiving feedback is seen as being the right thing to do. Perhaps not everyone will want it at that particular time. Therefore, the right to refuse should be given and allowed. The person charged with the task of providing feedback to the candidates should be sensitive to the possibility of peer group pressure, and give an individual the opportunity to change his or her mind, with out any loss of face. Respecting the individual's privacy and his or her right to refuse feedback is a key to the successful conclusion of the selection process.

Detailed advice outlining ways of providing feedback to aid development is given in Dale (1998). Lord (1994) also gives very practical and sensible advice on how to feed back the results of tests. There are some slight differences between providing feedback on day-to-day performance, and the feedback made available after a selection process. A main consideration is the individual's perception of his or her lack of success after the investment of time and emotion.

When applying for another job, applicants are processed. They are asked to expose their abilities, experience, attainments and personality to the scrutiny of others. They are asked to explain and justify their actions, and to demonstrate their future potential for a role about which they have only scant information, often to unknown people, in an unknown organization. Even if care has been taken to give the candidates choice in the process, they are still very much in the hands of the employer. The use of instruments, methods and techniques that are administered by experts and have a scientific basis gives the 'results' and outcomes high credibility. The results can appear to contain the whole truth (and nothing but the truth) about an individual.

Feeding back the results of psychometric instruments requires specialist training to ensure that the results are interpreted sensitively.

It is not unusual for the results to be given to the selectors before the candidate knows what the tests have revealed. In this case, it is virtually impossible for the candidate to deny or explain the outcome. If the information is used as part of the final interview to probe certain aspects of likely performance, individuals may find themselves on the defensive, not sure of their position. A fairer approach is for the results to be communicated to the candidates before the final interview so they are able to agree the report to the panel, explain any peculiarities in the results, and are prepared to discuss on a more equal basis the implication of the findings in relation to the role.

Care is also required to ensure that the recipient understands the context and the meaning of the results. Usually employers who use such instruments ensure that only trained and qualified practitioners provide feedback. The British Psychological Society has introduced levels of competence in an attempt to improve practice, recognizing the potential for damage to be done to individuals. The Chartered Institute of Personnel and Development has produced a code of practice and its journal, *People Management*, often contains articles discussing the practice and use of this mode of assessment. Reputable suppliers of the instruments also try to control their use by a system of licensing. Even so, there are employers who do not comply with acknowledged good practice.

The recent rapid expansion in the use of computer-based testing, and their availability on the Internet, have made psychometric instruments more accessible and simpler to administer. However, even though these packages may appear to be based on well-known tests, they are simplistic and at the very best can only been seen as indicative, in ways similar to those questionnaires found in popular magazines. Candidates should be told which instrument is being used and be made aware of its origin. They should be reassured about the competency of the person administering the test, and be given information about the instrument's validity in terms they understand. The codes of practice referred to above contain guidance on providing feedback after the administration of tests. The following checklist provides additional tips.

▌ The candidate should be allowed to ask for feedback. Offer the opportunity and encourage candidates to take it up but do not force it upon them. The impact on their well-being should be the main concern.

▌ The individual should have control over when the feedback is given. Remember that the candidate will return to his or her current job; ringing up and offering feedback may be a breach of confidentiality. If the candidate has not told anyone of the application before the selection process, having another employer make contact could make public a fact the individual would have preferred to keep private. In addition to constituting an invasion of privacy, it may be an unwelcome reminder of failure and unrealized ambitions.

▌ If individuals do want the feedback, begin by asking them to reflect on their own performance, and encourage them to identify gaps against the specification and criteria for themselves. Most people are aware of their own strengths and weaknesses, and only need them to be put into the context of the requirements of the job and organization. They do not want their failings paraded before them. Rather they would prefer guidance on how to improve. The use of exploratory questions can help the candidates reflect on not only their weaknesses but also on their strengths. Please do not tell candidates where they went wrong.

▌ Judge the amount of detail to provide. Some candidates will be very disappointed and will try to prove that the employer made the wrong decision. If too much detail is given, it is possible that the feedback session will become a fightback session and not be useful for anyone. If the person providing the feedback moves gradually, testing how much information the individual is able to accept, the risk of swamping the individual will be avoided. Remember the reason for offering feedback is to help the candidate move forward – if this is not the purpose, it should not be given.

▌ Provide indications of what was being sought. If it is appropriate and helpful, the specification, role requirements and selection criteria can be used to give practical examples of the sorts of skills, behaviours and standards being sought. However comparison between the individual and any other candidate, particularly the person appointed, should be avoided.

▌ Focus on behaviour that can be changed by providing evidence and offering examples of alternative approaches. Suggest ways in which improvements could be achieved. However, make sure any evidence presented is factually accurate and demonstrable.

▌ Do not pass judgement. Adjectives such as 'poor', 'good' or' better' are comparative and are difficult to substantiate. What may be good in one context could be awful in the opinion of another employer.

▌ The amount of feedback given should be limited. There is no point in overloading the candidates with detail. Broad indications of areas of mismatch between their abilities and experience – as assessed during the selection activities – with the criteria and requirements only should be given. Improvement that would have increased their chances of success can be suggested, but this can be dangerous ground. It may be better to encourage individuals to identify these factors for themselves, rather than tell them what they should have done or should do in the future.

▌ Make use of the positive. Make sure the candidates understand that they have strengths as well as shortcomings. Another employer might think they are the best candidates for a job.

▌ Candidates have the right to disagree and not accept the feedback. After all, they decided to submit an application for a job; they did not ask for an in-depth analysis of their personality and its shortcomings.

▌ Leave the candidates with a sense of the future. No one is unemployable and everyone has a future. Give positive indications, and if the individual asks, offer suggestions about ways, in your opinion, he or she could develop his or her career. Remember your opinion may differ from that of other employers – and the candidate.

The feedback will only relate to the demonstration of skills as evidenced against the criteria and specification at the time of the assessment. If the candidate did not do very well in according to the assessors for one particular employer, this does not necessarily mean that individual is not able to perform to the standard required for another. All that can be said is that under the circumstances and at the time, the assessors were not satisfied that the individual had the level of competency required for that particular role.

Even though the chance of an individual taking out a complaint against an employer can be reduced if the candidates have been respected and treated fairly throughout the process, candidates still have the right to register their dissatisfaction if they feel they have the grounds. This needs to be remembered during the provision of feedback. If there is any indication of this, or if the individual is getting upset or angry, the person providing the feedback should tread carefully. This is where preparation and training for the person charged with the task of providing the feedback comes in. He or she should be made aware of the warning signs and helped to develop techniques for withdrawing. Above all, he or she should be advised against getting into an argument with the candidate.

CORRECTING MISTAKES

Even when the processes have been very carefully designed and executed, it is always possible that the decisions made during the final stages of the selection process are not good. Improving the processes used to aid human decision making can only help to minimize some of the known inherent flaws and errors in judgement. Perfect decision making is a dream, not a reality, and even the techniques known to be the best predictors only have a validity coefficient of around 0.6. There will be times when the wrong person is offered a contract of employment and accepts it.

While is important to understand how and why this happened, it is more important to work out what to do about the situation. Regrettably, many poor appointments are not dealt with. People may mutter, and the individual continues in blind ignorance of his or her failure to match up to expectations. Alternatively the person may be told clearly that he or she is not up to standard, and is left to get on with the job as well as he or she is able. Failure to tackle this type of situation is an example of poor management, yet dealing with poor appointments is not straightforward. Assuming everything reasonable has been done to match expectations and clarify objectives and required standards of performance, the first step to take to correct a poor appointment is the admission of a mistake. Not many managers relish this. However, once this step has been taken it is possible to devise suitable action to rectify or at least improve the situation.

The developmental approach

If the employing organization makes use of appraisal or performance review schemes as part of its human resource management practices, and has used the results of the assessment carried out during the selection process, which can be used in the early stages of development planning, it can be comparatively easy to pick up any shortfall in performance.

▌ The criteria used for selection will have been explicit and behaviourally defined.

▌ The events or activities will have provided evidence of performance as assessed by competent assessors.

▌ Feedback will have been given and the outcome discussed.

This assessment is perhaps one of the most rigorous undertaken in employment. It makes sense, therefore, to use the results as the platform from which to review subsequent performance.

Stephan was appointed as product development manager in July 1998, but the employer had found filling the post difficult. The first advertisement had failed to provide a strong field and so a second was attempted. These applicants seemed better and six were short-listed. The general manager decided to go ahead with the strict proviso that if none of the candidates met the criteria no appointment was to be made. This instruction created a certain amount of tension. The continuing vacancy was hampering other operations.

Four of the candidates were obviously not suitable. One was marginal and Stephan seemed fine. The two were recommended for final interview. There were one or two areas of doubt about Stephan's performance, but considering the circumstances, the assessors felt confident in their recommendation to the interviewing panel.

Stephan was duly appointed and given feedback. This indicated that the assessors had concerns about his abilities to forward plan and pull resources together to enact those plans. They felt that while he was very good at detail and interpersonal relationships, he might tend to be bogged down. These concerns were included in his early development plan, and a note made for his manager to check on progress at the first appraisal meeting which would be held in January 1999.

The boxed example demonstrates how areas of concern highlighted during selection assessment can be used to indicate areas in need of early action, and be the basis from which to review initial performance. Appropriate action can be identified, and developmental plans implemented to address specific issues. If, as the example suggested, Stephan became bogged down in detail and failed to address the longer-term issues, his manager could have pulled him out for training on one day a week, or given a deadline for the creation of a development plan. Alternatively if Stephan did not know how to construct such a plan, his manager could have carried out some coaching to help him learn how to do so.

The main point is the importance of facing up to problems quickly. Performance problems do not go away if they are ignored. They hide, fester and get bigger. As they get older, they change. This can make it difficult to get to their root cause. Other people get involved, and the whole situation eventually becomes such as mess that it is nearly impossible to untangle. If the issues are addressed early, they can be dealt with and resolved.

Job redesign

If a developmental approach is tried but does not resolve the problem, other steps need to be taken to resolve a poor appointment. The problem will not go away of its own accord. The reason the appointment is not good may not be the candidate's not being as competent as required. Even if the measures outlined in Chapter 1 were taken, the job might have been constructed in a way that inhibits rather than facilitates achievement. The job or role might be:

I   too big (with too many disparate activities to complete);

I   too complex (the context may be changing rapidly, with too many external factors impinging on the post-holder's performance);

I   dependent on others who do not deliver;

I   impossible (that is, have objectives that are not attainable).

Alternatively, the range of skills required may be too great, so it cannot be possessed by one human being.

Stephan was finding his new job more difficult than he had anticipated. He had known there would be two aspects to it which might cause conflict, but he had not expected the demands to be so contradictory. He understood that the main purpose of his role was to lead the development of products, liaising with R & D, production and marketing. To do this he had a small team of engineers, and was responsible for managing them. Technically these engineers were meant to act as project managers. Instead, Stephan discovered that they were involving themselves in the detail of the production processes.

Stephan decided he would need to win their trust and respect before attempting to move them back into their proper roles. However, this meant that he too had found himself involved in inappropriate detail. He found it difficult to get the support he needed to resist these pressures, and began to realize that one reason for the engineers' involvement in production was a lack of cooperation from the R & D scientists.

Redeployment

There are occasions when the individual, not the design of the job, is the problem. Some applicants are very good at convincing interviewers of their competence, and it is not unknown for some candidates to falsify background details. In the latter case, the position is quite clear – the individual has deliberately misled the employer and so fundamentally breached the bond of trust. In the former case, the fact that the candidate was a better interviewee than appointee does not make the appointment invalid. Nevertheless in these circumstances action more akin to discipline than initial training is needed.

The first steps in any disciplinary procedure should be designed to help the role-holder correct performance that does not reach the standards expected, or does not comply with the employer's procedures. However if all reasonable remedial measures have been taken to help the individual achieve the standards or objectives required, other steps can be taken as part of informal disciplinary procedures. One of these is redeployment.

Stephan discussed his early difficulties with his manager during his first appraisal meeting. The manager also shared his perception of these. Together they agreed a plan of campaign to deal with the problems Stephan had identified and enable him to move more into the planning work expected of him. They set a date to meet again three months later.

In April when they met, Stephan's manager expressed his disappointment in the progress made. Stephan had not done anything to build bridges with the R & D department, and his staff were still predominately involved in production issues. The development plan Stephan had promised to write was still in its initial draft. The reasons for non-achievement were thin, to say the least. The manager agreed to give Stephan another three months to get the plan into action.

By the time of the next meeting, Stephan's manager was beginning to wonder if the reasons given in January had really been excuses. He decided to look at other ways of dealing with Stephan's poor performance in these aspects. The manager was torn. Stephan certainly possessed qualities the organization could use, and some of his work had been really good. The problem was that it was the wrong work. The manager began to think about other parts of the organization that might be able to make better use of Stephan's talents.

Redeployment is one method an employer can use, with the employee's agreement, if the original appointment is proving to be unsatisfactory. In this sense, asking an employee to move into another post should not be seen as an easy alternative to formal disciplinary action. Nor should it be seen as a way of 'parking' the problem. Any move should be to a post at a similar level, and handled discreetly. The point of making the move is to enable both the employee and the employer to form a new working relationship that is more beneficial than the previous arrangement.

The danger of this approach for the employer is that the individual could attempt to claim constructive dismissal. To do this, however, the employee would have to resign and then demonstrate that the actions of the employer had broken the contract of employment, or that it was no longer possible for the individual to do the job for which he or she had been employed. Selwyn (1988) says that 'making unilateral changes in employment terms, such as a change in the job, a lowering of earnings or change in location, providing there are no contractual rights to do so, would entitle an employee to resign. However it must be borne in mind that although this may amount to a dismissal in law, whether the dismissal is fair or unfair has still to be determined by the facts of the case and whether or not the employer has acted reasonably.' If feedback on the areas of performance causing concern had been given, action taken to help the individual make improvements, time, support and resources made available and further review undertaken, any individual would have a hard time convincing a tribunal of his or her case.

Demotion

This step is serious and should be taken only after other measures have been tried and failed. Asking an individual to move to a post at a lower salary and lower status represents formal disciplinary action, so the possibility of demotion should be included in the employer's disciplinary procedures which accompany the written statement of terms and conditions given to new employees. Otherwise, the individual's agreement needs to be obtained.

In August 1999 the administration manager in Stephan's organization was forced to take ill health retirement unexpectedly. To Stephan's manager this seemed to be a godsent opportunity for both the organization and Stephan. The job demanded someone who was able to pay attention to detail and also able to marry a number of conflicting demands. During the time he had been with the organization, Stephan's good qualities had been seen as his abilities to get on well with people at all levels, produce reports to tight deadlines, and deal effectively with matters that demanded high levels of accuracy.

Stephan had fitted in well with the organization. He had played a useful role in re-establishing the staff association that had been floundering, and was generally liked. Since the administration manager's job needed to be filled, the general manager agreed that Stephan should be asked to move into the post.

By the New Year, the general manager was wondering if she had been wise. Stephan was still not achieving the objectives set for him. He was burying himself even more in detail, seemingly relishing the minutiae. The staff reporting to him appeared to be doing their own thing. Yes, Stephan was popular, but this was because he was more one of the gang than respected as a manager and leader. In February 2000 the general manager asked to meet Stephan's current and his former manager to discuss the problem of Stephan's non-achievement.

Dismissal

If it is not possible to remedy poor performance or the post-holder's failure to meet agreed objectives or standards through training and development, redeployment or demotion, the employer may be decide that the best course of action is to dismiss the employee. This is a regrettable state to have reached for all concerned, but sometimes rather than prolong the situation it is better to make a clean break.

If this has to be the conclusion, the employer must make sure that the decision to dismiss is made fairly and properly, and the correct procedures are followed. An employee can claim to have been unfairly or wrongly dismissed if specified steps have not been taken before and during the dismissal. It is wise to obtain proper advice before any action is taken, as employment legislation is complex and can change rapidly as a result of tribunal and court decisions. The following therefore should not be seen as legal guidance.

The Employment Protection (Consolidation) Act 1978 lays down five grounds or reasons when a fair dismissal can be made. These relate to:

■ the capability or qualifications of the employee;

■ the conduct of the employee;

■ the redundancy of the employee;

■ the employee's inability to continue to work in the position without contravening a restriction or duty imposed by or under a statute;

■ some other substantial reason such as to justify the dismissal of an employee.

The failure of an employee to perform the job to the standard required could fall into one or several of the above categories, depending on the circumstances. The most common is likely to be the first, if the employee demonstrably is not achieving the desired output. 'Capability' can include any assessment by reference to skill, aptitude, health or other physical or mental quality, and 'qualifications' means any degree, diploma or other academic, technical or professional qualification relevant to the position held by the employee.

If an employing organization concludes that a position cannot be found for the employee – because the appointment was not successful or that the employee's standard of work had deteriorated – the proper procedures should then be followed. These should be taken with professional advice. The reason for ensuring that the proposed steps are taken properly is not just to safeguard the employer against tribunal action. Wrongful and unfair dismissal will reflect badly on the organization and damage its reputation as a good employer. This will harm its ability to recruit good quality staff in the future. It will also harm the individual.

Getting dismissal right is not difficult. All that is required is that the individual is given:

▌ feedback and information regarding the inadequate performance;

▌ the chance to state his or her perspective;

▌ several fair chances to improve or rectify inadequate performance;

▌ support and further feedback;

▌ warnings of the consequences;

▌ rights of appeal;

▌ the right to be accompanied.

ACAS, through its local offices, provides an advisory service as one of its primary aims is to avoid complaints, mistakes and unnecessary conflict.

In April 2000 the general manager decided to act. Stephan would be offered a lower-paid post comparable with his level of performance. If this was not acceptable, he would be given formal warnings in accordance with the company's disciplinary procedure. The personnel manager was duly consulted and a meeting arranged with Stephan and, if he wished, a 'friend'. The meeting was intended to state the company's position and ask Stephan to explain his continued inadequate performance. Depending on his responses, the company's options would be presented.

Stephan was given two days to think about the situation. His options were to refute the company's position, make an alternative set of proposals to enable him to continue in his present post, or accept the offer of a lower-paid post. The general manager rehearsed each possibility with the personnel manager and planned appropriate responses to each.

Sometimes, obviously depending on the particular circumstances, it is better for everyone to terminate the contract. This enables the employee to leave the organization quickly, with little public exposure of the problem. This clean-break approach can save face for both the employer and employee, as it represents an acceptance on both sides of a genuine mistake. Demotion and dismissal may appear to blame the employee, but when a poor appointment leads to inadequate performance, it is rarely anyone's fault. Instead, it tends to be a combination of unfortunate, but difficult to forecast, circumstances. Examples of these include cases when the indications of weakness seen during the initial assessment were not heeded, reservations expressed by one of the team of selectors, the employee over-estimating and over-selling his or her abilities, and an employer anxious to fill an important post.

Great care is needed if the reason for poor performance is related to a health condition or disability. The Disability Discrimination Act requires the employer to make reasonable adjustments to enable the individual to remain in employment. In addition to professional advice, medical opinion will be necessary, and possibly lateral thinking about how the job could be done differently so that the person can carry on for as long as is reasonably possible.

It was July by the time the various hearings had been held and the final conclusion reached. Stephan would not accept the lower-paid job, and he refused to accept that he was not doing the job to the level he had been employed at. He argued that the actions he had taken after his first appraisal had been agreed, and claimed that he had reached most of the targets set. Where there had been failures this was the fault of others, not him.

The general manager had not been able to reach any common ground, and she finally decided that Stephan's employment would have to be ended. She was dismayed to find that Stephan had two years' service, and that it had taken the organization so long to deal with the problem. She wondered what the consequences of giving him notice would be, because Stephan had been so recalcitrant.

The matter was discussed with the personnel director, and together they concluded it was more than likely that Stephan would claim unfair dismissal. They agreed they did not want to face the time, costs and publicity of attending a tribunal, so decided to recommend to the finance director that if Stephan did file a claim, discussions be opened to see if a suitable settlement could be found.

Termination by mutual agreement

There are occasions when the employee realizes that the appointment has been a failure. He or she will want to find a route out that will maintain his or her dignity and self-respect. He or she will also want to safeguard the chances of finding alternative suitable employment. Ending a contract of employment on mutually agreeable terms is perhaps the best solution to an unsatisfactory situation. The integrity of both parties can be preserved, and a no-comeback agreement reached. Such compromise agreements can be reached so the individual can leave the organization with clear understandings on both sides. The agreement may include the provision of references, compensation pay (or goods of value such as a car or computer) and help in finding other employment, for example by engaging the services of an outplacement or search consultant.

The general manager arranged to see Stephan at the beginning of August 2000 to give him his notice of dismissal. She was surprised when he came in to announce he wanted to leave. He had suspected what was coming, but could not find a way to admit that he had been wrong to apply for the job in the first place. He told the general manager that he had been under a lot of pressure to earn more money, and had been really surprised when he had done so well at the selection event. The first few months had been a real struggle for him, he had not been happy and now wanted a way out.

It did not take long to find a suitable formula that enabled Stephan to manage while he found another job. The employer realized that it was better to pay to solve the problem and avoid possible embarrassment.

WORDS OF CAUTION

Poor operation of selection events, inadequate records and the provision of poor-quality feedback are risky actions. They can lay the employer open to accusations of unfair treatment. Post-hoc rationalization, as discussed above, means that someone who feels rejected may be inclined to find someone to blame. If the selection process has not been conducted professionally and feedback given in a clumsy, unskilled way, individuals are more likely to blame the employer organization for not letting them display their abilities rather than examine critically their degree of fit with the organizational requirements.

Muriel was a personnel professional with experience of policy development and implementation, organizational development and the management of change achieved over a number of years in several organizations. She applied for a new post with a major local employer, believing that she had demonstrated her abilities against the published specification. She went through the initial assessment confident that it was a formality. She was somewhat surprised to find that she was not invited for interview.

When she took up the invitation to receive feedback, she was even more surprised to be told that she did not have experience in change management and policy formulation. The person giving the feedback seemed a little vague and was not able to give any specific examples. When Muriel pointed to parts of her application that demonstrated her skills and expertise in those areas, the employer's representative agreed, admitted to being puzzled, and wondered why she had not been short-listed. He promised to look at her application again. Muriel heard nothing more and finally, after a few weeks, assumed that she would not do so. She was not surprised to hear later that an internal candidate had been appointed.

Was Muriel lacking when compared with the person specification or was the process a fix?

Sometimes the process is flawed, and unlawful bias influences decision making. In this country, the equal opportunities legislation describes what should not be done. Elsewhere laws encourage affirmative action to redress imbalance and previous inequalities. The US system, for example, has used targeting and quotas. This has led to backlash, litigation and counter-claims. However it has also resulted in the development of recruitment and selection practices that are demonstrably fair. In Britain, general practice appears to be concerned more with avoiding prosecution than with complying with the spirit of the law by encouraging improvements to the treatment of members of under-represented groups and widening opportunities.

Any applicant or candidate who feels that he or she has been subjected to discrimination or unfair treatment has the right of recourse to an employment tribunal. This right is not limited to people from black or ethnic minority groups and women. Men and white people have the same access to the tribunal if they believe they have been discriminated against on any of the grounds laid out in the relevant acts. Examples of discriminatory practice can include the selection of a member of one ethnic group in preference to members of another on grounds unrelated to the needs of the job, or the denial of employment to men in predominately female work groups. Changes to the law have recognized that proving cases of unfair discrimination is difficult for the individual, so the onus of proof has been moved onto the employer. Also the ceiling on payments has been increased, to make proven breaches of the law more punitive.

SUMMARY

This chapter has outlined how the final stages of the selection process can have beneficial outcomes for all candidates, regardless of whether their application had been successful or not. Taking a developmental approach from the outset can foster a climate in which the unsuccessful candidates are offered constructive feedback to help them move on positively. Rejecting this approach can lead to candidates experiencing feelings of disappointment, rejection and a loss of confidence. They could engage in post-hoc rationalization and feel they have grounds for complaint. Turning the process into a win/win one is not difficult provided the sensitivities of the individuals involved are respected.

Agreeing the terms of employment continues after the decision to offer employment to one candidate has been made. Contractual terms need to be agreed, and the terms and conditions of the employment, both explicit and implicit, need to be clarified. The unsuccessful candidates need to be offered feedback and treated in a way that enables them to retain their sense of self-worth. The provision of feedback should be a positive experience. On the other hand, crass handling of people after they have been turned down can cause a lot of unnecessary pain and even damage.

Sometimes even though good practice may have been used and correct steps taken, a poor decision is made. Often responsibility for making the mistake cannot be attributed to one party or the other; both the employer and the employee will have contributed in some way. It is possible to remedy a situation that is probably unsatisfactory for all concerned, but once the new employee has started work it can be difficult to rectify a poor appointment. Admitting to a poor appointment decision requires an uncommon degree of honesty. Nevertheless, this first step is essential if the other measures are to be applied.

Depending on the particular situation, several courses of action can be followed. All require confidence on the part of the manager, compliance with proper procedures and the use of professional advice. Once a contract has been made, both parties have rights and obligations that are enforceable by law. Failure to follow procedures, accepted good practice and statute could lead an employer into an employment tribunal.

An employer has nothing at all to fear from complaints, provided:

■ Good quality descriptions of the role, specification of the required competencies and clear selection criteria have been prepared and used.

■ The advertisement and supporting information reflect the needs and context of the job and do not contain features that are directly or indirectly discriminatory.

■ The criteria are used for short-listing.

■ The reasons for rejection are evidenced and recorded.

■ Selection activities are designed to elicit required behaviours and are relevant to the job.

■ Decisions are based on evidence assessed against the criteria and are recorded.

■ The candidates are informed firmly of the decision and are given access to feedback if they so wish.

■ Candidates are given factual information that can be checked and evidenced if they question why they have not been short-listed or appointed.

■ Feedback is related to the criteria used for decision making.

■ Feedback is factual and is based on evidence.

■ Developmental advice, if given, is separated and it is made clear that any subsequent advice proffered is not related to the decision.

8

Induction and inclusion

We tend to assume that if the recruitment process has attracted a number of strong candidates and the selection activities have resulted in the best one being offered the job, everything is set for a rosy future. Nothing could be less true. So many good appointees have been turned into poor employees because the induction phase has been ignored and they are not made welcome. In this chapter, we will examine the various stages of induction, and consider how some simple actions can make sure that new employees are introduced to their new role and including into the organization – quickly.

We know from research that if certain simple actions are taken in the early days, the chances of the appointment being successful (that is, the employee is able to work productively and obtains the rewards sought for a useful period) are greater than if the new starter is thrown in at the deep end. Most organizations believe that they welcome their new staff very well. However, when their systems are examined they find that they pay attention to only some of the needs of the new employees. Probably this is because these needs seem to be straightforward. New starters have to be told what will be expected from them, they need to be shown around their workspace and the location of facilities such as toilets, cloakroom and kitchen. They need to be given copies of the employer's rules and health and safety policies and told when they will get paid. What more is needed?

NEEDS OF NEW EMPLOYEES

Starting a new job is a strange time. Stresses and emotions interplay in ways that are unpredictable even for the practised job mover. The factors involved are different every time, because they are influenced by other people and the particular circumstances. Moreover, all individuals have unique needs and emotions that affect how they respond to the situations in which they find themselves. It is also possible that individuals will not know what kind of help they need to settle in to their new job quickly. Let us look at what will have happened to the newly appointed person in their recent past:

▍ The individual will have decided to apply for another job, possibly because his or her current position was not satisfactory.

▍ When making the application, the individual may have gone through some self-examination about his or her wishes and capabilities.

▍ A period of uncertainty will have followed. This time could have consisted of high expectations and ambition, doubts about the application's chances of success, and questions about the individual's ability to do the job if appointed.

▍ The individual will have had to cope with the stresses associated with the assessments made during the selection activities.

▍ When the post was offered, the individual may have to make decisions about moving house and consider the impact this would have on other people (such as the rest of the family).

▍ The existing job and colleagues have to be left, and a period of bereavement lived through. (Even if the job was hateful, a sense of loss can be experienced.)

▍ The existing home perhaps has to be sold and friends and routines left.

▍ When the new job is started, again the individual may experience some doubts about his or her abilities.

▍ New people have to be met, assessed, new friendships formed, and decisions made about who and who not to trust.

▍ A learning curve is started where a great deal is unknown and progress is expected to be rapid.

There is little wonder that moving jobs is regarded as a major cause of stress. The pressures listed above can lead to the new employee being very uncertain and lacking in self-confidence at a time when the opposite could be expected. After all the new employee has been successful, and by rights should be excited and ready to go. Why should new appointees need their egos to be bolstered? The answer to this question is that they often do. Good employers recognize that new staff experience these feelings, and make sure that the concerns experienced in the early days and weeks of a new job are taken into amount. One of the indicators of an employer achieving the Investors in People standard is evidenced by 'people who are new to the organization and those new to a job can confirm that they have received an effective induction'. Actions additional to those outlined in the general human resource management textbooks can be taken to ensure that the induction phase is effective and the new employees feel part of the organization.

STARTING WITH RECRUITMENT

Induction is generally regarded as a training need, but here we will look at it from an alternative perspective and treat it as part of the recruitment and selection process. If this approach is taken, what the person ultimately to be appointed needs to know will be considered at each stage of the process. The pressures on employers have led some to recruit staff with the experience and skills required to enable them to 'hit the ground running'. The new person is then placed under pressure to achieve early wins. But there have been times when those appointed in this way have been left to fall flat on their faces, as they have not fitted into the organization. Adequate planning, preparation and briefing for the new start and future colleagues is required, if competent staff are to put their abilities into use quickly and effectively.

Planning should start right at the beginning of the recruitment and selection process. This is likely to include a schedule of dates that specifies when each stage is to occur. From this it is possible to anticipate the likely start date. An example is given in Table 8.1.

This level of planning may seem mechanistic, but if some slippage is allowed for unforeseen events, it can make sure that appropriate action is taken to ensure that the new starter is included into the new organization efficiently. Preparation is the lynchpin, for this approach cannot succeed if material and people are not adequately prepared. For example, the role outline and description of responsibilities have to be written in a way that facilitates the identification and agreement of targets and key objectives. The specification of competencies has to be phrased to enable the assessment of performance on the job, as well as during the recruitment and selection process. The assessment process during selection needs to be rigorous enough to provide information to help the formulation of the development plan.

Moreover, the workload of other staff needs to be planned so they are able to support their new colleague, and have the time to explain and answer questions. They should be briefed so they know what is happening and what is expected of them, so that they do not make unreasonable demands or believe that the new starter is being given special privileges. The workload of the new starter needs to be phased to take account of his or her progression along the learning curve. It should also be flexible enough to reflect the growth of his or her abilities and increase in confidence.

Table 8.1 *Schedule for recruitment and selection*

Week	Action
1	Agree role outline, description of responsibilities, specification, selection criteria and the process to be used
2	Prepare recruitment stage, including drafting any advertisement and additional information
3	Place advertisement or commence search
4	Respond to enquiries
5	Receive applications. Closing date
6	Short-list. Invite candidates to selection event
8	Selection event and final interview. Obtain references and make other checks
9	Negotiate terms and conditions
10	Written contracts exchanged. Pre-appointment meetings and visits
*14/18	Start day. Agree initial training and meetings schedule. Start scheduled training, meetings and discussions
15/19	Allocation of initial assignments and tasks. Begin assessment of progress
16/20	Review progress. Include feedback from selection assessments in initial personal training and development plan. Schedule second round of training, meetings and discussions
17/21	Additional assignments and increasing number of tasks
18/22	Review progress. Agree initial targets, key objectives and development plan
20/24	Progress review against role outline, responsibilities and specification, and development plan
24/28	Repeat week 24 every four weeks
*	depends on the notice to be given to the former employer.

Fiona was appointed as quality control manager. The post had been vacant for several months before she started, and in that time some jobs had moved from being pressing to urgent. The MD had every faith in her abilities, but he resisted the temptation of asking her to clear the backlog. He planned her first month with the finance director thus:

Week 1

Day 1 Introductions to new team then the rest of the day to be spent shadowing the MD

Day 2 Shadow the finance director

Day 3   Shadow the company secretary
Day 4   Shadow the works manager
Day 5   Shadow the sales and marketing manager.

Week 2

Day 1   Mee with the MD and works manager
Day 2–4   The quality team on assignment 1 and familiarization
Day 5   The sales and marketing manager at a customer conference.

Week 3

Day 1–2   The quality team on assignment 1 and familiarization with
               procedures
Day 3   Computer system briefing
Day 4   The quality team on assignment 1 and familiarization with
               procedures
Day 5   Progress review with MD and explanation of assignment 2.

Week 4

Day 1–4   Assignments 1 and 2
Day 5   Progress review with MD and agreement of key targets,
               objectives and development plan.

The MD justified the objections from the quality team by assuring them that their new manager's planned assimilation into the company would enable her to become effective more quickly than through the more normal approach to induction. He assured then that in the long run they would all gain. Fiona was also anxious to get going with her real work, but agreed with the plan. At the end of the four weeks, she felt as though she had been with the company several months rather than just one. Everyone involved agreed that she certainly knew her way around the organization and its ways of working.

Effective induction, as will be explained, is more just ensuring the new employee has pens, paper, a desk, PC and phone. The way in which the new person is received and introduced to the organization can have a direct effect on his or her long-term success, productivity and happiness. Garratt (1987) draws attention to two distinct processes that occur during a new employee's early days. These he calls induction and inclusion – hence the title of this chapter. The former is when 'people are introduced to their new organization or job, the people with whom they will be working and given some clues as to what is expected of them in terms of the technical side of their jobs'. The latter is 'about building up rapport, trust and credibility so that we can be accepted by and work with our fellows'. Most organizations assume that inclusion will happen somehow, and put little energy or time into ensuring that it is effective.

INDUCTION METHODS

Despite the assertion made by Garratt (1987) to the contrary, most employers do not organize the induction of new staff very well. Most are welcomed to their desk then effectively abandoned, left to make sense of their new world the best way they can. The inclusion of induction in the Investors in People standard reflects both its importance and the need to encourage employers to take the process seriously. When induction is organized, it is usually a series of visits and meetings and newcomers are bombarded with vast amounts of information in their first few days. The common outcome achieved by taking this approach is a new member of staff who has forgotten much of what he or she has been told, and is left with a confused and partial picture of the employer and its world.

A better approach is to make use of a structure that allows new employees to assimilate information at a rate they can absorb. They are provided with aides memoire and sources of reference to enable them to access what they need to know but cannot retain in their memory. The following describes some of the techniques that can be used to speed learning and aid the retention of information. Some form a record of progress and become a personal source of information. Some employers are making use of information technology to help new starters progress at their own pace and structure their own induction. E-learning is a tremendous development in this respect, but relies on exactly the same underpinning philosophies – the importance of induction, planning, and the systematic breakdown of the information to be provided so that it is provided in a logical order and chunks of comprehensible size.

There is a real dilemma at the start of any employment: there is a large amount of information, but with differing degrees of importance, to be transmitted by the employer to the new employee. The information also has two forms – what the employee needs to know and what he or she wants to know. The sheer quantity of information can lead to mental overload, and result in individuals being unable to distinguish the degree of importance of what they have been told. In addition the stress inherent in starting a new job can make it difficult for the new person to sort out peripheral from the important information, never mind remember any of it.

Checklists and handbooks

A practical approach to overcome these difficulties is to make use of a checklist supported by a handbook or guide. Salthouse (1995) describes the value of employee handbooks, and ways of producing them. They also have a role in supporting the written statement of terms and conditions, as discussed in Chapter 7.

A checklist can ensure the full range of topics a new employee needs to be told about is covered. These topics include:

▌ the employer's rules, including health and safety, standards of behaviour and expectations;

▌ places and facilities the individual will need to visit and use;

▌ key people including those the employee will be working with;

▌ basic administrative systems.

The guide or handbook will provide the written back-up. This will enable the individual to re-read the information, and so help the new employee remember what he or she has been told. The handbook can also contain supplementary and background information.

In addition, an employer may wish to explain to new (and existing) employees its vision, core business, strategic priorities, markets and values. A handbook provides a means of giving this information to new employees. In addition, it can contain information that helps employees put their role into context within the whole organization. This can be of particular value when the organization is large, has several outlets, locations or sites, or has a large range of activities in its operational portfolio.

The guide or handbook can also include or summarize policies and procedures. Many large employers produce these in published form – either in manuals or on their own internal network – as it is unreasonable for all employees to have their own copy. However, all should know what those key policies cover and where to find them.

The use of an induction checklist helps the manager make sure nothing is missed; it also indicates to the new starter what he or she should know. After the induction, the list serves as a reminder, and if space is provided it can allow the individual to make notes. It can also form a record to demonstrate that the employee has been told about certain rules and regulations. While this should not be the primary motivation for the use of a checklist, its existence can be of value if for any reason the employer wishes to demonstrate the employee has received information, has been trained to work to the desired standard, or has been made aware of rules.

The sample list in Figure 8.1 indicates possible topics that might usefully to be covered, and shows how the induction can be scheduled. It also references other documents or sources of information. Space can be provided for each item to be signed off once it has been explained to the new employee.

Many employers produce lists such as this, in paper or electronic form, but they are often unused. A reason for this is the lack of knowledge on the part of the manager and others responsible for carrying out the induction. Most trainers

Before the start date

1. Decide who is going to induct the new employee. If several people are to be involved, ensure everyone knows what they are to cover and who is going to be the main 'inductor'.
2. Ensure that the new employee knows where and when to report, who to meet and what to bring (for example documents to be checked, refreshments, safety clothing etc).
3. Make sure the main inductor is ready and prepared to meet the new employee.
4. Check that the necessary facilities (eg desk, telephone, computer, parking place, keys) are ready.

Topic	Reference	Initials Employee	Initials Inductors	Date
Day 1 Introduce the inductor and explain his or her relationship to the new employee (eg supervisor, manager, mentor)				

The job Check the new starter has a copy of the role outline and description of responsibilities, and understands:
● his or her duties and responsibilities;
● the expected results and standards;
● the reporting lines and other relationships with key others;
● general issues that affect the job;
● possible early problems and how to deal with them;
● details of protective or special clothing;
● rules about safe working practice and conduct;
● arrangements for working hours and overtime:
  ● time sheets;
  ● sickness, holidays and other absences;
  ● mealtimes;
  ● leaving the workplace;
	Safety manual Safety manual Handbook Forms available from Office			

Figure 8.1 *Induction checklist*

Topic	Reference	Initials Employee	Initials Inductors	Date
• storage and use of personal property; • social rules of the workplace (eg tea clubs)				
Contract of employment Check understanding of terms and conditions and period of probation, notice and main procedures	Personnel Office Handbook			
Payment Complete necessary forms for payroll, tax and pensions Explain arrangements for pay and layout of payslip	Personnel Office			
The workplace Make sure the new employee is shown around and knows the location of: • entrances, exits and emergency assembly points; • cloakrooms and toilets; • cooking facilities; • rest room; • first aid facilities and fire fighting equipment; • notice boards and use of intranet; • supplies; • telephones and the Internet – their availability for private use; • car parking	Safety manual Safety manual Handbook Handbook			
Key others Introduce to immediate colleagues. Indicate the significant others and explain their importance. Make arrangements for initial meetings and visits	Organization structure in Handbook			

Figure 8.1 *(Contd.)*

Topic	Reference	Initials Employee	Initials Inductors	Date
First week Tour of main site(s) Explain how the work of the individual fits into the work of the section Explain how the work of the section fits into the work of the organization and contributes to its primary purpose	Business Plan and Annual Report			
Who the main internal customers of the section are What services are provided for them	Internal directory			
What quality standards exist What performance indicators are used	Quality procedures			
How complaints and feedback are handled	Complaints procedure			
Checks Check understanding of: ● individual's expectations of the job, boss and employer; ● lines of communication; ● role purpose; ● priorities; ● standards of work; ● reporting relationships; ● working relationships; ● main policies, procedures and operating rules; ● working arrangements, hours, conduct and safe practice; ● source and use of forms Does the new employee know how to discuss problems and with whom?				
Within first month *Relationships and memberships* ● organizational structures;				

Figure 8.1 *(Contd.)*

Topic	Reference	Initials Employee	Initials Inductors	Date
• key relationships between the employee and the rest of the organization; • social clubs; • staff associations; • trade unions.				
Organizational communications *Formal:* • newsletters and employer's magazine; • intranet; • e-mail; • notice boards; • meetings. *Others:* • informal; • reliability; • main sources of gossip. Sources of information describing: • formal decisions; • procedures; • employment matters; • pay matters; • personal advice.	Handbook			
Employment conditions Training opportunities Location of terms and conditions of employment and sources of advice	Training plan Handbook			

Figure 8.1 *(Contd.)*

can point to well-produced, but seldom used, guides for managers explaining how to make sure new employees are welcomed and assimilated into their new workplace quickly and easily. However, horror stories abound. Real examples include the new employee who found she had no place to work as no one had made any arrangements for a desk to be provided. Another new starter had to wait six weeks for a key to the building, and had to wait outside every day until someone arrived. Worse still was the new person who was shown to her private office by a secretary, and found that there was a phone and an unconnected PC. The boss arrived after an hour, said hello and told her to get on with it. New colleagues introduced themselves as they passed in the corridor. Introductions like this are unlikely to produce enthusiastic employees who feel a high level of commitment to their employer.

Checklists such as the one in Figure 8.1 can be a big help, but their value is totally dependent on the way in which they are used. Usually the manager is responsible for inducting new employees but sometimes, even though the boss should always welcome the new person, it may be more appropriate for another member of staff to carry out the detail of the induction. The manager rightly might not know about the workings of the tea club or how the trade union communicates with its members. There are also other aspects of employment better dealt with by others. For example, the details of pay and the contract of employment are too important to be left to the vagueness of an uncertain manager. Health and safety rules also need to be communicated accurately. Even though the manager should know and endorse safety rules wholeheartedly, the safety officer or fire marshal may be the best person to explain evacuation procedures. An experienced work colleague may be able to demonstrate most effectively safe working practices.

Buddying

Some employers have introduced a 'buddy' system in which the new person is assigned to an experienced (and possibly trained) employee who in effect befriends them. The buddy understands how the organization works, is willing and able to be of assistance to the new person, and will be a good role model. Typically for the first few days in the new job the new employee shadows the buddy, and thus has ready access to someone who knows his or her way around. The new employee learns about the job, is introduced to colleagues, and finds out what it is like to work for the employer.

The induction checklist provides a link between the manager, the buddy and appropriate others. It ensures that everything the new employee needs to know will have been explained satisfactorily, or at least steps have been taken to help him or her to obtain the information required. (Finding out can also benefit those carrying out the induction.)

As new employees become more confident and are able to take charge of their own learning, their dependence on the buddy can decline. Even so, if the relationship has been productive, the new starter will have acquired a 'sympathetic ear' for future use.

Mentoring

A similar but different approach that has gained popularity as its value has been proven is mentoring. A mentor is usually a more experienced employee who is able to help new person learn about the job and the employer. The role of mentor is more extensive and long-lasting than simply helping the new person settle in. A mentor can help the new employee learn by reflecting on his or her progress, and question initial perceptions and assumptions. The mentor can form the sort of close relationship that enables him or her to challenge, in a friendly and non-critical way, the appropriateness of the new person's expectations and ambitions. The role of a mentor is described more fully in Dale (1998 and 2002).

INCLUSION

Most organizations assume that inclusion will happen somehow and put little energy or time into ensuring that it is effective. I believe that it is an important developmental state which needs managing because, without it, it is impossible to become competent in an organization or job.

(Garratt, 1987)

Prem was the first management accountant the organization had employed. The other professional staff in the finance department were qualified chartered accountants. Prem's appointment signalled that the change in accounting methods, discussed for months, was about to become real. Some people viewed the change with excitement; others believed it was bound for disaster and were suspicious of Prem. The finance manager was nervous yet hopeful. She expected Prem's appointment to be successful even though she knew that some obstacles would have to be overcome. Prem was very well qualified, enthusiastic, and seemed to appreciate some of the problems he was likely to encounter.

For the first few weeks everything seemed to be going well, and the finance manager started to relax. Then the first indications of problems began to emerge. Staff, including those who were initially supportive, began to complain about Prem's attitude to his work. They said he was not fitting in and was slow. The finance director was puzzled. Prem's work seemed to suggest that he was getting to grips with the organization and had some good ideas. She decided to ignore the moans and hope that they would go away. They did not. Prem, despite his cheerful attitude, was becoming more isolated. His colleagues were excluding him more, not just from the social chit-chat of the office, but failing to give him the business information he needed to do his job.

Eventually the finance manager felt the situation had deteriorated far enough. She asked Prem what was going on. Prem said that he was very unhappy and did not understand why his colleagues were failing to accept him. He had tried, he said, to be sociable and to make friends in his early days. At first he had thought he was succeeding, and had started to build a productive relationship with one person in particular, but suddenly that person had started to back off. The lunchtime walks they had begun to share stopped abruptly. Prem had not felt able to question his colleague about what had happened, but from then on things had got steadily worse.

The finance manager asked to see Michael, the colleague in question. Michael was hesitant at first and denied knowing about the problem, but the finance manager pressed on. Eventually Michael blushed and began to tell his manager what had happened. Prem never washed up, and left his mug and plates in the office kitchen for others to clear. One or two heavy hints had been dropped, but Prem had not taken any notice. His failure to comply with normal office customs had become the favourite topic of conversation. One or two people had made some remarks about Prem's ethnicity that were close to being racist. A very bitter argument had followed in the office, and the atmosphere was tense. Prem was held responsible for causing the argument between people who had previously had good working relationships. Even those people such as himself who did not like what was happening had decided the best course of action was to stay away from the source of the trouble.

The finance manager was faced with a very difficult situation to resolve. It was all caused by the fact that no one had told Prem properly about the agreed practice where everyone was responsible for washing up their own crockery.

As can be seen from the boxed example, including a new member of staff requires more than hints. It is essential for new employees to be accepted by existing staff if they are all to work productively together. We looked earlier at how existing staff could be involved during the recruitment and selection process, for appropriate participation can contribute to the achievement of successful inclusions and acceptance of new employees. However, other action is needed to make sure that this important aspect of induction is not left to chance.

> *Buddies and mentors can help new employees be accepted by the work team, but only if they understand the importance of making explicit the unspoken rules and rituals.*

Socialization

A new member of any group goes through a period of initial socialization. This is a normal part of group formation and development. The consequences of the new person not being accepted can lead to that person being isolated and sidelined, becoming a rebel and disrupting influence, or being rejected. The example of Prem demonstrates how these phenomena easily occur. Rebellion can take place when the new group member is allowed to have a role in the group but does not accept its norms fully.

The aim of socialization is to obtain conformity to the group's existing culture. The dynamics strive to reinforce existing behaviours and enable the new member to acquire the assumptions that underpin the group's working methods, practices and value systems. Peer group pressure is a compelling force, and its processes are subtle and strong. Refusal to comply can make the situation exceedingly uncomfortable for the new person. Pressure to conform can include flattery and special treatment, allocation or withdrawal of privileges, dumping of the worst tasks on the newcomer and ostracizing him or her.

Groups strive hard to hang on to their existing behaviours, values and assumptions, and efforts to introduce change to the status quo can be resisted fiercely. A newcomer wanting to bring in ideas from his or her previous experience or develop new working methods may be faced with, 'Yes, that might have worked there but it won't here because Mary in Customer Accounts won't accept it', or, 'Our systems are more complicated that the ones you used before.' Resistance can take the form of, 'We have tried that before and it didn't work then', 'We are too busy this week, but we will try next', 'Have a go if you want (but we won't help you)', or, 'It won't work.'

When appointing a new employee whose task is to bring about change, the employer should think about the power of group pressure and processes of socialization. People new to an organization need support and the opportunity to form good working relationships. Therefore their need for inclusion and acceptance by colleagues will be high. They will also need to understand the culture of the organization to be able to work effectively within it. But if the reason for appointing that person is to bring about change to that very culture, the employer will need to consider how best to manage the contradictions that will arise during the inclusion phase.

While the new employee will go through the induction and inclusion processes, steps will be required to avoid drawing them into the existing culture. Failure to achieve this end can be seen in the attempts made by the public sector, particularly the health service, to bring in people with experience acquired in the private sector to change management practices and increase efficiency and effectiveness. Many times these attempts have resulted in failure.

There are examples of when the people newly appointed did not find the experience positive. They found it difficult to understand the culture of their new organization, their attempts to introduce change were frustrated, and they met with opposition. Many have left their jobs after comparatively brief periods in the post. Others introduced inappropriate methods, hoping to translate working practices from one culture into another that were totally alien and failed to achieve their purpose. There have been times when the transfer of experience between sectors was very positive, but these are not as well known or apparent as the failures. The lack of success should not be attributed to the individuals or to the principle of cross-sector employment, but to the poor quality of the induction and inclusion programmes used by the employers.

CELEBRATING THE NEW EMPLOYEE'S APPOINTMENT

Mostly, a new employee just starts work. After all it is almost an everyday event, especially in large organizations. But everyday for whom? Certainly not the new employee. Starting a new job is a new beginning, a new way of life, a make or break opportunity, the beginning of new relationships. In other words it is a major life event. If the employee expects to stay in the job for five years, in most working lives first days will happen only eight or nine times at the most. Consequently starting a new job is cause for celebration.

This can occur in various ways. Some employers report starters and leavers to their major decision-making body such as the board of directors, but this is usually done as numbers not names. If names are reported at all, it is normally confined to senior posts. Another medium for the announcement of appointments is the employer's internal newsletter or e-letter. Photographs of new employees may augment brief biographies, but again this practice tends to be restricted to senior staff. Some employers arrange receptions at suitable points in the year to enable the new staff to meet 'important' people such as the chief executive or the managing director. If the employer is large enough and recruits enough new employees, it may run formal induction courses. These can involve senior staff so they can formally welcome the new employees and outline the employer's priorities. Courses of this nature can help the new people fit themselves and their roles into the wider context. They also have the opportunity to discuss priorities with a senior manager; this will help them understand matters of importance.

Methods such as these may seem excessive if turnover is high. However, if the point of good quality induction is to achieve rapid assimilation into the organization and high affiliation with the employer's aims, perhaps the productivity gains outweigh the cost. Moreover, actions such as these demonstrate a greater commitment to staff than do bland words in the Annual Report about caring employment practices. Demonstrating this commitment in practice may contribute to reducing turnover as well as enable new employees settle in more quickly than would otherwise have been the case. Induction is included in the Investors in People standard because it is shown to have bottom-line benefit.

PROBATION AND TEMPORARY CONTRACTS

All employees on permanent contracts have the right to appeal to an employment tribunal after 12 months in employment if they consider their contract has been ended unfairly or wrongly. This right includes part-time employees, and the rights of those on fixed or temporary contracts are being extended. This is an area of employment law undergoing change in response to the harmonization of practice across the European Union, therefore the detail regarding the meaning of the legislation to a particular context will need to be checked. One implication of the changes has been the increased use of probationary periods. These provide the employer and the new employee with a breathing space during which both are able to place the other on trial before the permanent contract of employment is confirmed. There is by far greater benefit to the employer from this approach, but its use can also ensure that the new employee is provided with training, feedback and support.

Mary started work with a major retailer on 4 January, and for her first two months she was placed with a manager in the customer sales and invoice office. On 4 March the manager asked to see her, to review formally her first eight weeks. She was asked to reflect on what had gone well and what had been not so good. She was given feedback and suggestions were made about which areas of her work needed further improvement. Her subsequent two months were spent on the shop floor. At the end of this period her work was again reviewed, this time by the merchandising manager. She was also required to complete a self-assessment form.

A discussion was then held between Mary and the store's personnel and training manager to decide whether she should go on to the training scheme, whether she needed more general office experience, or whether she needed to spend more time on the shop floor. A move onto the training scheme suggested that initial progress had been satisfactory. More time in either the office or on the shop floor would have indicated a cause for concern. If Mary did not achieve a satisfactory report at the end of a further month, she knew she would not be confirmed as a permanent employee. If she were confirmed as a permanent employee she would join the training scheme.

A probationary period is in effect a work sample. These and job trials are regarded as the best predictors of subsequent performance. Both Cook (1988) and Smith, Gregg and Andrews (1989) give them a predictive validity of over 0.5. One would hope that work samples and trails lasting this length of time would achieve a better coefficient.

Even though a probationary period is not long enough to give employees rights to complain to an employment tribunal for wrongful or unlawful dismissal if their contract is terminated, employees may be protected by disciplinary and grievance procedures, as provided in their written statement of terms and conditions of employment. If Mary felt that the training she was given was insufficient to allow her to achieve the required standard and she was disciplined, if the specified procedure was not followed, she might have grounds for complaint to a tribunal even if she did not have the necessary qualifying employment period, currently 12 months.

The use of contracts other than those of a full-time, permanent nature has increased considerably as working patterns have altered. While full-time permanent contracts are by far still the most common, part-time, temporary, fixed-term, and home-based employment have increased. Also there is a trend towards the use of self-employed contractors who provide services. One of the main reasons for these shifts in working practices is to provide employers with increased flexibility. Torrington and Hall (1995) describe the mechanisms companies were using in the mid 1990s to achieve flexibility in employment. This was due to the pressure they were under to develop their workforces so they were able to respond more quickly, cheaply and easily to unforeseen changes. Two aims of this new flexibility were to enable the employer to increase or reduce the size of the workforce in response to requirements, and maintain tight control over unit costs. The way this was achieved was by restructuring the workforce into three groups:

First are core employees who form the primary labour market. They are highly regarded by the employer, well paid and involved in those activities that are unique to the firm or give it a distinctive character. These employees have improved career prospects and offer the type of flexibility to the employer that is so prized in the skilled craftsworker who does not adhere rigidly to customary protective working practices.

There are then two peripheral groups – first those who have skills that are needed but not specific to a particular firm, like typing and word processing. The strategy for these posts is to rely on the external labour market to specify a narrow range of tasks without career prospects, so that the employee has a job but not a career . . .

The second peripheral group is made up of those enjoying even less security, as they have contracts of employment that are limited, either to a short-term or to a part-time attachment. An alternative or additional means toward this flexibility is to contract out the work that has to be done, either by employing temporary personnel from agencies or by subcontracting the entire operation, as has happened so extensively in office cleaning and catering . . .

To most people it may be an unwelcome development as it provides few safe havens for people seeking security. For others, however, it provides the attraction of being one's own boss, having a variety of work experiences and being able to organize one's life to accommodate, for instance, periods of several months away from work to take a long holiday, renovate the house, update skills or simply to have a break.

These changes were not universally welcomed, as the increased numbers of part-time jobs have been filled mainly by women. While this has provided routes back into the workforce, many of these jobs are regarded as low paid, with few prospects and limited futures. However, since then there have been changes to employment rights. These now provide all staff with employment contracts, and the qualifying period of 12 months' service have gone some way toward protecting employees from unscrupulous employers who were trying to use temporary or fixed-term contracts as a means of avoiding redundancy payments. Part-time employees have also been provided with other rights such as parental leave and sick pay and access to equal pay for work of equal value. The high levels of employment seen in the late 1990s have also driven out some of the examples of poor practice, as employers compete for employees rather than employees competing for jobs

An interesting development is the increased trend towards self-employment. This is currently a grey area of employment law, as the differences between a contract of service and a contract *for* services can be subtle. The use of outsiders to provide services that are not part of the employer's core business appears to be a mutually beneficial arrangement. The employer benefits from the work being done but does not have the full-time or permanent commitment to the individual. The individual has the flexibility and can chose whether, when and where to do the work. However the employer has little immediate control over standards, and the self-employed worker can be isolated and be excluded from the wider life of the organization.

INITIAL TRAINING

If it is rare for induction to be seen as part of the recruitment and selection process, it is even less common for initial training to be linked. Yet there are two reasons that this first phase of training should be seen as an integral part of the recruitment and selection.

First, when devising the role outline, description of responsibilities and assessing the competencies required to inform the selection criteria, consideration should be given to which elements would need to be competently performed immediately (that is, the skills and knowledge that are absolutely essential for effective performance) and which could be acquired or developed later. The absolutely essential criteria should not include organization-specific aspects unless the post in question is to be filled internally. If rapid acquisition of such specific knowledge or skills is necessary, this should be covered in the early training programme.

Second, the recruitment and selection process subjects individuals to rigorous scrutiny and a detailed assessment of their attainment, experience, skills and aptitudes. When else does such a detailed assessment occur during the normal course of employment and involve so many other people? This assessment provides a rich source of information, which can contribute to an initial training and longer-term development programme.

If the recruitment and selection process is regarded as one in which candidates' experiences and capabilities are being matched against the requirements of the employer and the job, the type of punitive judgement that detracts from learning can be avoided. Rather than dismiss some applications as not good enough, the assessment can be used to identify gaps in skill, experience and competence. This alternative view of recruitment and selection is of particular importance and value when internal appointments are being made. This mode of thinking need not, and indeed should not, be confined to large employers. To the contrary, smaller employers depend just as much, if not more, on the goodwill and continued commitment of their staff. Thus using the full range of opportunities to contribute to their development and invest in their future will be of benefit to employer and employees alike.

The assessment, if aimed at assessing levels of competence and degree of fit, can give candidates whose applications have not been successful valuable information about what to do differently, or do more or less of, to aid their future career prospects. The information gained during the assessment process can be used in two ways, as described in the examples that follow.

Comparison of the individual's profile to the role outline, description of responsibilities and specification of competencies required for the post

The post of operations director had become vacant when the current holder decided to set up his own consultancy business. Turnover at this level had been low, and the chances of promotion for the middle-level managers had seemed like waiting for the 'shoes of the dead'. This vacancy therefore represented a golden opportunity for all the production plant managers. The managing director and human resources director were very aware what could happen unless they handled the process very carefully. Competition already existed between the plants, and they felt that if the promotion process was seen as a point-scoring exercise several undesirable outcomes could result.

They were also fearful of any negative competition that might develop between the managers, and concerned about the rivalries that might grow as each candidate attracted a team of supporters. They felt that the criteria for selection used by the workforce, would not match those of the management. If that happened, the person appointed would be not be generally accepted as the best candidate. The new operational director would then find him- or herself in an almost impossible position, with the difficult task of trying to heal the schisms that had been created by the process.

The HR and managing directors planned a normal process and then considered how it could be transformed into a team development event. They saw this as the chance to upgrade the overall management skills available at the level of plant manager. Currently the managers' focus was on the engineering aspects of the job rather than their role as managers. The process they used comprised the following steps:

1. Draw up a specification that would describe the operations director role as a leader and senior manager. While it included some attainments as an engineer, the focus was shifted towards outlining skills and distinct competencies. Leadership (defined as guiding, directing and enabling), communication skills, negotiating, dealing with conflict and team building were weighted more highly than the skills previously stressed. These (customer and market relations, business skills and strategic planning abilities) were rated as still important but less critical to success.

2. Potential candidates were asked to register their interest in the post by agreeing to participate in a diagnostic process. After this, those who wished to become candidates would be asked to submit formal applications.

3. It was made clear that everyone would come out of the process with a personal assessment to inform a development plan. They would be expected to agree to a learning contract with the managing director and the operations director.

4. The diagnostic process was designed by the HR and managing directors with assistance from a specialist consultant, and the MD invited the chief executive of a major customer to be an assessor and ultimately act as a mentor for the operations director. The diagnostic process comprised a battery of activities:

   - A series of work-based activities drawn from the role outline, designed to elicit the skills outlined in the competency specification.

   - A self-assessment questionnaire. This was based on a repertory grid, which used the description of responsibilities as the elements in the grid. The participants were asked to compare the responsibilities in groups of three, and identify which skills were common to two and which was needed by the third alone. They were then asked to weight the skills they had identified in order of importance for each responsibility. The results were analysed and contrasted with those of the managing and HR directors.

- Staff drawn from each of the plant's sections were asked to give confidential feedback about their managers' performance against the relevant criteria, using a 360-degree feedback questionnaire.

- The main customers (internal and external) were also asked to contribute to the questionnaire, based on their experience of the manager in question.

This process may seem excessive, but the MD believed that the appointment of a new operations director represented more than the person's salary for at least five years. It was being used as an opportunity to upgrade the management skills of a level, and getting the promotion process right involved more than simply appointing the best candidate. Consequently, the MD decided to gather information in the same way as would be done for any other significant investment decision.

5. The information gathered from all modes of assessment was analysed by the consultant (to ensure impartiality) and then discussed with each participant. This was to give the participants some control over the information before it was passed on, and to give them the chance to add any comments and explanations about their performance in the activities.

6. The participants were then asked to declare if they wished to make a formal application. Out of the group of 15 plant managers, only three decided that they wanted to go on to the next stage. The remaining 12 recognized their development needs and agreed that they wanted to concentrate on enhancing their skills in their current positions. The challenges this would present them, they agreed, would provide them with enough career advancement for the time being.

7. The three candidates were asked to make a presentation to members of the company's board, in which they were to 'sell' themselves as if they were a service. This approach was intended to allow the board members to make the decision as if they were deciding to invest in some major capital expenditure. The MD and HR director were conscious that the board members knew some of the candidates personally, so wanted to control, as far as possible for any halo effect. It was also thought that taking this approach would help the unsuccessful candidates feel less rejected personally.

8. The board was asked to assess the strengths of each presentation, based on the criteria. The results of this assessment were combined with the previous assessments so each candidate could be offered feedback and a personally designed learning contract. This contract including mentoring arrangements between the candidates not offered the post and two of the non-executive directors. The development plan for the new operations director would be designed more to fit the immediate needs of the post.

9. Throughout the whole process everyone on the site was kept fully informed of what was happening via the bulletin boards.

10. The final appointment was announced with an atmosphere of celebration, which resulted in:

   – General sympathy for the candidates but a recognition that the process had been open, fair and testing.

   – All those who had participated in the diagnostic process gained from the experience and their learning contracts.

   – Because of the use of very specific criteria, the two candidates not appointed could see very clearly the differences between their performance and that of the person offered the post.

   – Even though they were disappointed, they knew they had the chance to make a different sort of impression on the members of the company's board. In addition, they had learning contracts that were qualitatively different from the rest of their colleagues.

   – A new management process had been introduced and the learning culture had been reinforced in the plant.

The individual's application and behaviour throughout the selection process can be used as the basis of feedback to be offered during a debriefing

One of the candidates for the operations director post, Maurice, gave a really disappointing presentation. The managing director had thought he would deliver the best sales pitch as he had worked for a time in sales, but on the day Maurice did not deliver. Perhaps it was nerves, but a more likely explanation was that he had misjudged the situation.

His presentation had not been professional. He had not interpreted the brief correctly. He had seen the opportunity as a chance to tell the board what he had done throughout his career; in effect, he had presented a verbal CV. He had used the presentation to project himself as a person rather than treating it as a sales event, as requested. The audiovisual aids had been used poorly. Although he had been trained in PowerPoint, the slides had been prepared as typed lists. The content was totally historic, concentrating on his past achievements. There was only a passing reference to what Maurice intended to do in the future, and no mention of what benefit would accrued to the company from his appointment.

The managing director was to debrief Maurice after the appointment had been made, but knew he had some stark messages to convey. The main mistake had been Maurice's failure to think himself into the position of his audience. Maurice had thought merely about what he wanted to tell the board. He had not considered what they wanted to hear from someone selling a service to a board ready to make an investment decision. This had reflected on his abilities to relate to his customers and markets and to plan strategically. But the MD did not want to tell Maurice this. He knew such a message would be hard for him to hear and could do further damage to his self-confidence. Therefore he opened the session by asking Maurice how he had seen the presentation and what he thought the board had been looking for. This approach was chosen to enable the MD to encourage Maurice to recognize how he could have take a different approach to the presentation. At the end of the debriefing the MD arranged, as part of Maurice's learning contract, for him to spend some time in the company's main marketing and business planning departments.

The assessment carried out during recruitment and selection need not be limited to the unsuccessful candidates. The chances of making a perfect appointment are slim, and it is likely that the person appointed will have some gaps between his or her current level of competency and that required for the performance of the role's full range of requirements. The opportunities presented by the rigorous examination of an individual's skills, experience and capabilities can be used to indicate which areas:

▌ need initial work on appointment;

▌ would benefit from longer-term development;

▌ need to be watched, as they may be indicative of areas that may be a cause for concern.

Bruce was over the moon when he was appointed to the post of operations director. He had worked really hard throughout the appointment process, and felt he had earned his achievement. Nevertheless he was somewhat daunted by what he knew faced him in the coming years. The company's future was far from secure. Competition was hotting up on a global level, and the need to keep costs and prices down would become even more critical than it had in previous years. The workforce was good and a high spirit of cooperation existed, but Bruce knew that some hard and perhaps bitter decisions would have to be taken.

The managing director debriefed him after the board presentations. Bruce was told that the board felt he would be a good appointment, and his popularity with the other managers and workforce would be a positive help in the future. As they reflected on what Bruce's learning contract needed to contain to help him prepare for what was to come, the MD asked what aspects of the role Bruce felt would cause him the most difficulty. Bruce initially identified internal communications. The presentation itself had not been easy for him. He was not used to public speaking, and felt his performance could be improved. Skills in this area would be essential if he were to make an early impact on the works council meetings. The MD readily agreed to Bruce's suggestion that he should receive some training and support in this area.

Bruce went on to think about how he would manage the team. He told the MD that going through the assessment process had given them all a common experience that had cemented their working relationship. A strong team spirit had developed. However, even though he wanted to continue in this vein, he was not sure how to do it. This, he felt, was not an immediate development need; rather it was an aspect of the managers' work that would continue to develop as they worked together on the issues common to all their learning contracts.

'But', asked the MD, 'what will you do when you are required to implement a decision that is opposed by the rest of the managers?' This question took Bruce by surprise, as he was developing a mental picture of the team making decisions based on consensus. He had not considered that his colleagues and good friends would not agree with him. The idea that they might try to undermine his authority had not entered his head. The MD explained that the board was a little worried about Bruce's ability to deal with conflict and rise to the position of being a leader of those leading others. The board recognized that they simply did not know how Bruce would face with such conflict, as to their knowledge he had never dealt with this type of situation before. Nevertheless, they felt he had the potential to bring about the necessary changes.

Bruce agreed that he did not know either how he would react. He began to realize that he could not be an equal member of the team – he would need to be both part of it and able to stand back. Especially if times became difficult as was predicted, hard choices that might not be to the liking of some would be necessary. Bruce and the MD therefore agreed that team leadership and conflict handling would be part of his longer-term plan. If a really difficult situation arose and if Bruce did not feel as though he had the abilities to handle direct conflict, the MD promised that he would have the necessary support to enable him to manage and learn from it.

The examples above show how the recruitment and selection process can be used to provide some tangible spin-offs for those who are not appointed. This can take the form of structured and informed feedback, which includes recognition of strengths as well as weaknesses against the competencies. The feedback can also give the applicants good-quality information about the action they can take to improve their performance in their work-related skills and gain in experience, and to develop the standard of their applications if they decide to apply for jobs again. The action plan can contain elements for them to take forward privately, and others that should be supported by the employer.

The assessment provides information about the person appointed to the role. It would be a mistake for anyone in such a position to sit on the glory of his or her success and think it the end of his or her learning. The opposite is the truth: new jobs always present new challenges. Even if the person appointed is superbly qualified and equipped to carry out the role, there are bound to be some areas where learning is essential. Seeing the assessment as an opportunity to obtain some good-quality information that identifies areas critical to performance can speed up induction and inclusion into the new role, and increase the chances of long-term success.

DEVELOPMENT

In the above example, Bruce's immediate need was identified as the skills needed for making presentations. More significant for the long-term success of his appointment, and for the company, were the abilities needed to keep his team together during difficult times. Both these needs could be addressed by creating a development plan with key objectives against which progress could be assessed and further need identified.

The days following the appointment tend to be euphoric and optimistic, especially if the successful candidate is a popular choice. One or two people may have axes to grind or scores to settle, but these tend to be held in abeyance, as those individuals wait to see how the new appointment shapes up. The postholder will be full of enthusiasm, energy and commitment, ready to make changes and get going. Wise individuals, particularly in senior posts, build in time, but not too much, to take stock and plan how they are going to approach the new role. They will identify where changes need to be made quickly, what can be left alone, and which aspects will need action later on. In effect, they will develop a change programme. Part of this programme should include actions to gain commitment and take everyone along willingly, including those who may see themselves as 'losers' from the selection process.

Bruce's change programme included making improvements to stock management, purchasing and waste control, energy efficiency and the employment conditions of supervisory staff. The last was known to be sensitive and probably the most difficult to achieve, especially since Bruce suspected that not all of the managers agreed with the need to make these changes. He decided this would merit discussion with the managing director.

During their next meeting, Bruce broached the topic. The MD agreed with Bruce's diagnosis and saw the problem as an initial test of Bruce's team-building skills. Team leadership is easy when times are good, but not so when hard choices have to be made. The MD suggested Bruce should explore the problem in greater depth by listing the forces in favour of the change and those opposing it (these forces should include circumstantial factors as well as people). He was then asked to consider how best to mobilize the forces in favour and to deal with the opposing forces. At their next meeting, they discussed the product of Bruce's deliberations. The MD had some additions to suggest, and offered ideas about the tactics Bruce could use to make progress.

Meanwhile Bruce was maintaining a diary of his learning in the form of a folder, which contained his learning contract, copies of the notes he was producing as his early plans for the production plant were being developed, and a notebook containing his thoughts and reflections on his experiences. Even after only three months, the way his plans were shaping up showed interesting evidence of his progress. His thinking was becoming clearer and his understanding of the plant's market was deepening. When he read back through the papers, he could also see indications of where he was not so confident. The same sort of difficulty was presenting itself. He had not got to grips with the inconsistent flow of information from the external sales force.

His notebook was the most valuable part of his folder, and he carried it at all times in his jacket pocket. This was where he jotted down the ideas and insights he was gaining. Gradually the picture was making sense to him. No one knew exactly what went into the book, but his scribbling in it had been noticed. He had developed a habit of taking it out of his pocket and making the odd jotting now and again. Bruce's red book was becoming the centre of jovial speculation – and some of the other managers had started to copy him.

A development programme drawn up as part of the recruitment and selection process can be used to inform subsequent progress and performance reviews. If the initial performance objectives were derived from the role outline and description of responsibilities, and the specification of competencies needed to achieve those objectives, it makes sense for the work of the person appointed to the role to be focused towards the realization of these words. The review of performance should concern the progress made towards achieving them and the development of the individual's abilities. The identification of areas in need of further development should also stem from them. Any initial training programme drawn up from the selection process should reflect these needs as well as the aspirations of the individual. The longer-term development programme should do likewise, but should be contingent enough to allow for future change. If this approach is taken, the early months will automatically prepare for subsequent performance reviews and appraisals.

Six months after Bruce's appointment, the managing director arranged for a formal review of progress. The agenda contained the following items:

I business plan;
  - current situation;
  - market share;
  - financial performance;
  - current and planned production volume;
I business development;
  - current customers;
  - new markets;
  - competitors;
I internal management;
  - health and safety;
  - operational state of plant and equipment;
  - stock levels and work in progress;
  - energy utilization;
I human resources;
  - morale;
I management;
  - skill levels;
  - internal communications;
I team development;
I Bruce's development.

While the above may seem like a lengthy agenda, it focuses on all aspects of the 'business' and areas directly within Bruce's influence and control. In effect, they are all his responsibility as defined by the role outline. Using the selection criteria as the basis for performance review makes them clearly relevant. The relationship between the activities used during the selection stage and the realities of the role will be clear and will serve to prepare the person subsequently appointed. The use of 'games' or irrelevant techniques can reduce the potential of the whole process. Thus using recruitment and selection as an integral part of human resource and personal development can be a very powerful contribution to the growth of an organization and the people within it.

SUMMARY

This chapter has dealt with an area of human resource management most often treated as a training activity. It was discussed here to demonstrate that if induction and inclusion are considered as part of the recruitment and selection process, it is possible to integrate all aspects into holistic human resource development.

Any new employees, if they are to apply their skills effectively and quickly and develop their potential in the context of their employer, need to be respected as individuals. Taking on a new role contains stresses and pressures that are often ignored in the euphoria of success and a new beginning. Some of these have been listed, but it must also be remembered that the needs of an individual will be unique to that person. Moreover, perverse as it may seem, it is possible that the successful candidate will experience some lack of confidence despite his or her success. It is therefore important that the actions needed to deal with induction and initial training needs be considered and planned into the recruitment and selection schedule.

Even though the best candidate is the one offered the role, it is highly unlikely that the person appointed will be fully competent in every aspect. Although it may be believed he or she is able to 'hit the ground running', inevitably there will be some things to be learnt. Effective induction makes sure individuals know the necessary details concerning their employment and employer. An induction checklist, such as the one described, can help a manager create a 'route map' for the new employee. As well as being a vehicle for providing the necessary information systematically, the list can also act as a source of reference and as a record, evidencing what was covered. The latter can facilitate other processes such as probation and subsequent performance management.

Deliberate efforts to ensure the full inclusion of the new person take account of the normal socialization processes that occur when any new member is introduced to a group. If new employees are to be effective, they need to be competent at the job; they also need to 'fit'. Even when a key part of the role is to bring about change and to challenge the status quo, the individual will require some insight into the rules, customs and underpinning assumptions, and needs to be able to build effective working relationships. Often the importance of inclusion goes unrecognized. Many promising appointments fail due to lack of understanding, lack of acceptance by the people with whom the person needs to work, or just failing to fit.

The inclusion of the new person into the team can be assisted if the appointment is seen as an occasion for celebration by the employer and existing staff, and if new employees can be feted in some appropriate way. At the very simplest of levels, a formal welcome from an 'important' person can make a new employee feel part of the organization. It also helps if new employees understand the employer's priorities and its key policies, so they are able to put their role into context. This applies to temporary, probationary and part-time employees just as much as to those on full-time and permanent contracts of employment. Those acting as contractors would also benefit, as feeling part of the team helps the individual understand important matters such as standards of behaviour and quality.

The rigour of the assessments carried out during recruitment and selection is often left behind once the person has accepted the post. Yet it is seldom that such a rigorous assessment of an individual's skills and abilities is carried out at other times. If the assessment has been made against the criteria drawn from the role outline and description of responsibilities, the results can be used to provide high-quality feedback and inform a development plan. The latter will include information about initial training and longer-term development needs which can be used as a basis for performance review.

Use of the results of the assessment need not be confined to the successful candidate. The candidates not appointed have the right to be offered feedback. If these are current employees, it is in the employer's interest to treat these people with respect so that any negative feelings or sense of rejection are minimized. The offer of a development plan can help to retain their commitment and motivation by outlining positive action. This may go some way toward preventing their feeling as though they are 'losers'.

The recruitment and selection process is too expensive to seen as a one-off event that finishes once the new employee is established in post. The whole process consumes considerable time, resources and money, yet, often what happens within it goes unevaluated. We know the validity of selection methods has been researched, as described in Chapter 5, but the overall effectiveness of the other stages is rarely questioned. The main measure to judge success or failure is the achievement of the person appointed to the post. However, this can be influenced by many factors beyond the appointment process. We will therefore examine next what other information is needed to assess the value of the approaches taken at the various stages of the process, to determine what needs to be improved and assess the value of their contribution to getting the right person for the job.

9

Evaluation

The theme of this book has been getting the best person into the right job. We have discussed some of the ways we can describe the best person, and how best to recruit and select this candidate. But how do we decide, after the event, whether the *best* candidate has been appointed? Is it possible that there are people even better out there, who did not apply and were not given the chance to demonstrate their abilities? Can we be certain that the person who would have really been the best was not rejected in the early stages of the process?

After the offer of employment has been made, the contracts signed and exchanged and the person has started work, definitions of what is best might change. Therefore, how can we be sure that the definition of the role requirements and competencies were right in the first place?

How do we know that all the effort has been worthwhile? Could the same end have been achieved with less effort and cost? Was the whole thing a waste of time and money because the person appointed was not up to the mark? Who decides if the best person was employed? The person him- or herself, the employer (and in the case of large organizations, who is this?), the people who work with the new person or the customer?

Some of these questions are impossible to answer with any degree of accuracy. It must be remembered that conditions are changing, and even the very fastest recruitment and selection process takes some weeks. During that time, something will have changed that will have altered the definition of 'best'.

This chapter explores rather than answers these questions. One of the biggest shifts in human resource management has been the need for the function to demonstrate that it is adding value to the organization's effectiveness. Human resource accounting is still in its infancy. In its 14 October 1999 issue, *People Management* reported the work that had been done up to that date. This demonstrated the link between good human resource practice and profitability, and recognized the need for further research and greater understanding of this relationship. The 12 October 2000 issue contained a report of field research into the causal links between HR practices and organizational performance. Linda Gratton of London Business School was quoted as saying, 'It's true that the effect of HR on the bottom line is very difficult to measure but it is not impossible . . . The issue is information.'

One of the examples given in the article demonstrated the effect staff turnover had on productivity. Many of the actions taken by the particular company to reduce turnover resulted in changes to selection practices. 'We found that a pretty high number of people left in their first year. We weren't doing a good job in selection so we focused on presenting the job more clearly and improving promotion prospects.' In a year the company had halved its turnover.

A further report, *Human Resources* for December 2000, described how companies can increase shareholder value, and claimed that resource management practices, including recruiting excellence, can add over 7 per cent. This required 'effectively planned recruitment that supports the business plan by placing the right people with ready to use skills in the right roles'. Demonstrating these links, as stated by Gratton, requires the collection and use of information; this will help possibly sceptical managers understand the importance of applying good practice to the process of attracting and selecting the best candidate.

EVALUATING THE TECHNIQUES

We examined some of the flaws of decision making in Chapter 3, and concluded that making decisions free from subjective influences is virtually impossible. People who make judgements about others do not make dispassionate assessments; the mental processes used when making decisions are prone to errors; we all make prejudgements and hold erroneous assumptions. Nevertheless there is a compelling desire to demonstrate that selection decisions are objective; subjectivity has no place in modern management.

As many selectors believe their decisions to be rational and logical, they also believe that the outcome should be capable of being evaluated scientifically and the results counted. While this may be true for many areas of business – the importance of accounts, statistics and ratios as performance indicators demonstrates this – human resource management does not lend itself entirely to the use of numerical values to assess value. Some areas, such as turnover and attendance levels, are suitable for counting, and in some industries it is possible to quantify productivity, but other aspects require the use of qualitative measures.

Herriot (1989a) suggested that evaluation of recruitment and selection processes can be assessed against two dimensions. The first is effectiveness – 'selection procedures should yield the right type of information and lead to correct decisions' and the second efficiency – 'every step taken within a selection procedure and any instrument used may add to the procedure's utility as well as its cost'.

Smith, Gregg and Andrews (1989) and Cook (1988) are perhaps the main British sources of information on ways of assessing quantitatively the worth and value of human resource methods. The former use two main quantifiers, validity and utility.

Validity

We considered the main types of validity in Chapter 5. These can be summarized as:

I Face validity: are the techniques and methods appropriate to those involved?

I Content validity: are the contents of the process appropriate for the job or role in question?

I Construct validity: do the methods and techniques examine relevant aspects of behaviour for the job and organization?

I Criterion validity: do the methods and techniques do what they claim, and nothing more?

I Reliable validity: do the techniques and methods do the same job every time they are used?

I Impact validity: is the effect on the people involved beneficial?

However before we even start to assess the validity of the techniques used, we must ask if engaging in a recruitment and selection process was a valid action to take in the first place.

In June 1999 the managing director had had enough of the squabbling between the production manager and the marketing manager, and decided to take after-sales support away from them both. A year earlier, a training room had been set up and an engineer from the production department had been asked to train customers' staff to maintain the company's products. The move was beginning to pay off, and the time spent by the company's engineers on site had reduced. Mistakes and misdiagnosis had reduced as the abilities of the customers to analyse faults had improved. Customer satisfaction had increased and the working relationships had become stronger. By the end of 2000, the training service had begun to pay its way and was proving to be a real boost.

When the MD reviewed progress midway through 2001, a different picture emerged. The managers had started to argue again. The production engineer was not being allowed enough time to prepare for the training sessions, and the dedicated room was being used by other staff for everyday jobs. The engineers were leaving the room in a mess and were not helping. The marketing manager was being supportive but the sales representatives were not passing on queries from customers.

The MD decided to appoint a customer training manager. The engineer was dreadfully disappointed. The marketing manager argued that the appointment would not make any difference, and in any case the income gained from the training service would not be enough to cover the additional salary costs. The production manager sulked.

A recruitment consultancy was engaged to find the right person, and within two months a superb appointment was made – a real find. The training manager was well qualified and very skilled. He left after a year, after becoming very frustrated by the lack of cooperation from most of the production staff and the production manager. Meanwhile the engineer had also left to take a better-paid job in the local college.

The decision to appoint a training manager rather than deal with the conflict between two managers had cost over £40,000 (£30,000 for the salary and employment costs plus £10,000 for the consultant's fees) and had lost the company's capacity to provide training to customers. Was the decision to engage in recruitment and selection a valid one to take?

Utility

Utility is defined as the 'condition for being useful or profitable'. In the context of recruitment and selection, it is generally used to calculate the robustness and comparative worth of various recruitment and selection techniques. The results of utility analysis can be used to support the case for changing and improving practices, as well as supplying indicators to judge the overall value of the process. Smith, Gregg and Andrews (1989) argue 'investment in selection procedures has been shown to be one of the best investments an organization can make . . . utility analysis has now developed to the point where different strategies of selection can be compared and an informed choice of the most effective strategy can be taken'.

They demonstrate how the utility is calculated:

▌ Estimate the selection ratio: that is, how many applications are received for every job. If this is 10 per job the ratio is 0.1, if it is 50 the ratio is 0.5.

▌ Apply the validity coefficient. This is an estimate of the predictive validity of the particular technique being scrutinized, as described in Chapter 5.

▌ Estimate the percentage of applicants who can adequately perform the job. For example if the job is easy perhaps 50 per cent of the applicants could be expected to do it. If it is complex and requires a lot of specific knowledge, this might be 3 per cent.

This analysis relies on the use of the formula and subsequent calculation, and is limited to estimating the inputs (qualified applicants, validity of techniques) rather than estimating the worth of the outcome (the value of the end result).

The managing director needed a new PA. Because the company had a good reputation in the town and such senior secretarial positions were rare, the personnel officer predicted a large response unless clear criteria were included in the advertisement. Even then, 66 applications were received.

The MD insisted that the PA should be able to take fast, accurate dictation and produce a finished document, ready to go out, without any further checking being needed. However she did not want to be bothered with any fussy selection activities, claiming she would know the best person for the job from an interview. The personnel manager, on the other hand, argued that for only a small extra cost and effort, a work sample would be a more effective way to assess the short-listed candidates.

Creating the short-list was not be a problem, as the personnel manager anticipated that only 30 per cent only of the applicants would meet the criteria. Using these parameters and a simple formula the personnel director was able to calculate the comparative effectiveness of the two selection methods, in relation to their cost and the size of the salary investment. Using this approach enabled her to present the case in the sort of numeric terms the MD was used to, and she found it easier to convince the MD the fuss would be worth the effort.

Cascio (1987) takes this approach further and makes use of decision theory to include other factors that affect the process. He says:

> The utility of a selection device is the degree to which its use improves the quality of the individuals selected beyond what would have occurred had that device not been used. Quality may be defined in terms of
>
> a)   the proportion of individuals in the selected group who are considered 'successful'
> b)   the average standard score on the criterion for the selected group
> c)   the payoff to the organization resulting from the use of a particular selection procedure.

To obtain a reliable result from these calculations, extensive investigations are required to determine the monetary equivalents of the individual parameters used. The methods proposed are very similar to the work-study procedures once used to determine efficiency levels and fix productivity pay. For the findings and results to be valid and robust, a large sample drawn from the target population is needed for the database. A degree of stability is required so the findings can be repeated and checked, and measures of subsequent job performance need to be developed and agreed. Inevitably the results of these investigations are based on historic data. Moreover the effort needed to gather and test the data is considerable, requiring the outlay of expertise and time, and access to a large number of employees and managers. This means that these techniques are most valuable to very large employers who recruit large numbers of people to very similar jobs. They are less useful for small organizations, or when conditions are changing rapidly.

Cook (1988) also suggests some (more simple) means of evaluating selection techniques:

▌ **Validity:** 'unless a test can predict productivity, there's little point in using it'.

▌ **Cost**, but this is 'often given too much weight by selectors . . . It isn't an important consideration, so long as the test has validity.'

▌ **Practicality:** 'a reason for not using a test'.

▌ **Acceptability** to the candidates.

▌ **Legality:** 'another reason for not using something'.

Obtaining the necessary information for assessing the quality of a particular set of actions may seem awesome and excessive for an individual appointment. It may be more worthwhile to evaluate the techniques used as part of an overall review of practices. In this case, the effort required to carry out a systematic evaluation may be justified. It is interesting to note that many of the criteria recommended for assessing the worth of a selection method involve the use of subjective judgements. The thinking underpinning the quantitative modes of analysis described above has some value, for they provide ways of estimating benefit and providing numeric values to facilitate comparison between otherwise incomparable processes.

However, they are limited, for they do not tell the manager how effective the recruitment and selection process has been. This can only be achieved, after the event, by assessing the accuracy of the process and the quality of its outcome against a number of predetermined criteria. The main test is the performance and achievement of the post-holder. However, the effect of filling the post on the rest of the organization should also be considered.

EVALUATING THE APPOINTMENT

We discussed the ways in which the assessment opportunities presented during the recruitment and selection process can be used to inform induction, initial training and longer-term development in Chapter 7. The criteria used to make the selection decisions can be applied when assessing whether the candidate appointed was the 'best' person for the job in the longer term. If the role outline, description of requirements and specification of competency were carefully written and forward-looking at the outset, they will provide an enduring basis from which to evaluate the quality of the outcome from the process.

However, it is very rare for events to be predicted fully. Therefore when the selection documents are used to support the assessment of the performance of the person appointed to the role, some account will need to be taken of the changes that have inevitably occurred subsequently. These will include:

▌ Internal changes in the structure and operation of the organization and in the context in which is operating.

▌ Alterations in market conditions as customers, competitors, and suppliers change.

▌ People with whom the role-holder works will acquire skills, knowledge and experience. Their level of motivation and job satisfaction will vary, and changes to personal circumstances will influence attitudes to work and working relationships.

▌ The person appointed will affect the dynamics of the work group. His or her output will contribute to the work of the team and should add to the achievement of the employer. The person will have made the new role his or her own by focusing on different aspects and including priorities in the key objectives agreed with his or her manager.

Evaluation of the effectiveness of an appointment will therefore need to include a number of measures in addition to the criteria used for the selection purpose. These may include the following.

Trainability

▌ How quickly can the individual progress up the learning curve to attain the status of a competent employee? This will depend on prior skills, knowledge, and the relevance and applicability of previous experience.

▌ How steep is the learning curve? This will be influenced by the individual's ability to assimilate information and comprehend the new role and its environment. The effect of the environmental factors must not be taken lightly. Take for example individuals who have always worked in a closely regimented environment. When they move into one in which individuals are given targets and expected to organize their own work, they will need time to adjust.

▌ Level of achievement. Some people's learning curve flattens out before others' as each individual reaches his or her ceiling. Even though the prediction of ultimate performance should be part of the selection decision, estimating what that will actually be is far from straightforward. (Remember the frailty of the best predictive validity coefficient.)

Performance

The actual performance of individual employees should be assessed all the time. Many employers have recognized the importance of holding formal appraisal meetings once a year, and have developed systematic processes to ensure they are held. They help to ensure that all employees understand how they contribute to the organization, are given feedback on their achievement, and their ongoing learning needs are identified. These processes are taken as evidence of achieving the Investors in People standard. Some mechanism is needed to ensure these assessments are made fairly and consistently between employees, and have some link to the work they are expected to perform. Without such a mechanism, the process is open to judgements being made on the private, idiosyncratic prejudices of a particular manager, with all the difficulties this may create.

If a systematic approach is taken to the design of recruitment and selection processes, performance management and appraisal can be based on the documents developed to support their operation. Assessing performance is relatively straightforward if the role comprises responsibilities that can be counted such as sales made, widgets built or customers served. It is also possible, though perhaps more difficult, to assess less tangible aspects. It is necessary for good quality objectives to have been agreed, and in their drafting, account to have been taken of how achievement is to be assessed, as can be seen in a simple example. A catering manager's main responsibility might be defined as 'To maintain and improve customer satisfaction'. This could be assessed by:

▌ the level of litter;

▌ the amount of graffiti;

▌ the number of thefts;

▌ levels of complaints;

▌ the number of letters of appreciation;

▌ the amount of spend per customer,

▌ the volume of repeat business.

The level of performance can also be assessed by comparing performance against the behavioural criteria set out in the specification, but again allowances must be made for changes that have occurred since the appointment. These will have occurred in the organization, the work of the individual and other people who have an influence on the role-holder, as noted above. We should also remember how we tend to attribute events to the behaviour of the person who is centre of our attention at a particular moment of time. When we focus on one individual's behaviour, we tend to attribute the cause of that behaviour to one or more of the following three sources:

- the individual (the actor);
- the target of the behaviour (another person or item);
- the circumstances surrounding them both.

Information is needed to explain the behaviour, as witnessed, so that the real cause can be identified. The following example shows that more explanation is needed to answer the question, 'Why did X behave like that?'

Belinda does not talk to her co-workers. Why? The answer might be:

- Belinda is moody and anti-social.
- Belinda's co-workers are offensive.
- The employer for whom Belinda works does not encourage social inter-action.

Even though the root cause of behaviour is usually a combination of factors, we tend to regard the central person as being responsible. This tendency is known as the fundamental attribution error, and is thought to be generally pervasive. The value of this theory here is as a warning to those appraising the behaviour of others. When there is little experience of that person (for example a new employee) the tendency to focus on that individual, see them as the cause of events and to ignore or minimize the importance of the other factors is likely to be greater.

Weiner (1974) has developed a 2 x 2 matrix to demonstrate how the factors can influence an individual's level of performance: see Figure 9.1.

This matrix clearly demonstrates the dangers of making judgements without allowing for other causes. Proper performance management methods designed to involve the 'actor' fully are the simplest way of ensuring that the effects of biases and assumptions are reduced. The individual can be involved in the assessment, and diagnosis of reasons for his or her behaviour that involve using shared and explicit criteria, as in Figure 9.2.

If a rating scale was used to inform the selection assessments, this too can contribute to a later performance review. Care should however be exercised to

	Temporary behaviour (likely to change)	Stable behaviour (unlikely to change)
Internal to the individual	Effort, mood, fatigue	Ability, intelligence, physical characteristics
External to the individual	Luck, chance, opportunity	Task difficulty, environmental barrier

Figure 9.1 *Weiner's matrix of factors affecting the level of performance*

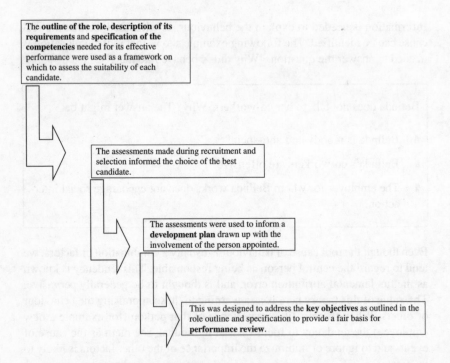

The **outline of the role, description of its requirements** and **specification of the competencies** needed for its effective performance were used as a framework on which to assess the suitability of each candidate.

The assessments made during recruitment and selection informed the choice of the best candidate.

The assessments were used to inform a **development plan** drawn up with the involvement of the person appointed.

This was designed to address the **key objectives** as outlined in the role outline and specification to provide a fair basis for **performance review**.

Figure 9.2 *Assessment and diagnosis of reasons for behaviour*

ensure that subsequent assessment takes account of the changes and other casual factors, as outlined above, that may influence the individual's performance. This is especially important if the rating scale was numeric and based on absolutes (above average, good, excellent). Cold numbers tend to have a permanency which in reality is fallacious. What was seen as 'excellent' performance in the context of a selection event may seem ordinary in the cold light of everyday work. For example, if an individual achieved a rating of 4 for planning and organizing during the selection exercises, one would reasonably expect that individual to maintain or increase the rating as a result of additional experience. A subsequent rating of 3 or less would raise questions about what was happening.

An alternative is the use of behaviourally anchored rating scales. These use numbers to symbolize a statement describing a level of performance in a particular area of competency. Thus, if the individual's rating was 'skills used with positive impact some but not all of the time (development is needed in some but not all aspects)', the subsequent review allows greater opportunity to explore which aspects of the individual's performance have improved and which still require attention.

If the review of performance and assessment of progress are used to determine the allocation of rewards, for example by giving additional pay or access to training schemes, permanent employment or other opportunities, extra care needs to be taken to ensure both fair treatment and that unreasonable sources of bias are reduced.

Fit into the organization

If the ability of each candidate to 'fit' into the organization and with the existing workforce was a factor considered during the selection decision, this too can be a useful dimension against which to evaluate the quality of the recruitment and selection process. This criterion should only be used with the greatest of care if the dangers of cloning and stereotyping are to be avoided.

We discussed in Chapter 7 the dilemma of appointing someone who would be assimilated easily into the existing culture, against someone who would challenge it. Of course how well an individual fits with existing staff is partly within his or her own control, but it is also dependent on the quality of the induction process and the attitude of significant others. Nevertheless it is reasonable to expect that if the various phases of recruitment and selection process have been effective, it will be possible to judge whether the individual is able to work productively within the organization after a reasonable period of time in post.

Achievement

Productivity by definition implies that some measures of achievement are available to calculate actual against desired and specified output. Achievement is also dependent on the clarity of the role outline and agreement of key responsibilities and objectives. The recruitment process is intended to attract individuals who are able to perform the role to the standards required and in the conditions unique to the employer. The selection process aims to discriminate between those who, the employer believes, will match the criteria and those believed not able to meet the requirements. During the course of both processes, information is supplied to the candidates about the role and employer. This enables them to decide whether the job is one they want to and feel able to do.

If these processes have been effective, the individual and the employer should have reached a good understanding about the nature, key aspects and purpose of the role. This understanding should have included agreement on the main responsibilities, priorities and the desired level of achievement.

The key features of the role used during recruitment and selection should be used to assess achievement of the person appointed to the post and thus the effectiveness of the processes used to select the individual.

Considering the amount of effort that goes into these processes and achieving a good level of understanding, it makes sense to use achievement of the agreed objectives and responsibilities as the main measure to judge the effectiveness of the recruitment and selection process, as well as the performance of the individual. If the desired levels of achievement are not being obtained, a well-planned and documented recruitment and selection process should make it possible to trace the reasons for non-achievement and identify where remedial action is needed. Remembering what we have learnt about fundamental attribution error, these reasons may be not always be the responsibility of the individual appointed.

During the assessment centre, Jackson was by far the best of the candidates. Depending on the judgement of the final interview panel and references, the assessors were sure he would be offered the post.

The assessment centre, however, had not been entirely satisfactory. The candidates had completely misinterpreted the topic for the group exercise, and had pitched their discussion at an operational level, focusing on local issues rather than seeing the strategic implications their brief contained. This meant the assessors had found no evidence on which to assess the strategic thinking skills of any of the candidates. Even though Jackson's performance in the group in this dimension was better than the others, he had not acquitted himself particularly well in the two other exercises designed to explore strategic thinking. Notes of these weaknesses were made in the overall report submitted to the selectors. However the need to appoint to the post was high, none of the other candidates was thought to be as good, and it was felt that Jackson's weakness could be addressed in the development plan.

Jackson started work and quickly found himself immersed in the operational demands of the role. His development plan had been agreed but good reasons were found for not completing its various stages. As time passed, his manager became more and more worried about Jackson's performance. While he was good at the detail he was not planning ahead, his lack of foresight was beginning to show, and he was not reading the signs around him. Even though procedurally the section was working well, a sense of uncertainty about the future was beginning to reduce productivity and effectiveness.

Jackson's manager decided to review his performance formally after nine months rather than wait for the full first year to be completed. She retrieved his personnel file, and the comments of the assessors made sense in the light of actual performance. She saw with hindsight that she should have taken more directive action to ensure that the perceived weakness in strategic thinking skills was addressed. The organization of Jackson's work should also have been more tightly planned, so the development needs could not have been sidelined so easily. Rather than blame Jackson, wisely she saw that she too had some responsibilities for his level of performance.

She decided to restructure the work of the section on a temporary basis, to take away long-term planning until Jackson's abilities in this dimension had increased sufficiently for it to be returned. A work schedule was arranged, to include regular meetings between Jackson and his manager. These were to be coaching sessions, using the planning responsibilities as vehicles for learning. While initially the manager would take the responsibility for this area of work, it would be gradually transferred back to Jackson, provided he made satisfactory progress.

The manager was aware that if Jackson did not achieve the desired level of progress, she was doing everything right to start formal proceedings towards dismissal on the grounds of lack of capability. Jackson, too was aware that unless he made the required effort and changed his behaviour, he would need to be looking for another job that suited his actual abilities better.

Even though the full implications of predictions made during the recruitment and selection process are not always seen until later, they need not always be negative. Sometimes people outstrip the assessment of their abilities and flower under the conditions offered by a new role. The opportunities for growth can unleash latent potential and start an exponential learning curve. The adage 'nothing succeeds like success' can be very true, for achievement leads to growth in confidence; this encourages individuals to try more difficult or complex tasks and learn other skills. The halo effect also favours them, as others increase their trust in them and allow them to take more risks. This phenomenon does not happen that often (but about as often as the example given above). But, when it does, it gives those involved in the appointment their own satisfactions and a sense of achievement.

OUTCOME MEASURES

The aim of recruitment and selection is to appoint the best person, in a cost-effective way that suits the employer's standards and values. Deciding whether this has been achieved requires the application of value and qualitative judgements as well as quantitative measures. The aspects of the process that can be counted include:

I How many suitably qualified applicants expressed their interest?

I What was the cost of attracting this number of applicants?

I How much did the selection process cost?

I Did the selection methods provide enough information to support decision making?

I Were all the vacant posts filled?

I How long did it take to fill the post(s)?

I Was the person appointed at a cost (in terms of salary and other benefits) that the employer wanted to pay?

However these measures tell us little about the quality of the outcomes. The application of less tangible measures is needed to determine whether:

I the process produced the desired outcome (the appointment of the 'best' person for the role);

I it gave value for money;

I the overall standard desired was achieved.

The evaluation of these is an assessment of quality – was the process 'fit for purpose'? This therefore must beg the questions who decides whether the desired outcome has been achieved, what measures can be used and what the individual's purpose is in making this evaluation. We will answer these questions next, taking the standpoint of the key stakeholders involved in the process.

The post-holder

This central person is often forgotten in the evaluation of the success of the recruitment and selection process, except as the object of the evaluation. The most common measures used to assess the quality of the appointment are those discussed above:

I Is the person trainable?

I Does he or she perform to the desired standard and achieve his or her objectives?

▌ Does he or she stay long enough, but not too long, in post?

How frequently do employers assess the quality of the recruitment process from the post-holder's perspective? It is often assumed that because the person was successful, his or her view of the process will be seen through a rosy haze of glory, and because the employer was generous enough to offer him or her a job, he or she will not have (nor have the right to have) any criticisms. In fact the people subjected to the process will possess a great deal of information about its quality, based on their own real experiences, that will help the employer with the evaluation. The sorts of question that could be posed could include, for example:

▌ Was the information supplied relevant, accurate and realistic?

▌ Do the work conditions match those contained in the glossy brochure?

▌ Were the initial impressions created confirmed by later experiences?

▌ Were the expectations created in the mind of the applicant about the nature of the role made real after the appointment?

▌ Was the level of responsibility and workload as described?

▌ Were the training opportunities promised delivered?

▌ Were on-target earnings and commissions really obtainable?

▌ Does the role-holder actually have the promised authority to decide and freedom to act?

▌ Are working relationships as conducive as suggested, and so on?

▌ Does the role and organization offer realistic opportunities for obtaining the achievement of the role-holder's aspirations (for example career development, status, job satisfaction, further advancement)?

Asking newly appointed staff during induction about their experiences can be revealing. It can be better if these questions are asked by someone outside the management line or not connected with the process. This helps the new staff to be open and more honest than perhaps they would be with the people who were responsible for the appointment. Employee attitude surveys have been used more extensively in recent years, but many do not include questions about the recruitment and selection processes to which employees are exposed.

Human resources

The human resources function can assess the effectiveness of the recruitment and selection against several measures, including:

I   The cost of the various stages used, such as consultants' fees, the size of the advertisement, printing costs, the number of people involved.

I   The size of the outcome. Did an adequate number (not too many and not too few) of suitably qualified applicants come forward?

I   Did the selection stage run smoothly?

I   How much did the selection stage cost?

I   Were the various activities valid and did they contribute to the overall goodness of the process:

 –   Did each stage fit into the cohesiveness of the whole?

 –   Did they make sense separately?

 –   Did they combine to add value to the information being exchanged and the final decisions of those involved?

I   Was the person appointed as good as had been hoped, or was the appointment made because there was no one better at the time?

I   Could the same result be achieved in ways that were easier, simpler, cheaper, faster? Was the process cost-effective?

I   Did the process contribute to the development of the human resource management function and its reputation within the organization?

I   Did the process aid the implementation of other policies such as equal opportunities, skill enhancement and development?

I   Did the process aid the achievement of the employer's strategic plans, undergo change and attain its overall goals?

It is very common to find each of the different functions within human resource management separated out, with dedicated sections of responsibility for employee relations, development, reward and resourcing. Alternatively they can be integrated. This can achieve a greater good additional to the benefits supplied by each specialization alone. Using the sort of linked approach proposed here can contribute to the achievement of meta-goals. Evaluating recruitment campaigns and selection events, in the light of the employer's strategic needs and business plans, can be a valuable way of integrating the different functions of human resource management as well as adding to the quality of recruitment and selection.

The employer

The use of strategic planning and business plans to inform business and operational decision making has increased. Most employers, even small companies, have adopted this approach as an indicator of good management practice. A central part of drawing up such plans is the SWOT analysis of the organization's environment, its operations and resources. The strengths and weaknesses of the workforce can have a direct bearing on the employer's ability to achieve its goals and ambitions. Recruitment and selection activities, even if the post in question is the most junior, should aim to minimize weaknesses and augment the employer's strengths.

When evaluating the process from the employer's perspective, the assessment should judge the contribution it has made to overall performance and achievement of the strategic plan.

▌ Will the processes used and the person appointed help with the achievement of the desired performance and business outcomes?

▌ Can clear links be seen between the competencies, as outlined on the specification, the role, as defined in the outline, and the achievement of business and strategic plans?

▌ Have the process and appointment avoided creating new and helped to resolve old problems? (Some appointments can cause more damage than benefit, and if the process is handled badly, the resentment caused can lower productivity more than that gained from the employment of another body.)

▌ Have the employer's ethical considerations been taken into account, and has the employer been helped in the discharge of its social responsibilities? (The way in which recruitment and selection decisions are made can be at odds with the employer's espoused values. For example, an employer that prides itself on openness will not be seen as consistent if the appointment process is conducted in secret, and commitment to improving the job prospects in the locality is not fully discharged – say, if local people are appointed only to lower-paid posts and the better-paid ones are filled by people attracted from elsewhere).

▌ Has the employer's reputation been enhanced? (Recruitment and selection are normally public activities. Discriminatory advertisements, poorly produced inaccurate information, mistakes in letters, breaches of confidentiality, badly organized selection events, absence of feedback or follow-up information are all known examples of poor practice. None of these paint a picture of a professional or business-like organization.)

The manager

Most managers want to fill the vacant post in their section quickly, with the least disruption to their existing staff and with a minimum amount of effort and cost. They hope the person appointed will become effective quickly and cause no trouble. Most seem to realize that they are taking a risk, but it seems that few appreciate the size of the risk, or how proper planning can help to reduce it. The challenge to those helping managers discharge their responsibilities for recruiting and selecting the best person is how to increase their understanding of the endeavour. One way of doing this is to consider how managers decide whether the recruitment and selection process has been successful. The following questions might figure in their assessment of the process:

▮ Was it easier to get the vacancy advertised than expected?

▮ Did the advertisement result in at least one application from someone who could be appointed immediately?

▮ Did the expected disagreements fail to materialize?

▮ Was the person appointed capable of 'hitting the ground running'?

▮ Did everyone approve of the appointment?

▮ Did the person appointed solve all the problems in his or her first month in post and turn the section around in the second, without making any waves?

Perhaps these are extremes, but most human resource practitioners would recognize these motivators and the perhaps unexpressed fears of managers. The anxiety and stress levels of candidates are recognized and taken into account. For example, it is common to hear assessors comment on the nervousness of the candidates, but how often is acknowledgement given to the anxieties of managers and assessors? The chances of getting an appointment wrong have been discussed earlier. The manager has responsibility for failing to get it right (whatever this means). Unpicking an unsuccessful appointment can be enough to cause even the most experienced manager to quake.

It is no wonder that most view having to fill a vacant post with some trepidation. Even though their own success depends on the effective recruitment and selection of staff, how often does any one manager have to fill a post? Perhaps more account should be taken of managers' stress levels as they go through the process, and perhaps they should be given more guidance and support in carrying out the critical tasks of describing the role and specifying the competencies. They are often expected to know how to do it, and are left to get on with it. Interview skills training is common for managers, but how many employers train managers in these other essential tasks?

Colleagues

Much of the success of appointed individuals depends on their abilities to build good working relationships with their new peers and colleagues. This requires commitment from both parties. Most people coming in to a new role are filled with enthusiasm and the wish to make a good impression. Very few people start with the intent of making enemies. To the contrary, we looked at the hygiene factors above; one of these concerns the quality of working relationships with managers and colleagues. However, not all existing employees view their new colleague with the same degree of enthusiasm.

Part of the manager's responsibilities, after an appointment has been made and before the new person starts, is to prepare the team. Any group of people naturally views a new member with suspicion. The status quo is being disrupted, and the new person will inevitably have an impact on normal custom and practice. The existing staff will want someone who will fit in and make a positive contribution to both the work of the unit and the life of the team. Different teams will define what constitutes a positive contribution in different ways, and the local meaning should have been taken into account during the preparation of the specification and the recruitment process. Initial questions asked when the role is being analysed should include, 'What will tell us the post-holder has been successful in a year's time?' This question could well include the reply, 'The quality of the working relationships with . . . and . . .'

From the point of view of colleagues, the best way of finding out whether an appointment will be successful in their eyes is to ask them what they expect the outcome to be. It is also worth asking them what would constitute a successful recruitment and selection process from their perspective. Anticipated responses might include:

▌ Transparency of the process to all concerned.

▌ Openness and clarity of the selection criteria.

▌ Fairness and reasonable treatment of the candidates.

▌ Opportunities to be involved, appropriately. This does not necessarily mean being involved in the decision making. The opportunity to show the work place to candidates might be sufficient.

▌ The speed of decision making. No one likes not knowing for long periods of time.

▌ Appropriate communications of the results. (White puffs of smoke from the board room, plums from the grapevine, are not really adequate ways of telling existing staff about a major investment decision.)

▌ Good quality feedback to the unsuccessful candidates, with some benefit accruing to them. (The vine can bear sour grapes as well as plums.)

Existing employees are justified in expecting that the new role-holder will be someone willing to contribute from his or her previous experiences and knowledge while learning about the employer's history and current ways of working. 'New brooms' might sweep clean but they are seldom very popular. Someone who is prepared to listen, learn and then share is more likely to be well received.

The best way of finding out how colleagues will decide if the best person for the job has been picked is to ask them – before the event.

Customers and suppliers

The supporters of total quality management stress the importance of working closely with customers and suppliers. The degree of involvement varies considerably. Some employers, especially those in service and care businesses, see the customers as being integral to the organization and are prepared to involve them in decision making. Student representatives on the boards of governors in educational establishments, residents' and patients' associations, tenants groups, fan clubs and car owners groups are all examples of customer groups who can be actively involved in decision making. These valued customers may also have views on the success or otherwise of the recruitment and selection process. However they may have their own individual criteria and expectations about the appropriate level of involvement. Similarly, the employer and its managers will have views on how much involvement by these groups is appropriate, particularly in the recruitment and selection of new staff.

Regardless of the degree of participation, acceptance of the new post-holder by customers and suppliers will have a positive or detrimental effect on that person's ability to perform the duties effectively. Again it is worth considering and asking, at the beginning of the recruitment and selection process, what criteria will be used by these and other key stakeholders to evaluate the end product.

Recruitment consultant or advertising agency

Recruitment consultants and other agencies have their own criteria that will inevitably be different to those of the other stakeholders. Their reputation and the possibility of repeat business will depend on reaching a satisfactory outcome. However, this satisfactory outcome may be very different from that desired by the employer. The boxed example demonstrates how easy it is for different agendas to influence the quality of the outcome.

Philip's earnings in the agency were determined by the number of posts filled. His job was to find clients, find candidates, make a match and achieve an appointment. His on-target earnings were set in terms of completed assignments. The agency's client base was made up of large organizations, and its particular speciality was senior management and board level appointments. Consequently the chances of repeat business were slim. Most clients were seeking to fill a single post, and came to the agency as a result of seeing advertisements for similar vacancies to their own in the press, or hearing of the agency through word of mouth. The agency's reputation was built on two factors – speed and confidentiality.

It was therefore important to Philip that he got someone in post – fast. If they did not stay in the job for very long, it did not really matter. Appointment 'failures' could usually be attributed to the employer (for example, poor induction or bad decisions) or to the individual (inability to transfer, or ability in an interview that did not translate into delivery). Rarely was it seen as the fault of the agency for putting forward low-quality candidates. To Philip, the fact that a post-holder left quickly meant there was the chance of repeat business. He always made sure that his clients thought that the process had been handled smoothly and professionally.

Most reputable recruitment agencies follow up with both the clients and the people appointed, as they realize that their business cannot be built on quick fixes alone. Nevertheless, when appointing consultants it is worth discussing at the start of the assignment what constitutes a satisfactory outcome, and building evaluation into the contract.

Advertising agencies are usually anonymous. Their work appears under the banner of the employer and their reputations exist in their own industry more than in the market. Nevertheless they have distinctive styles that can be recognized by those who watch the situations vacant columns. Their desired outcome, unlike some recruitment consultants', is the establishment of long-term working relationships with their clients. Short-term gains (such as oversizing advertisements, not passing on commissions obtained from publishers, poor quality control) tend to negate the renewal of contracts, and so are counter-productive in the end.

Employers usually form contracts with agencies after a process of tenders and presentations. These may include displays of work followed by contractual negotiations. Some better agencies undertake to monitor the effectiveness of advertisements and recruitment campaigns at the time of agreeing the initial contract. Their measures will include the cost of the advertisement and production of additional material, the number of enquiries received and the number of enquiries translated into candidates. They will monitor the effectiveness of different media for different types of job, and will be able to advise on other recruitment methods from their experience and databases.

USING THE NEED TO FILL A POST AS A STRATEGIC OPPORTUNITY

The only real measure of success is the contribution the process and appointment make to achievement of the employer's strategic plans and operational imperatives. There is little point in doing something that does not add value to the organization's operations and take it closer to realizing its ambitions. The size of the investment required to fill and fund any post, even at the most junior level, was described earlier. The recruitment and selection process can thus be paralleled with any other investment decision. However because it directly affects the lives of people, it must be seen as having consequences that are more serious.

The following steps indicate the distinct stages in the recruitment and selection process, and include guidelines that should ensure the process contributes to strategic achievement. They also take into account the needs of the people involved in the operation of the process and those being processed.

1. Define and design the job to be done or role to be occupied.

2. Identify the requirements to:

    –   achieve the employer's objectives;

    –   meet needs – fill gaps, enhance strengths, minimize weaknesses;

    –   carry out the responsibilities of the role;

    –   contribute to the employer's society.

3. Develop a profile of a competent performer, describing the abilities, attainments, achievements and attributes required to perform the full range of responsibilities at a level above that deemed to be satisfactory.

4. Attract candidates using cost-effective means (that is, applications are received from an adequate number of suitably qualified individuals to enable a choice to be made).

5. Supply candidates with good-quality information so they are able to form a realistic picture of the organization and its requirements.

6. Devise a selection process that obtains enough accurate information to enable all parties to make the best decision for them.

7. Assess the competencies of candidates against the criteria and requirements so that potential performance may be predicted and development needs identified.

8. Provide sufficient information to support the negotiations about the explicit contract of employment and clarify the expectations contained in implicit terms.

9. Draw up an orientation and initial training programme to enable the appointed candidate to become effective quickly.

10. Inform the early stages of the training and development programme to help the new role-holder move from adequate to competent and beyond.

11. Complement the initial induction with inclusion activities designed to help the existing team assimilate its new member quickly, and to regain and enhance the level of the whole team's performance.

SUMMARY

We have discussed the sometimes disparate and conflicting needs of the employer, the manager, colleagues and the person wishing to be appointed to a job. The employer's long-term requirements are usually paramount in any examination of the recruitment and selection process, for unless the organization continues to exist no one will be employed within it. Nevertheless this overriding factor does not negate the importance of considering the needs of the people who are subjected to the chosen procedures, nor should it provide excuses for sloppy practice.

The way people are treated during the recruitment and selection process, and the way decisions taken about them are made, lay the foundations for the success or failure of any appointment. An employer's reputation can be severely damaged, and therefore its ability to attract good-quality applicants in the future can be adversely affected. The images created in the minds of candidates during the recruitment stage inform the expectations of the person appointed, and once an offer of employment has been made and accepted, it can be difficult to change the explicit terms and conditions of the contract. It is even more difficult to alter the understanding of the implicit terms and aspirations of individuals enthused by the opportunities offered by the organization in its attempts to sell them the job.

There is no excuse for creating misunderstandings. Establishing a clear expression of role requirements and the criteria to be used in making the final decisions will make the other stages of the process straightforward. If these critical stages are missed out or inadequately completed, those following can be difficult and stressful for all concerned. If on the other hand care is taken on the preparation of these documents, the chances of the process running smoothly and even being fun are greatly enhanced. The selection activities can provide the opportunity for the candidates to demonstrate their abilities. Their competencies will be assessed by people who are competent at assessment. Useful criteria and relevant activities will mean that very helpful feedback is available. The process can lay the foundations for the creation of good-quality learning contracts and development plans. Those not offered the post will be able to understand why their application was not successful, and they will have learnt how to improve their chances of success for next time.

Recruitment and selection is a major investment that affects an employer's ability to succeed and implement strategic plans. It also comprises a series of decisions that influence the quality of the lives of others. We know the processes used by human beings to make these sorts of decision are prone to errors and biases. It is possible to introduce methods and aids to reduce the negative effect of these and improve the overall quality of the processes.

The final note is to remind us all that:

▌ Assessing the performance of other people and being assessed is stressful and demanding.

▌ Making sure that the needs of the role are identified and translated into good-quality selection criteria is essential, for all other stages depend on these.

▌ Planning the processes in advance and scheduling the time will enable the evidence needed to be gathered and assessed. It also makes it easier to give the details the attention they deserve.

▌ Decisions should be made by people trained to do so, against the criteria and based on the evidence.

▌ People involved should be treated with respect, and their applications should be assessed fairly and consistently.

If the advice and suggestions offered in the preceding pages are applied, the chances of matching the right people to the right role by the right employer will be increased. Using good practice can change this aspect of employment from one dreaded by all concerned into one that produces benefits and the opportunity for all to learn.

References

Alban-Metcalf, B and Nicholson, N (1984) *The Career Development of British Managers*, British Institute of Management, London

Alimo-Metcalfe, B (1994) Waiting for fish to grow feet, in M Tanton (ed), *Women in Management: A developing presence*, Routledge, London

Armstrong, M (2001) *A Handbook of Human Resource Management Practice*, 8th edn, Kogan Page, London

Audit Commission (2002) *Recruitment and Retention: A public service workforce for the twenty-first century*, Audit Commission, London

Bazerman, M H (1994) *Judgement in Managerial Decision-Making*, Wiley, Chichester

Belbin, R M (1981) *Management Teams: Why they succeed or fail*, Heinemann, London

Bevan, S and Thompson, M (1992) *Merit Pay, Performance Appraisal and Attitudes to Women's Work*, Report no 234, Institute of Manpower Studies, Brighton

Boyatzis, R E (1982) *The Competent Manager*, Wiley, Chichester

Broverman, I K *et al* (1975) Sex-role stereotypes: a current appraisal, in M T Schuch Mednick, S S Tangri and L W Hoffman (eds), *Women and Achievement: Social and motivational analyses*, Hemisphere Publishing, New York

Cascio, W F (1987) *Applied Psychology in Personnel Management*, Prentice Hall, Englewood Cliffs, NJ

Chambers, H E (2001) *Finding, Hiring and Keeping Peak Performers: Every manager's guide*, Perseus Publishing, Cambridge, MA

Child, J (1984) *Organisation: A guide to problems and practice*, 2nd edn, Harper and Row, London

Cook, M (1988) *Personnel Selection and Productivity*, 3rd end, Wiley, Chichester

Cook, M (2001) *Personnel Selection: Adding value through people*, 3rd edn, Wiley, Chichester

Dainty, P (1987) Work motivation and job design: is progress over? *Journal of Occupational Psychology*, (28), pp 59–78

Dale, M (1992) *Why Do Women Decide Not to Submit Applications for Management Jobs?* MSc dissertation, Huddersfield Polytechnic

Dale, M (1998) *Developing Management Skills*, 2nd edn, Kogan Page, London

Dale, M (2002) *The Learning Dimension*, Blackhall, Dublin

Dale, M and Iles, P (1992) *Assessing Management Skills*, Kogan Page, London

Deaux, K (1976) *The Behaviour of Women and Men*, Wadsworth, Florence, KY

De Witte, K (1989) Recruiting and advertising, in P Herriot (ed), *Assessment and Selection in Organisations: Methods and practice for recruitment and appraisal*, Wiley, Chichester

Fyock, C D (1993) *Get the Best: How to recruit the people you want*, Business One Irwin, Homewood, IL

Garratt, B (1987) *The Learning Organisation*, Fontana, London

Grout, J and Perrin, S (2002) *Recruiting Excellence: An insider's guide to sourcing top talent*, McGraw Hill, Maidenhead

Guest, D E *et al* (1996) *The State of the Psychological Contract in Employment*, Chartered Institute of Personnel and Development (CIPD), London

Hackman, J R and Oldham, G R (1980) *Work Design*, Addison-Wesley, Reading, MA

Handy, C (1985) *Understanding Organisations*, 2nd edn, Penguin, Harmondsworth

Handy, C (1989) *The Age of Unreason*, Business Books, London

Handy, C (1994) *The Empty Raincoat*, Hutchinson, London

Herriot, P (1989a) *Recruitment in the 90's*, IPM, London

Hertzberg, F, Mausner, B and Snyderman, B (1959) *The Motivation to Work*, Wiley, Chichester

Hunter, J E and Hunter, R F (1984) Validity and utility: alternative predictors of job performance, *Psychology Bulletin* (96), pp 72–98

Iles, P A and Robertson, I T (1989) The impact of personnel selection procedures on candidates, in P Herriot (ed), *Assessment and Selection in Organisations: Methods and practice for recruitment and appraisal*, Wiley, Chichester

Institute of Public Policy Research (2000) *Wanting More from Work?* Department for Education and Skills, London

Kakabadse, A, Ludlow, R and Vinnicombe, S (1987) *Working in Organisations*, Gower, Aldershot

Kelly, G A (1955) *A Theory of Personality: The psychology of personal constructs*, Norton, New York

Lord, W (1994) The face behind the figures, *Personnel Management* (December)

Mabey, C and Iles, P (1991) HRM from the other side of the fence, *Personnel Management* (February)

Makin, P J (1989) Selection of professional groups, in P Herriot (ed), *Assessment and Selection in Organisations: Methods and practice for recruitment and appraisal*, Wiley, Chichester

Marshall, J (1994) Why women leave senior management jobs, in M Tanton (ed), *Women in Management: A developing presence*, Routledge, London

Maslow, A (1954) *Motivation and Personality*, Harper, New York

McClelland, D C (1953) *The Achievement Motive*, Appleton-Century-Crofts, New York

Nicholson, N and West, M (1988) *Managerial Job Changes: Men and women in transition*, Cambridge University Press, Cambridge

Pedler, M J and Boydell, T H (1985) *Managing Yourself*, Fontana, London

Robertson, I T and Smith, J M (eds) (1988) Personnel selection methods, in P Herriot (ed), *Assessment and Selection in Organisations: Methods and practice for recruitment and appraisal*, Wiley, Chichester

Roe, R A (1989) Designing selection procedures, in P Herriot (ed), *Assessment and Selection in Organisations: Methods and practice for recruitment and appraisal*, Wiley, Chichester

Salthouse, M (1995) *A Guide to Staff Handbooks*, Croner, Kingston on Thames

Schein, V E and Mueller, R (1990) Sex role stereotyping and requisite management characteristics: a cross-cultural look, Paper presented to the 22nd International Congress of Applied Psychology, Kyoto, Japan

Selwyn, N M (1988) *Law of Employment*, 6th edn, Butterworth, London

Smith, M Gregg, M and Andrews, D (1989) *Selection and Assessment: A new appraisal*, Pitman, London

Sternberg, R J (1988) Sketch of componential sub-theory of human intelligence, *Behaviour and Brain Sciences* (3)

Taylor, F W (1991) *The Principles of Scientific Management*, Harper and Row

Taylor, S (2002) *People Resourcing*, 2nd edn CIPD, London

Torrington, D and Hall, L (1995) *Personnel Management: A new approach*, 3rd edn, Prentice Hall, Hemel Hempstead

Weiner, B (ed) (1974) *Achievement Motivation and Attribution Theory*, General Learning Press, Morristown, NJ

ADDITIONAL READING

Boot, R Lawrence, J and Singer, M (1993) *Fairness in Personnel Selection: An organisational justice perspective*, Avebury, Hampshire

British Qualifications (2002) *British Qualifications: A complete guide to educational, technical, professional and academic qualifications in Britain*, 33rd edn, Kogan Page, London

Chandler, P (2003) *An A–Z of Employment Law*, 4th edition, Kogan Page, London

Conlow, R (1994) *Excellence in Management*, Kogan Page, London

Corfield, R (2003) *Preparing Your Own CV*, 3rd edn, Kogan Page, London

Corfield, R (2003) *How You Can Get that Job! Application forms and letters made easy*, 3rd edn, Kogan Page, London

Edenborough, R (1999) *Using Psychometrics*, 2nd edn, Kogan Page, London

Edenborough, R (2002) *Effective Interviewing: A handbook of skills and techniques*, 2nd edn, Kogan Page, London

Farbey, D (2002) *How to Produce Successful Advertising*: *A guide to strategy, planning and targeting*, 3rd edn, Kogan Page, London

Greenwood, D (1999) *The Job Hunter's Handbook*, 2nd edition, Kogan Page, London

Lewis C (1985) *Employee Selection*, Hutchinson, London

Pearn, K (1998a) *Tools for Managing Diversity*, CIPD, London

Pearn, K (1998b) *Tools for Assessment and Development Centres*, CIPD, London

Ryan, C (1996) *The Master Marketer: How to combine tried and tested techniques with the latest ideas to achieve spectacular marketing success*, Kogan Page, London

Skeats, J (1996) *Successful Induction: How to get the most from your new employees*, Kogan Page, London

Smith, P R and Taylor, J (2001) *Marketing Communications: An integrated approach*, 3rd edn, Kogan Page, London

Taylor, S (2002) *People Resourcing*, 2nd edn, CIPD, London

Wilson, E (ed) (2001) *Organisational Behaviour Reassessed: The impact of gender*, Sage, London

SOURCES OF INFORMATION

Rather than risk giving outdated information only the titles and location towns of organizations are given below. Current addresses and telephone numbers may be obtained from local reference libraries, the Internet or directory enquiries.

Association of Search and Selection Consultants, London
British Institute of Graphologists, Weybridge, Surrey
British Psychological Society, Leicester
Chartered Institute of Personnel and Development, London
Commission for Racial Equality, London
Employers Forum on Age, London
Employers Forum on Disability, London
Equal Opportunities Commission, Manchester
Institute of Employment Consultants, Woking, Surrey
Institute of Employment Studies, Brighton, Sussex
Investors in People UK, London
New Ways to Work, London
Recruitment and Employment Confederation, Guildford

TRAINING MATERIAL

Fletcher, J (1997) *Effective Interviewing* (audio cassette) Kogan Page, London
Lowe, P (1993) *Recruitment and Interviewing Skills* (workshop package), Kogan
   Page, London
Video Arts family of training videos and briefcase booklets

The major producers of psychometric instruments and tests (especially Saville
and Holdsworth, Oxford Psychologists Press Ltd, the Psychological Corpora-
tion and ASE) provide training and information.

REFERENCE SOURCES

The *Personnel Manager's Yearbook* is a useful source of information, and
contains contact details of professional bodies, publishers and consultants as
well as major employers. This can be found in most major reference libraries or
obtained from the publisher, AP Information Services.

Local reference libraries and the Internet maintain up to date information on
employment law and recent judgements. The most comprehensive service is
published by Croner Information Services. Other Web-based sources include:

Disclaw: wwwemplaw.co.uk
EORdirect: http://rimerbutterworths.co.uk/eordirect/
Freelawyer: wwwfreelawyer.co.uk
IRS Employment Review: www.irsemploymentreview.com

Index

ACAS   256
achievement   301–03
activities   173–81
advertisement   57
    language   60
    location   58–60
    presentation   58
    press   67–69
    repeat   216
advertising agencies *see* recruitment
        agencies
agencies *see* recruitment agencies
applicants *see* candidates
application
    forms   134, 135–38
    letters   134, 140–41
applications   62, 124–56
    assessing   8
    online   134, 142–43
    submitting   7
appointment
    evaluation   296–303
    failure to make   217–19
    wrong choice   215–16
appraisal *see* development
Advisory, Conciliation and
        Arbitration Service *see* ACAS
assessment centres   186–88
assessors   166, 225–27
assumptions *see* bias

attracting candidates   5–6
    see also recruitment

behavioural anchored rating scales
        301
benefits *see* rewards
bias   7, 46, 60–62, 82, 83, 87, 104,
        105, 130, 160–64, 234–35
    see also discrimination
biodata 144–46
brochures   74–75
buddying   272
candidates
    considerations   197–204
    domestic considerations   201–02
    effects   203–04
    impact   195
    personal disclosure   199–200
    power to refuse   224–25
    rejection   204
    rejection of offer   216–17
    treatment   219–28
    uncertainty   202–03
    unsuccessful   196, 242–45, 309

capability   255
case studies   176–77
checklists   266–72
childcare   208
choice of media   54–56

cognitive ability tests *see* tests,
    cognitive ability
colleagues
    leaving   211–12
    outcome measures   308–10
competency   24, 151–53
    frameworks   188
confidentiality, lack of   200
constructs   129–30, 161
contracts, psychological *see* psycho-
    logical contracts
contracts of employment *see*
    employment contracts
costs   62–63
Council for Race Equality   6
culture, assumptions   209–10
curriculum vitae   134, 139–40
customers, outcome measures   310

decisions   7, 93, 95, 101
    frames   129–34
    making   191–93, 227
    matrix   192, 232
    over-confidence in quality
        102–03
    poor   2
    theory   295
    trees   192–93
    win/win   231–35
demotion   254
development   250–51, 286–88
disability   210–11
    see also bias
    errors
    discrimination
    stereotyping
discrimination   60, 61–62, 204–13,
    259
    indirect   45
    statistics   205–06
discussions, informal   113–14
dismissal   255–57, 278
    constructive   253–54
diversity   206–07

domestic responsibilities   207
employee
    achievement   301–03
    celebrating appointment   276
    fit   301
    needs   261–63
    outcome measures   304–05
    part-time workers rights   279
    performance   298–301
    specification   44–47
    trainability   297–98
    treatment   241–42
employer
    objectives   312–13
    outcome measures   306–07
employment contracts   235–38,
    277–79
    explicit terms   236–37
    implicit   238–39
    see also psychological contracts
    probation   277–79
    short term   237–38
    termination mutual agreement
        257–58
    see also dismissal
employment
    offer   10–11, 235–39
    mistakes   250–58
Equal Opportunities Commission   6
equal opportunity   206
equity   222–23
errors   7, 84, 87, 100–08, 130,
    160–64, 234–35
    see also bias
    discrimination
    stereotyping
escalation of commitment   101–02
ethnicity
    see bias
    discrimination
    errors
    stereotyping
evaluation   12, 109–10, 291–314

events, social   114–15, 180–81
expectations   32
    see also psychological contract

failure   211
feedback   84, 245–49, 285
fit   301
fliers   72–73
functional analysis   27

gender   239
glass ceiling   209
graphology   137, 146–47
group discussions   178–79, 180
groups   212–13

Hackman and Oldham   24
halo effect   162
handbooks   238, 266–72
handwriting   105
    see also graphology
Hertzberg   21–23, 34
    see also motivation
honesty checks   190
Human Relations School   19
human resource
    accounting   291–92
    outcome measures   305–06

image   57
impact on applicants   9–10
impressions   104–06, 160–61, 163
inclusion   10, 263–76
induction   10, 261–90
    methods   266–73
    planning   263–66
    see also training
information
    additional   108
    availability   103–04, 200–01
    flow   93–95, 97–100
    needed   95–100
    packs   110
interactions   179

internet   55, 69–71, 111
interviewers, training   130
interviews   167–72, 231
    behavioural event   170–71
    competency based   169–10
    final   172
    focused   170
    informal   171–72
    one to one   82, 167
    panel   167–168
    preliminary   115–16
    situational   171
    structured   168–69
in-tray exercises   176
investment   3

job   30–31
    as a product   56–57
    centres   52, 55
    characteristics   24, 27
    description   4, 5, 16–30, 35–42,
        51–52
    design   16, 17–30, 31, 36–39
    redesign   251–52
    satisfaction   24, 28, 33–34
    seeking, reasons   63–64
    trails   277
    see also role
        work
job-holder *see* employee

knowledge workers   213–14

labour market   52–53
learnt incapacity   33
long-listing   84

mail shots   74
management by objectives   24
manager, outcome measures
        307–08
market research   59
marketing   51–66
Maslow   20–21, 34, 63

see also motivation
McClelland   24
measures of success   90–91
measures, outcome   303–11
meetings, preliminary   82
mentoring   272–73
milkround *see* recruitment fairs
motivation   19, 29, 33
   to change jobs   63–64

negotiations   239–42
newspapers   55

objectives   34, 38, 286
open days   114–15
organization goals and objectives
   30–31

pay *see* rewards
performance   33, 298–301
   management   300
      see also development
   related pay   26
   review   287
person specification *see* employee
      specification
personal construct theory   129–30
personality questionnaires   184–86
   see also tests, psychometric
positive action   83–89, 134
post-holder *see* employee
prejudice *see* bias
presentations   175–76
privacy   222
probationary periods   277–79
problems   178
productivity   301–03
psychological contracts   95–97,
      235, 241–42
   see also employment contracts,
      implicit
   expectations
psychometric tests *see* tests,
      psychometric

quality   295

race, assumptions   209–10
   see *also* bias
   discrimination
   errors
   stereotyping
radio   55, 71–72
rating   188
records   131, 227, 232–34
recruitment   54, 90, 117
   agencies   56, 70–71
      outcome measures   310–11
   consultants   79–88, 118, 202–03
      briefing   80
      choice   86
      management   86–88
      outcome measures   310–11
      search   81–82
   fairs   76–77, 111–12
   methods   66–92
   see also attracting candidates
redeployment   252–54
references   83, 119, 121, 188–89
relationships   33, 37, 211–12, 309
   see also socialization
reputation   117–20, 150–51
rewards   11, 26, 29, 34, 38–39,
      240–41
risk   2
   averse   163
role   30–31
   description *see* job description
   design   31, 36–39
   outline   42
   profiles   42–43
role-holder *see* employee

scientific management   18–19, 27,
      29
screening   113, 115–16, 143–53
   see also shortlisting
search *see* recruitment consultants
search committees   88

selection 3–9, 85, 173
  activities 173–81
  benefits 196–97
  events 196–97
  methods 157–94
    choice 158, 190–91, 220
    operation 223–28
    prediction of success 159–60
  process 220
self efficacy 35, 195–96
self-esteem 246
shortlisting 125–29, 153–56
  see also screening
socialization 274–76
speculative letters 89–90
stereotyping 45, 60, 82, 105,
  162–63
strategic opportunity 312–13
stress 35
substance abuse checks 190
success 211
  measures *see* measures, outcome
    prediction 106–08, 118,
    159–60
suppliers, outcome measures 310

talent, loss of 214–15
Taylorism 18, 26–27
telephone calls 134, 141–42
television 71–72
terms and conditions of employment
  see employment contracts
tests 147–49, 174–75
  cognitive ability 149–50, 183
  feedback 247–48

psychometric 181–83
work-related 147–49
Trade Union Reform and Employment Rights Act 236–37
trainability 297
training 279
  assessors 279
  initial 11, 279–85
  interviewers 279
  schemes 90
  see also induction

utility 294–96

vacancies
  publishing 65–66
validity 83, 131, 160, 165–67,
  221–22, 293–94
  see also types of selection
    method
visits 112, 114–15, 179–80

women
  glass ceiling 209
  participation 208
  see also bias
  discrimination
  gender
  stereotypes
word of mouth advertising 117–18
work 32–33
  design 23–26, 27
  see also job design
  placement 90
  samples 173–74, 277